D1616374

BASIC PRIVATE INVESTIGATION

BASIC PRIVATE INVESTIGATION

A Guide to Business Organization, Management, and Basic Investigative Skills for the Private Investigator

Edited by

WILLIAM F. BLAKE, MS, CPP, CFE

CHARLES C THOMAS • PUBLISHER, LTD.
Springfield • Illinois • U.S.A.

Published and Distributed Throughout the World by

CHARLES C THOMAS • PUBLISHER, LTD.
2600 South First Street
Springfield, Illinois 62704

© 2011 by CHARLES C THOMAS • PUBLISHER, LTD.

ISBN 978-0-398-08642-8 (paper)
ISBN 978-0-398-08645-9 (ebook)

Library of Congress Catalog Card Number: 2010053971

With THOMAS BOOKS *careful attention is given to all details of manufacturing
and design. It is the Publisher's desire to present books that are satisfactory as to their
physical qualities and artistic possibilities and appropriate for their particular use.*
THOMAS BOOKS *will be true to those laws of quality that assure a good name
and good will.*

Printed in the United States of America
MM-R-3

Library of Congress Cataloging-in-Publication Data

Basic private investigation : a guide to business organization, management, and basic investigative skills for the private investigator / edited
by William F. Blake.
   p. cm.
Includes index.
ISBN 978-0-398-08642-8 (pbk.) – ISBN 978-0-398-08645-9 (ebook)
1. Private investigators–United States. 2. Private security services–
United States. I. Blake, William F. II. Title.

HV8088.B375 2011
363.28'90973–dc22

                                        2010053971

CONTRIBUTORS

Andrew C. Albright, MS
Outsource Investigations, Inc.
Castle Rock, Colorado

Andrew C. "Skip" Albright is a former Special Agent with the Air Force Office of Special Investigations. He owns and operates Outsource Investigations, a Colorado-based private investigations firm specializing in insurance claim surveillance. He has more than thirty-four years of law enforcement and investigative experience.

William F. Blake, MS, CPP, CFE
Blake and Associates, Inc.
Littleton, Colorado

Mr. Blake is a retired United States Army Criminal Investigation Command Special Agent and has more than fifty years' experience as a military, corporate, and private investigator. He is a member of INTELLENET.

Gregory J. Caldwell, BS, VSM
White Hat Solutions, LLC
Marysville, Tennessee

Gregory J. Caldwell owns and operates White Hat Solutions, LLC, licensed in Florida and Tennessee. He has been a private investigator for more than thirty years and specializes in corporate work. A member of INTELLENET since 1991, he was on the Washoe County Homeland Security Council and is a member of the Florida Association of Private Investigators, the Florida Association of Licensed Investigators and National Council of Investigation and Security Services, Investigative and Security Professionals for Legislative Action, Tennessee Professional Investigators, and The Vidocq Society.

James P. Carino, Jr.
Executive Security Consultants
Gladwyne, Pennsylvania

James P. "Jim" Carino, Jr., is a former Special Agent with the U.S. Air Force Office of Special Investigations. He owns and operates Executive Security Consultants, Gladwyne, Pennsylvania, specializing as an expert witness in premises liability and negligent security litigation. He has over 50 years of investigative and security management experience.

Jack Chu
R.A. Consultants, Ltd
Hong Kong, Hong Kong

Jack Chu has thirty-five years of experience in law enforcement, security, and private investigations. He served more than twenty years in law enforcement in China and Hong Kong. He is an acknowledged expert in Chinese law and foreign policy.

Frederick H. Coward, Jr., BS
Investigative Services International
Honolulu, Hawaii

Frederick H. Coward, Jr., is a retired Supervisory Special Agent and Legal Attaché with the Federal Bureau of Investigation and former police officer with Long Beach, California. He is the owner of Investigative Services International (ISI) Corporation with offices in numerous international locations. He has over 45 years of investigative, managerial, and administrative law enforcement experience.

Christopher Finley, MS
Finley Consulting and Investigations
Pittsburgh, Pennsylvania

Christopher Finley has been a private detective since 1997 and has practiced in several states. He is currently the owner and president of Finley Consulting & Investigations, Inc., with offices in Philadelphia and Pittsburgh, Pennsylvania. Mr. Finley specializes in physical surveillance.

Mary Clark Fischer
Business Security Consultant
Berlin, Germany

Mary Clark Fischer is a Business Security Consultant with the Berlin, Germany office of Jell, a United Kingdom investigative and security management firm. She is fluent in several European languages and has over 20 years investigative and intelligence experience and management of international operations.

Diana L. Garren
True Perceptions, Inc.
Atlanta, Georgia

Diana L. Garren is the founder of True Perceptions, Inc.® and a leading business image consultant, strategist and perception management specialist with more than twenty-seven years of experience.

Thomas Miles
Hawk Security Company
Germantown, Tennessee

Thomas H. "Tom" Miles is a retired U.S. Army officer with over 40 years of investigative, law enforcement, and intelligence experience. He is the owner of Hawk Security Company, a Tennessee-based private investigation and security consulting form. He has numerous years of security management and investigative experience with major international and Fortune 500 companies.

Reginald J. Montgomery, CLI, CPP, CFE, CST, CFC, CP
RJ Montgomery Associates
Allendale, New Jersey

Reginald J. Montgomery has over 40 years of law enforcement, investigative, and security management experience in the corporate and private sectors. He is a certified expert witness and polygraph examiner. He has many years of experience as a trainer in investigative and security matters and as an adjunct professor at several colleges. He is also a prolific author of investigative and security management publications.

Dale J. Seymour, CPP, CAMS
Seymour Investigative Services, LLC
Trumbull, Connecticut

Dale J. Seymour has owned and operated Seymour Investigative Services, LLC, since 1998. He has a Bachelor of Arts degree in Speech and Drama. He holds a Certified Protection Specialist® designation from ASIS International and holds a Certified Anti-Money Laundering Specialist designation from the Association of Certified Anti-Money Specialists. He began his law enforcement career with three years of service at the Hartford, Connecticut, Police Department and then served as a Special Agent with the Drug Enforcement Administration in Hartford and Bridgeport, Connecticut, retiring after twenty-three years of Anti-Terrorism Advisory Council at the United States Attorney's Office in New Haven, Connecticut for two years.

Warren J. Sonne, CPP, CLI
Sun State Investigations, Inc.
New York, New York

Warren J. Sonne is a retired New York City Police Department detective with 21 years of law enforcement experience and also has over 21 years' experience as a private investigator. He is the owner of private investigation companies in New York and Florida. He is the author of numerous investigative articles in professional journals.

Michael J. West, MS, CFE, CLEI
Arkansas Investigations
Little Rock, Arkansas

Michael J. West has more than thirty years' law enforcement experience at the local, state, and federal levels.

PREFACE

Today's private investigator comes from two primary sources: (1) law enforcement agencies and (2) academic environments. As a result, the experience gap varies widely. Those coming from law enforcement agencies normally are retirees, and private investigation is a secondary full- or part-time occupation. They normally have a minimum of twenty years' law enforcement experience. These are the most experienced individuals. Those coming from the academic world have the advantage of exposure to the latest in investigative techniques and legal knowledge. They only lack in the application of their knowledge to real-world situations. Each group comes with a different outlook, perspective, and set of values as well as experience. To be successful as a profession, these groups must be melded to a common group of values and objectives.

The purpose of this book is to provide the private investigator, regardless of experience, with information that will result in business and personal success. It is not our purpose to make an individual a highly skilled private investigator in every conceivable investigative arena. We only want to provide information that will lead to success in a particular chosen area of interest. It is impossible to be an expert in every possible investigative area, but with some general knowledge in a specific area, the private investigator will be able to better determine the qualification of associates who have the necessary expert skills.

The authors of this book are a unique group of professionals. Each author has a minimum of ten years' investigative experience, and there is an average of at least thirty-five years of experience in the private sector and with various military and governmental investigative units. They have extensive expertise in many areas. The professional certifications earned by the authors demonstrate their quest for professionalism and current knowledge due to the requirement for continuing professional education.

The book is divided into two parts. Part I discusses basic business organization and management subjects applicable to those who desire to be a successful business owner. It covers material for those just starting a business as well as information that is of value to those who want to better organize and manage their current business.

Part II discusses basic investigative skills applicable to all levels of experiences and areas of personal interest. This information comes from experienced private investigators and takes a step beyond the traditional "school solution." These are the skill sets normally used by an investigator who is just starting out in business. These are normally considered as general investigative skills that serve as a foundation for more specialized experiences.

Success as a private investigator is influenced by two different business options. An individual may portray his activities from a business perspective and dispense investigative services to all possible clients through the use of his own skills augmented by investigative resources of other qualified associates. Second, an individual may rely strictly on current skills and operate within a limited scope of activities.

W. F. B.

INTRODUCTION

The world of the private investigator has evolved from a very simple to a very complex business. In our early history, the private investigator primarily operated like a law enforcement officer but was employed by an individual or corporate entity. The basic qualifications of the private investigator were being able to find people who may or may not have committed a crime and, when the circumstances required, being able to shoot first and accurately. There were no legal restrictions on the activities of the private investigator, and in some cases, their activities were clearly criminal violations of law. There was no public outcry for restrictions on their activities because there was a general public opinion that the perpetrators probably deserved what happened to them. There was also a common opinion that a person had a right to protect his personal reputation and business interests by any means possible. This attitude was portrayed in the early Western movies where John Wayne, Hopalong Cassidy, and Gene Autry portrayed the white hat savior of the common person being persecuted by the black hat bad guys.

When the possibility of being a viable business opportunity became apparent, individuals put together business ventures advertising their skills, resources, and abilities to operate in numerous geographical areas. In 1850, Allan Pinkerton established what is purported to be the first nationwide detective agency in the United States. Originally known as the Pinkerton National Detective Agency, it later became known solely as Pinkertons. Pinkerton became famous when he foiled a plot to assassinate President-elect Abraham Lincoln, who later hired Pinkerton agents for his personal security during the Civil War. At its height, Pinkerton employed more agents than there were members of the standing army of the United States, causing the state of Ohio to outlaw the agency due to fears it could be hired out as a private army or militia. Pinkerton's operations moved into the areas of infiltration of labor unions, strikebreaking, securing property, and interference with work disputes. Currently, Pinkerton has business operations in a number of investigative and security functions on an international basis.

Through evolution, private investigation companies proliferated and engaged in many diverse activities. Some companies involved in strikebreaking and protection of corporate interests freely used deadly force to obtain their objectives. These private security guards and investigators were responsible for many deaths. These forces also engaged in the apprehension of wanted persons, as well as the protection of valuable shipments of gold, silver and other valuable commodities. Because of conflicts with labor unions, private security guards and investigators continue to be associated by labor organizers and union members with strikebreaking.

The actions of the original private investigators were not without an influence on our current-day law enforcement and investigative operations. In 1871, Congress appropriated $50,000 to the new Department of Justice (DOJ) to form a suborganization devoted to "the detection and prosecution of those guilty of violating federal law." The amount was insufficient for the DOJ to fashion an integral investigating unit, so the DOJ contracted out the services to a private agency. Private investigation work suffered from the police modernizations movement that saw the rise of the Federal Bureau of Investigation and the bolstering of detective units and resources of public police.

The successes as well as the problems of earlier private investigators have had a significant influence on the modern-day private investigators. Most state governments have instituted legal requirements for private investigators, among which are minimum experience, and insurance and educational requirements. These actions were undertaken to protect members of the public. Current and pending legislation will also have an impact on what can be accomplished by the private investigator. These restrictions are a result of the outcry for personal privacy and the inappropriate and highly publicized criminal activities of a small number of private investigators.

The role of the current private investigator primarily encompasses those areas that are not criminal in nature or are of sole interest to the business community, such as internal matters and civil litigation. There are also situations in which the private investigator may become involved in criminal matters because of jurisdictional problems and financial limitations of public law enforcement. This has created a wide variety of business opportunities for the qualified private investigator.

Because of the ever-increasing public outcry and governmental legislations, the private investigator must develop a recession- and legislative-proof business niche to remain a viable business entity. One example is the current and pending limitations on obtaining personal information from public records. The private investigator whose business is primarily based on obtaining personal information will find ever-increasing difficulty in obtaining the desired information. Now is the time to reevaluate business opportunities and identify goals for the future. At this point, the individual is no longer just a private investigator but a business person who provides investigative services. The emphasis is on "business."

WHAT IS INTELLENET?

International Intelligence Network–Intellenet–is a worldwide network of private investigators and security consultants. Intellenet's membership is by invitation only and is restricted to highly qualified individuals with extensive experience in law enforcement; intelligence; private security; and public, private, and corporate investigations. Intellenet offers an extensive array of diversified services and operational scopes that are virtually unlimited throughout the United States and the international community. Members represent some of the most competent investigators available in the world. Many members have served in highly sensitive supervisory and management positions in government and corporate business entities. Regardless of client needs–regional, national or international–Intellenet members provide unique services to individuals and businesses.

Intellenet operates as a closely knit association. It is an alliance of experienced professional investigators and security experts adhering to a set of bylaws and a code of conduct that stresses ethical, professional, and expert business conduct. Member's many-faceted skills are acquired or enhanced through seminars, conferences, and training experience available through Intellenet training activities.

Intellenet members number over 400 individuals, with at least one member in every state and virtually every country throughout the world.

Unlike the majority of private investigation and security associations, Intellenet membership is not a right and is by invitation only, which allows for maintenance of high standards of professional experience and conduct by the members. Membership requires a personal recommendation by an Intellenet member in good standing. Possible candidates must have a minimum of 10 years' experience and comply with all state/country licensing and business requirements.

The membership selection process is structured to ensure the professionalism and ethical conduct of the membership. Secondarily, it is designed to maximize the specialized expertise of the membership while ensuring that any one area of professional expertise or geographical area is not oversaturated with members. This is designed to ensure an equitable distribution of work for each member.

MEMBERSHIP CRITERIA

1. Each prospective member must have a minimum of ten years of verifiable experience in investigative or security activities with emphasis on increased responsibility of the member's years of experience.
2. Each prospective member must be personally recommended by a member of Intellenet in good standing who must attest to the personal and professional experience, conduct, and reputation of the proposed member.
3. The prospective member must complete an application that documents the prospective member's professional employment and experience. The applicant must provide three character references who have known the prospective member for a minimum of five years and can attest to the prospective member's personal and professional qualifications.
4. All prospective and active members must be currently licensed in those jurisdictions where licensing is required. Failure to maintain current licensing will result in immediate termination of membership.
5. Annually, all prospective and active members must agree in writing to abide by the Intellenet code of ethical standards and conduct and the Intellenet bylaws.

Selection Process

Verification of the prospective member's application will be conducted by a designated Intellenet member appointed by the executive director.

1. The scope of the background check will include record checks as appropriate. Conviction of any felony or major misdemeanor offenses will be disqualifying.
2. In those jurisdictions where licensing is not required, criminal record checks will be conducted.
3. Interviews of the applicant's references will be conducted. Additional reference interviews may be conducted at the sole discretion of Intellenet.
4. Any material or deliberate falsification or omission of fact will be disqualifying.
5. Upon completion of the background screening, the application will be forwarded to the Intellenet Executive Director, other designated individual, or the Membership Committee for determination of the applicant's qualifications for membership.
6. The applicant may be approved; disapproved for failure to meet the required minimum professional, ethical, or experience requirements; or placed in abeyance to a later date due to oversaturation of members, expertise, or experience in a geographical area.

FORMER AGENCY AFFILIATION

The breadth of the former agency affiliation of Intellenet members demonstrates the varied experience background available for consultation by all of the membership. In addition to various local and state law enforcement agencies, Intellenet members have served, *inter alia,* with British Customs, Canadian Intelligence, Central Intelligence Agency, Federal Bureau of Investigation, Hungarian Intelligence Service, Immigration and Customs Enforcement, Israeli Mossad, Italian Carabinieri, New Scotland Yard, Royal Canadian Mounted Police, Russian KGB, U.S. State Department, and various military intelligence and investigative agencies.

LANGUAGE SKILLS

The many language skills of Intellenet members include Arabic, Bosnian, Cantonese, Chinese Mandarin, Czech, Farsi, Guarani, Hungarian, Lithuanian, Pashtun, Russian, Serbo-Croatian, Slovakian, Tagalog, and Urdu.

AREAS OF EXPERTISE

Members' areas of expertise include accident reconstruction, arson investigations, asset tracing and recovery, computer forensics, corporate investigations, document examination and analysis, due diligence, executive protection, expert witness, forensic accounting, insurance investigations, litigation support, and missing persons investigations.

ACKNOWLEDGMENTS

I want to express my sincere thanks and appreciation to all of the authors who took valuable time out of their workday to assist with this project. Each author is a member of Intellenet and an experienced professional. This project was undertaken following numerous comments and discussions, and, in some cases, complaints about the problems encountered in transitioning from positions as investigators in various agencies where there was no need to be concerned with marketing, developing clients, and other business activities. We never worried about these issues—work always came to us, sometimes in far greater quantities than we could control. If there was an administrative concern such as getting new equipment, there was always someone to take care of it. Over the years we have all developed our own niche of expertise, thanks to the training programs someone else paid for us to attend.

When we started our private investigation business, we wasted many hours and large sums of money taking a "hit or miss" approach to business requirements. It soon became obvious that we needed a basic education to enter the business world. Over the years, many of us learned expensive lessons and this led to our desire to impart our experience and knowledge to those who will follow us. Each of the authors developed his or her own way of doing business and adopted some strategies that only work for him or her. Others used the more traditional business approach.

There are no written plans or programs designed for organizing a private investigation business. The important thing is to identify a business goal or objective, choose parts of some existing concepts, and do not be afraid to alter your operational plan as necessary changes are identified as you move ahead in your business venture.

The authors' unanimous judgment was that one method for sharing what we learned from our mistakes would be through this publication. There are more comprehensive tomes written on business organization and management but we wanted to provoke the reader's thinking and encourage further inquiry into those business and administrative areas for your success. You are also encouraged to contact the authors for further advice.

CONTENTS

PART II
BASIC INVESTIGATIVE SKILLS

BASIC PRIVATE INVESTIGATION

Part I

BUSINESS ORGANIZATION AND MANAGEMENT

Chapter 1

PRIVATE INVESTIGATION AS A SECOND CAREER

WILLIAM F. BLAKE

Individuals entering the private investigation career field come from many different backgrounds. The vast majority come from law enforcement agencies within the federal and local governments as well as the military services. In recent years, many have come directly into the private investigation market from colleges and universities where they have received degrees in criminal justice, forensic science, or related fields. The influx from the college environment has been greatly influenced by the proliferation of forensic science and investigative television shows. Each of these groups has unique advantages and disadvantages.

Experienced investigators, frequently retirees entering a second career either for additional financial resources or for the love of the business, normally have many years of investigative experience. Depending on the organization from which they retired, they may not have the appropriate management skills for business success. During their career prior to retirement, the organization with which they were employed had a support staff to take care of all of the noninvestigative matters, such as financial administration, supply acquisition and personnel management. Retirees desiring to be business owners must acquire these skills to be successful.

Newcomers from the academic environment may have developed some theoretical skills but lack practical application of these skills. Many of these individuals have been exposed to the latest information and techniques–these they can share with their associates. Some may have been exposed to business subjects while in college but again they lack practical experience in business and personnel management.

The world of private investigation is unlike public law enforcement or corporate investigations. The public law enforcement investigator primarily deals strictly with violation of criminal laws. The corporate investigator may investigate some criminal acts occurring with the corporate environment but may also be involved with inquiries into violation of corporate policies not resulting in criminal acts. The corporate investigator may also be involved in litigation actions for the in-house or outside counsel.

The private investigator may be involved in criminal investigations, corporate internal investigations, and litigation support. The private investigator probably does not have the financial and investigative support resources of the public agency or corporation. This will cause the private investigator to depend frequently on business associates in areas where the investigator does not have appropriate skills.

The philosophies of private investigation and law enforcement are different but also interrelated. Law enforcement investigators are primarily oriented to identifying someone who may have committed a criminal violation. They normally do not look into the cause of the problem or identify measures and strategies to prevent recurrence. The goal of criminal action is to punish or rehabilitate depending on the court philosophy. Restitution is not normally a viable goal. A court may order restitution, but there is little reasonable chance of recovery because of the defendant's prison term and inability to repay.

The goal of the private investigator is multipurposed. It includes identifying the individual responsible for a criminal act or violation of corporate policies. It also includes identifying what precipitated the problem and what strategies can be employed to prevent recurrence. The corporate client will normally be concerned with public relations problems and a desire to recoup financial losses rather than initiate criminal action. Private investigators are frequently tasked to provide investigative and litigation support in legal matters affecting their employer or client.

There are several major differences between private and public sector investigations. In the public sector there is normally a formalized rank reporting structure, with the role of the investigator defined in a bureaucratic manner with strict supervision. In this environment there is normally no maximum cost restriction placed on investigative effort. The goal is the solution of the problem and the identification of the responsible party. No one ever told a law enforcement investigator that he or she must solve a serious crime within a strict budget.

In the private sector, the investigator may be subordinate to an executive who has little or no investigative knowledge. These executive positions may range from chief executive officer to human resources (HR) manager or director of maintenance. This type of organization requires an education and training process for the investigator to achieve appropriate corporate objectives. In the corporate or private environment, cost is always a factor and the bottom line is the only goal. The corporate goal is normally recovery of loss and not referring a matter to law enforcement with the resultant public relations issues.

In simple terms, the law enforcement agent operates in a reactive mode and the private investigator is expected to be proactive. There may be a problem with changing investigative philosophies and actions.

The role of the private investigator in the corporate environment is varied. In addition to the investigation of criminal acts and internal problems, the investigator may become involved in conducting background investigations for executive and sensitive positions as well as conducting due diligence inquires on corporate business associates and vendors.

Another role of the private investigator may be that of executive protection for at-risk individuals. This includes planning, management of, and performance of activities to protect individuals while at home, in the office, or traveling. This activity requires an awareness of risk assessment strategies and interaction with law enforcement in the United States and international venues.

The myriad business possibilities for the private investigator are only limited by the desire to expand business horizons. It is impossible to be an expert in every possible area of private investigation. It is necessary to identify a few areas for concentration of effort where the investigator has special expertise. Expertise in other investigative areas can be developed through association with other investigators with the necessary skills.

An offshoot of the investigative association process is the ability to say "I can do it" to any client request. This allows the investigator to subcontract work to another investigator and still receive a management fee for controlling the investigation. It also increases the probability that your client will request additional work from you instead of going to someone else recommended for lack of expertise.

There are numerous desirable skills that the investigator should have to be successful as a businessperson and to increase investigative knowledge. Initial exposure to these skill sets mandates that investigators remain knowledgeable of new trends and concepts. These desirable skill sets include accounting, business management, criminal and civil law, interpersonal relations, psychology, written and oral communications, computer and information management, investigative techniques, HR, fire and life safety, and professional certifications.

The attainment and maintenance of professional certifications is a vital marketing tool. These professional designations, as long as they have a continuing education requirement, demonstrate that the investigator is keeping up with current information and trends. Professional designations with minimal requirements and lacking a requirement for continuing education are primarily an income-generating process with little professional value.

Starting a private investigation business requires a comprehensive inspection of numerous personal and business skills. The actual process of starting a business will be discussed in more detail in Chapter 2. Some initial considerations include providing answers to the following questions:

1. What are the future opportunities? Can you provide a significant service with an adequate market potential?
2. What is the level of your computer literacy? How competent are you with various business-oriented programs, such as accounting, word processing, database use, and contact management?
3. Is there a willingness to develop a business niche and become an expert in this area? Is there a willingness to avoid a "shotgun" approach to providing business services?
4. Is there a willingness to self-promote and sell investigative services? Can your services be marketed without being labeled as obfuscation?
5. Are you a motivated self-starter? You get what you work for. There will be no one to provide incentive or motivation.

6. Do you have the financial and physical resources to set up an office? What equipment and facilities will be needed?

7. What are the fee and expense schedules of your competitors? How will you set your fee schedule to remain competitive while promoting a professional image?

8. What market areas should be targeted for business opportunities? What is your competition in these areas?

9. Do you have the necessary skills to publish marketing material for your business? Are you willing to be a public speaker as a marketing tool? Publishing and public speaking are the best marketing tools available. Do not "preach to the choir"–get exposure to potential client groups.

10. Are you willing to put in the effort of developing a business plan? A business plan is essential to identify needs, markets, services, and business goal benchmarks.

Developing personal information to provide to potential clients is essential. Among everything else, honesty and integrity must never be compromised. You must always present a professional image. Without a doubt, your personal and business reputation is your most important professional asset. If your reputation is compromised, your investigative skills will never offset your reputation.

Promoting your professionalism takes many roads. The primary information tool is a professional appearing résumé. The content of any résumé is normally suspect because of the tendency of some individuals to prevaricate and embellish their accomplishments. It is cost effective to utilize a competent professional to develop a résumé. You should emphasize your supervisory and management skills. An "accomplishments" résumé is a better format to use. This format identifies the various tasks that you have accomplished and is not just a restatement of work assignments and employers. It is important that you will be interacting with business executives and not office clerks. The executives are interested in how your skills and accomplishments fit into their corporate structure and philosophy.

Networking among various professional and business groups is essential to business success. It is often said that it is not what you know but who you know that will make you successful. Serious consideration should be given to developing alliances with other independent private investigators to identify mutual resources and assist in establishing your reputation.

Depending on your professional background, difficulty may be encountered in interacting at the corporate executive or decision-making level. It is necessary to be comfortable with executives and not be intimidated by their name or position. Remember that "time is money" for the executive, and there is no time for extended personal conversations. When interacting with executives, it is important to remember that they have extensive experience in evaluating individuals. Their evaluation will include your appearance, what you say, and how you interact with the executive. A poor evaluation can be expected if your appearance is not similar to that of the executive or if you make derogatory statements about another individual or business. Younger people must remember that they are not trying to impress their peers but rather the executives. The moral attitudes and opinions of the executives will be generationally driven and normally more formal than those of younger persons.

A significant influence in business marketing is the ability to "think outside the box." It is best to avoid traditional thinking, but it is also extremely important to justify actions based on a "return on investment" for your client. This demonstrates to the executive that you are a professional businessperson with a product or service that will be of value.

A plan must be made for financial resources during the business start-up phase. Many private investigator businesses do not achieve financial success adequate to support personal and business needs for two or more years. Optimism is a virtue and pessimism will defeat your purpose. A long-range vision will justify your early efforts.

The transition from a salaried worker to private businessperson can be challenging. It requires detailed planning, consistent dedication, and a professional attitude to achieve success. Getting established in the private investigation business can be daunting, but the rewards are many.

Chapter 2

ORGANIZING YOUR PRIVATE INVESTIGATION BUSINESS

WILLIAM F. BLAKE

As seen from the experienced eye of another, organizing a personal business can be complicated for many diverse reasons. Integrating previous investigative skills into a successful business is not as easy as we would like it to be. If your prior experience has been with a governmental entity, you will find that governmental and business environments are different. In the governmental environment, there is an administrative structure created by those before us, requiring no action on our part but to follow organizational policy. As we enter the business environment, we discover there are numerous business areas in which we may be lacking in necessary skills. The former organizational environment did not require a specific return on investment—no one required that a serious crime be investigated only to a point where the costs reached a defined limit. There was no concern for legal costs. A private business venture would make cost controls and return on investment new areas in which to develop skills and knowledge.

With the move into the private investigation business, several basic decisions must be made to guide your efforts. One basic decision is "How much money must I make to meet my financial goals?" For some, the amount needed will be a minimal amount; for others, it will require a significant amount of income. Another key concern is "How hard do I want to work?" These two questions will reappear at each stage of your business organization and development.

11

There are certain issues that must be resolved regardless of your business style. The business planning process can be informal or formal depending on the decisions made about your basic financial concerns. Based on the experiences and numerous mistakes of others, it is strongly suggested that anyone starting a business seriously consider developing a formal business plan. Developing a business plan requires that you identify and analytically review the various components required to be a successful business. Prior to retirement or career change, you were considered an investigator; after moving to the private sector you are a businessperson who owns a business selling investigative services. This requires knowledge of basic business skills.

WHO AM I?

The first step in developing your business model is an analytical and realistic evaluation of your investigative and business acumen. As a minimum, you must answer the following questions in great detail:

1. What are my special skills? Example: *I have extensive experience and knowledge in the investigation of financial crimes, homicide, property crime, and traffic accidents, and I am fluent in Spanish.*
2. What are my general investigative skills? *I have above average computer, crime scene processing, interview, and interrogation skills.*
3. What are my investigative interests? *I prefer investigating financial crimes.*
4. What are my business goals? *I want to have a successful business that I can pass along to my children at a later date.*
5. What are my personal goals? *I want to make enough money each year so my wife and I can take a month's vacation and travel to other parts of the world.*
6. How much do I want to work? *I want to work no more than thirty hours per week and never work on weekends or holidays.*
7. How much money do I need to make per year? *I need to make a sufficient monetary profit each year to allow us to travel and to increase my savings for when I quit work completely.*
8. What is the extent of my networking capabilities? *I am an active member of two private investigation associations and expect to receive referrals from other association members.*

WHO ARE MY COMPETITORS?

After identifying your skills, knowledge, areas of expertise, and business and personal goals, it is necessary to determine with whom you will be competing for business opportunities. Your competitors will vary with the size of their organization, financial resources, specific skills and areas of expertise, and reputation. Do not get discouraged. You cannot compete with every investigative organization; you only have to find your niche in the general scheme of things and concentrate on developing your business reputation around this niche.

You can frequently identify your competitors from the telephone Yellow Pages or through local private investigation association membership lists. Once you have identified your competitor firms, it is wise to conduct some research to determine their impact on your business objectives.

Contacting the local Better Business Bureau and the local courts will assist in determining their business activities and reputation. If your competitor has been party to litigation, the court case file may provide you with valuable information. *Is this company a defendant because it did not conduct its activities in a professional and ethical manner or does it have problems with creditors?* These activities will give you a "feel" for the competitor and help you decide if this organization is actually one to be concerned with as a business competitor.

Another area of concern is the geographical area of interest for your competitors. *How does this geographical area overlap with the area in which you would like to concentrate?* Do you have the resources, either as part of your business or through associates, to compete in this geographical area?

It is also important to identify regional and national firms that conduct business in your geographical area of interest. The large national and regional firms normally have contracts with a national business because of the perceived value of having one firm to handle all matters within the corporation. The same theory holds true for governmental contracts and organizations.

WHAT ARE THE INDUSTRY PREDICTIONS FOR THE FUTURE?

Market research is essential to determine the future business opportunities in the private investigation profession. Among several market research firms, the Fredonia Group (www.freedonia.com) conducts research in the private security industry. The following is a sample of their market research:

> U.S. demand to grow 4.7% annually through 2012. U.S. demand for private contracted security services is forecast to advance 4.7 percent per year to almost $66 billion in 2012. Growth will be spurred by a high perceived risk of crime and a belief that public safety officials are overburdened. Gains will also be fueled by an ongoing trend in the privatization of some public safety operations such as guarding government facilities and correctional facilities management. Continuing changes in regulations, including background search and training requirements, and change in security technology make the use of contract security services more effective and less expensive than in-house security departments.[1]

WHAT ARE THE GOVERNMENTAL INFLUENCES ON MY BUSINESS?

Because of public concerns for privacy and identity theft, as well as the publicized misdeeds by corporate entities and private investigators, federal, state, and local governments are reviewing access to information concerning individuals and incidents. The result has been many restrictions on information previously accessible through data research companies. These restrictions particularly impact attempts to identify and locate individuals and to obtain personal information without permission of the concerned individual.

Unfortunately, some states are not willing to require licensing for private investigators as a means of protecting the public from incompetent and unscrupulous investigators. Wyoming and Colorado are two examples of this problem. There have been examples in which the private investigator has been a convicted felon. The Professional Pri-

---

1. *Private Security Services: U.S. Industry Study with Forecasts for 2012 & 2017.* Fredonia Group, www.fredoniagroup.com, February 9, 2010.

vate Investigators Association of Colorado has lobbied for licensing legislation for many years. The Colorado legislature has failed to act, possibly due in part to lobbying efforts of some former investigators who do not see a need for continuing education and insurance. The lack of licensing has created a problem where access to information in another state is restricted to "licensed" private investigators. Additionally, many out-of-state investigative agencies refuse to conduct business with uninsured and unlicensed firms.

The increasing privacy concerns and resultant restrictions may have a serious impact on your future business capabilities. When choosing a direction for your business it is necessary to identify potential problems that could reduce your capability to address specific investigative areas.

WHERE CAN I GET ADVICE AND GUIDANCE IN STARTING MY BUSINESS?

An essential and primary element of starting a business is to get appropriate legal and business advice. Although this can be an expensive process, it is much less costly than trying to start a business while making bad decisions that will be very costly in the future.

It is strongly suggested that you find a competent attorney who practices in the business environment; you do not want a divorce or real estate lawyer to be your legal advisor on business matters. Remember, you get what you pay for! The money spent at this point on competent legal advice will save many headaches in the future.

The Small Business Administration (www.sba.gov) provides many business services to assist in starting your business. Along with documents, they frequently have business seminars that can be very valuable to the start-up business.

The RSVP Program of the Corporation for National and Community Service (www.seniorcorps.org) have experienced business retirees who can provide advice to business owners.

A great source of business advice is to talk with your contemporaries to identify the problems they faced starting a business and how these problems were solved. We may be competitors for investigative services clients, but, based on friendship and other personal concerns, we will normally be able to rely on our contemporaries for advice.

Regardless of the source of your advice, it is wise to analytically review the information and determine how it fits into your proposed business scheme. What works for one person may not be the best advice for another person to follow.

SHOULD I DEVELOP A FORMAL BUSINESS PLAN?

Formal business plan software is readily available and a wise investment. Using a business plan software program such as Planwrite© Business Plan Writer© Deluxe facilitates the compilation of information to develop a plan for your business future. A formal business plan is normally required when obtaining investment funds or subsequent additional financial resources. The plan demonstrates that you have conducted a thorough investigation to identify the potential for success of your business. Even if you do not produce a formal business plan, the software program will identify concepts and areas to be researched to provide guidance for success.

WHAT WILL IT COST TO GET MY BUSINESS STARTED?

Identifying your business start-up costs requires a realistic and analytical approach to determining your business financial needs. Among the many costs to be considered are the professional services of an attorney, a certified public accountant (CPA) and possibly a computer expert. Where your office will be located is a major cost consideration.

Establishing a functioning office can be very expensive. There will be a need for computers, printers, bookcases, copiers, office furniture, filing cabinets, fax machines, office supplies, telephones, equipment maintenance, website development, insurance, licensing, marketing material such as business cards and stationery, and reference material such as dictionaries and industry and legal publications. There should also be a supplemental cost estimate for unanticipated expenses. It is inevitable that you will discover the need for additional equipment and resources as you start your business operations.

If you intend to have employees, you must consider the salary and benefit costs as well as additional equipment needs for each employee.

WHAT IS THE BEST LEGAL STRUCTURE FOR MY BUSINESS?

The legal form of your business can be one of several possibilities based on your personal preference. It may be a sole proprietorship, partnership, limited liability company (LLC), or corporation. It is wise to obtain professional advice from an attorney and CPA regarding making a choice of your business' legal structure.

There are several ways you can structure your business and no one way is necessarily better than another. What suits you best depends on the size and expected profitability of your company, how many owners you have, and the risks involved. There are several options, which will be explained later, that include sole proprietorships, partnerships, LLCs, corporations, and cooperatives.[2]

LEGAL STRUCTURE OVERVIEW

Corporation

Each legal structure has advantages and disadvantages. Basically, a corporation is a legal entity. It is created under the laws of the state in which it is incorporated. The laws of each state vary, some more favorable than others. Federal law under the Securities Act of 1933 regulates how corporate securities (stocks, bonds, etc.) are issued and sold.

A corporation creates an "artificial person" or entity that can sue or be sued, enter into contracts, and perform other duties necessary to maintain a business. The major advantage of a corporation is that the entity shields the individual owners or shareholder from personal liability for the liabilities and debts of the corporation, with some limited exceptions (such as unpaid taxes). The legal "person" status of a corporation also gives it an indefinite life; the termination or death of certain individuals does not alter the corporate structure.

Persons trained in corporate law are responsible for bringing corporations into being. Corporate lawyers structure the stock and bond offerings and the bank and insurance loans that provide enterprises with capital. They also consult about the joint ventures, licensing arrangements, mergers, acquisitions, and the myriad of other transactions entered into by the corporation.

---

2. www.legal-definitions.info

Limited Liability Company

You have probably heard a great deal about LLCs and probably see that many of businesses are using this legal structure with good reason. LLCs have the advantages of a corporation and of a sole proprietorship and a partnership rolled into one. Many small business owners and entrepreneurs prefer LLCs because they combine the limited liability protection of a corporation and the pass through taxation of a sole proprietorship or partnership. The LLC is responsible for the debts and liabilities of the business, meaning you will not be personally liable, and taxes pass through like a partnership, for example, on your personal tax returns. You heard correctly: no personal liability and no separate business tax returns.

Until a few years ago, the LLC was not recognized in all states. Another downside to an LLC is that it does not offer the free transferability of ownership, perpetual existence, and the ability to be totally owned by a single individual that one gets with a corporation, although in many states, sole proprietors can form LLCs.

Another disadvantage is that forming an LLC is more expensive than a partnership or a sole proprietorship is. You have to draft articles of organization and file them with your state to get LLC status, and–in addition to the paperwork–this can be somewhat expensive, in the range of a few hundred dollars, depending on the state. If you are looking for the requisite paperwork, you can probably get LLC forms from a library or Internet source. These forms are basically templates you fill out and mail to your state's Secretary of State. It is wise to consider the old saying that a person who represents himself in court has a fool for a lawyer.

Partnerships

Partnerships are like sole proprietorships for two or more people. Normally there is no need to register your partnership with the state. Like the sole proprietorship, you are taxed individually, in other words, each partner is taxed on the partnership's profits, so there is no need to file separate returns for your business.

Although you do not have to register a partnership, it is well-advised to draft a written agreement laying out the terms of the partnership. The partnership agreement, at a minimum, should outline each partner's share of the profits and losses and the funding obligations. Furthermore, the partnership agreement should detail what happens to the business should one of the partners die or wish to leave the business.

The major disadvantage is that the members of a general partnership are fully liable for the debts and obligations of the partnership. If the company is sued, then each partner will have to pay the damages and attorney's fees. If the damages are steep, you lose your shirt and your house!

A limited partnership is similar to a general partnership except that the limited partners are only liable for what they put into the partnership. Limited partners are like investors in the partnership; they can only lose what they invest. However, limited partners are not allowed to have any say in the management of the partnership.

Sole Proprietorship

If you are starting a company on your own, you may be best off going with a sole proprietorship as long as you are aware of the disadvantages of this structure. With a sole proprietorship, you need only two things: a business license, if required and—unless you are using your own name—a DBA ("doing business as") fictitious business name statement, which you file with your state. Otherwise, this method requires little or no paperwork and can be conducted swiftly. You do not have to register your company. You are, however, personally liable for the company's debts and liabilities. Sole proprietorships should also only be used if your business is owned by one person. For tax purposes, your sole proprietorship is no different than you are: you file your business taxes on your personal tax form.

Doing Business As

Companies file DBAs with the state in which they are doing business under a particular business name. This serves to protect the identity of the company within the state. To apply for a DBA, you must contact your Secretary of State's office, and there is a small fee.

Subchapter S Corporation

A Subchapter S Corporation is a corporation that has elected a special tax status with the Internal Revenue Service (IRS). The main advantage associated with the S corporation is that the income passes through to the shareholders, thus avoiding the double taxation of a C corporation. S corporations are most appropriate for small business owners and entrepreneurs who want to be taxed as if they were sole proprietors or partners; this is a pass through tax structure, meaning you file profits and losses on your personal tax returns.

Unlike an LLC, which can have an unlimited number of members, an S corporation is restricted to no more than seventy-five shareholders. An S corporation also requires formalities. At least one meeting of shareholders and directors is required each year, and meeting minutes are required to be kept with the corporation's records. Furthermore, an S corporation is perpetual in existence, whereas LLCs are limited to the lifespan of the members. With an S corporation, ownership can be transferred through stock; in an LLC, ownership is fixed.

General C Corporation

Unless you are operating a huge business, C corporations are probably not for you. A general corporation is the most common corporate type used by larger businesses. A general corporation may have an unlimited number of stockholders. A C corporation is normally chosen by those businesses that are planning to have more than thirty stockholders or planning a large, public stock offering. These general corporations usually pay taxes at two levels. First, the corporation is required to pay taxes based on the corporation's profits. Additionally, the owner or shareholder is taxed when the corporation distributes profits, known as dividends, to the individual.

Closed Corporation

A closely held corporation usually limits the number of shareholders or owners to no more than thirty. Additionally, the transfer of ownership or shares of stock is restricted and most of the shareholders are actively involved in the management of the business. Closed corporations are generally run by family members. Shares of a closed corporation are not normally traded on a stock exchange.

Nonprofit Corporation

More often than not, a nonprofit corporation begins as a nonprofit association—a loosely constructed organization run by mostly volunteers. In a nonprofit association, the members can be held liable for the debts and liabilities of the organization.

If a nonprofit association stays afloat long enough, it often seeks to gain tax-exempt status and attract donors by becoming a nonprofit organization. Once incorporated, not only can the organization gain tax-exempt status from the IRS, but also the individual members will no longer be subject to the debts and liabilities of the organization.

Becoming a nonprofit corporation is no more difficult than registering as an LLC. You draft articles of organization and file them with the Secretary of State. You must then submit your incorporation papers to the IRS to gain tax-exempt status under IRS Section 501(c) (3). To gain tax exempt status, you must obtain and fill out (likely with the assistance of a lawyer and/or accountant) IRS Package 1023.

The caveat to being a nonprofit corporation is that the assets of your organization must be dedicated to charitable, educational, religious, or similar purposes. Moreover, nonprofit corporations cannot campaign or lobby for or against political candidates. Finally, taxes must be paid on any profits the nonprofit organization makes.

HOW DO I CHOOSE A BUSINESS NAME?

The name of your corporate entity must be chosen carefully because having a name identical with, or similar to, another business entity will cause you nothing but grief. Corporate names may be checked through the Office of the Secretary of State in the state in which your business will be established. Once your business name has been chosen, it is necessary to register your business with the Secretary of State and the applicable tax and employment units.

Care should be taken when choosing a business name. The name will have an impact on your reputation and marketing efforts. When choosing a business name, consideration should be given to the salability of that name at a later date. Names such as "Madman Investigations" or "Killer Investigations" can be fatal if, in the eyes of the public, it represents a business that is more facetious than professional.

DO I NEED INSURANCE?

It can be business suicide to operate without adequate insurance to protect your investment. Errors and omissions (E & O) insurance protects you against mistakes that you make during your business operations. It does not necessarily protect you from the misdeeds of any subcontractors you may utilize. Therefore, it is important than any subcontractor be required to provide documentary evidence of E & O and workers' compensation insurance prior to conducting any work for you. E & O insurance providers frequently audit policyholders for evidence of insurance by subcontractors. If you have a subcontractor without insurance, your E & O provider may cancel or greatly increase the premium for your insurance. It is best to operate with a policy that there is no subcontracted work without insurance.

Another insurance issue is that of workers' compensation. Depending on the laws of your state, you may not be required to have workers' compensation insurance if you do not have employees. If your subcontractor does not have workers' compensation insurance and is injured doing work for you, he will be considered your employee. If you do not have workers' compensation, depending on state law, you may be liable for treble damages as a penalty for medical and rehabilitation costs as well as any legal settlement. As the owner or officer of a company, you can exclude yourself from workers' compensation insurance but it is wise to carry a policy just to cover your firm from a claim by a subcontractor.

Proof of automobile liability insurance required by the state should be another requirement for each subcontractor. If the subcontractor does not have the necessary insurance and becomes involved in an accident while conducting business on your behalf, you may find yourself as a defendant in civil litigation. It is important to develop a "hard-nosed" approach on the issues of insurance. You can either enforce proof of insurance or suffer the possible financial ramifications.

DO I NEED AN OFFICE STAFF?

Whether you need an office staff depends on some of your personal skills. If you have relatively good typing and computer skills, you may not need someone to do your typing initially. Not only will it be necessary to type routine reports, but also it will be necessary to prepare correspondence and other documents in a proper business style and format. With a little bit of effort on your part, you can easily develop the necessary skills.

Another area of administrative concern is an office accounting system. There are several accounting software programs that can be understood and utilized by anyone. An accounting or bookkeeping background is not necessary. Many private investigators use Quick-Books and find that it is easy to use and can be configured to meet your needs. It allows for the preparation of invoices, check payments, and receipt of income. It also allows for the preparation of financial reports, job costing, and payroll matters.

There is nothing more frustrating than to call an individual's office and not receive an answer. There are several means for responding to a caller when you are not available. One way is to have a good quality voice mail system that provides for the receipt of a message and also gives information for an alternate contact method, such as a cellular telephone number, that is continually monitored.

Telephone answering services provide a more personal response to calls in your absence. The caller can interact with the service operator in the same manner as an office receptionist. The personal touch with a human being instead of a voice message recorder is a more professional touch.

HOW DO I MARKET MY BUSINESS?

Using the services of a marketing expert is expensive but can be profitable in the long run. This person will be able to assist in developing your advertising, including business cards, stationery, and brochures. To assist in your marketing endeavors, "branding" of your business is essential. Branding, a commonly used term throughout the business world, essentially means to create an identifiable entity that makes a promise of value. It means that you have created a consciousness, an image, and an awareness of your business. It is your company's personality.

A brand is also a kind of promise. It is a set of fundamental principles as understood by anyone who comes into contact with a company. A brand is an organization's "reason for being." It is how that reason is expressed through the various communications to its key audiences, including customers, shareholders, employees, and analysts. A brand should also represent the desired attributes of a company's products, services, and initiatives. Many businesses try but fail to create a successful brand. Here are ten of the most common mistakes:

1. **Not thinking analytically.** Too many companies think of branding as marketing or as having a catch phrase or a logo. It is more than simply vying for attention. A brand warrants attention on a consistent basis, and represents something that your customer wants, but does not get, from your competitors. For example, it could be providing the best customer service in your industry—not just through your tagline or logo—but by actually providing the best customer service in your industry.

2. **Not maintaining your brand.** Too often, in a shaky economy, businesses are quick to change or alter their identity. Too much of this confuses your steady customers. For guidance, think of big brands: Nike, for instance has used "Just Do It" as a slogan for years. One rule of thumb is that it is when you have become tired of your logo, tagline, or branding efforts, that they begin to sink in with customers.

3. **Trying to appease everyone.** You will never be able to brand yourself in such a way that everyone will like you. Typically, the best you can do is to focus on the niche market for your product.

4. **Not knowing who you really are.** If you are not the fastest overnight delivery service in the world, do not profess to be. Too many business owners think that they are providing something that they do not provide. Know your strengths and weaknesses through honest analysis of what you do best.

5. **Not fully committing to branding.** Often business owners let the marketing and advertising departments handle such things as branding, while others work on sales and other important parts of the business. Sales and branding, however, are tied together as integral aspects of your business. Many Fortune 500 companies are where they are today because smart branding made them household names.

6. **Not sharing the joke.** If only the people in your office get a joke, it is not going to play to a large audience. The same holds true for branding. If your campaign is created for you and not "them," your brand will not succeed.

7. **Not having a dedicated marketing plan.** Many companies come up with ideas to market themselves and establish a brand identity but have neither the resources nor a plan for how they will reach their audience. You must have a well-thought-out marketing plan in place before your branding strategy will work.

8. **Using too much jargon.** Business-to-business-based companies are most guilty of piling on the jargon. From benchmark to strategic partnering to value added, jargon does not benefit branding. If anything, it muddles your message.

9. **Trying too hard to be different.** Being different for the sake of being different is not branding. Yes, you will be noticed, but not necessarily in a way that increases sales.

10. **Not knowing when you have them.** Companies that have succeeded in branding need to know when to spend fewer resources on establishing their brand, while continuing to maintain that which they have established. Monitor the results of your branding campaign. If your small business is a local household word, you can spend more time maintaining your professional image.

Not unlike a business plan, a marketing plan can play an important role in the success of your small business. Although the plan is primarily for your purposes, it should include

- your products and/or services
- your demographic audience
- methods of selling
- pricing
- your budget
- your geographic market
- your competition and your competitive edge
- an overview of the marketing tools available: media outlets, public relations (PR) possibilities, community activities, conferences, potential speaking engagements, and so on.

The final objective of your marketing plan is to define whom you are trying to reach, what you are selling, how you will reach this audience, and how much it will cost to do so. You will then devise a means of communicating your message to your audience.

Just as you do in your business plan, you will need to pull the many pieces together to demonstrate how you will reach your target audience. For example, if your plan is to increase the sale of your brand of healthy popcorn to a teen market, you might show how you will distribute samples at school activities, sponsor a series of events for teens, and propose articles on the health benefits of your popcorn to teen-oriented magazines and web sites.

Within your marketing plan, show how you will use diverse methods to get your message across, including different forms of media, product samples, sponsorship, and so on. Also, maintain a level of marketing at all times. In busier seasons, you will need a more aggressive approach; during the slower seasons, you may just want to keep your brand in front of your audience. Define such a strategy in your plan.

There are numerous cost-effective marketing tools. A goal of your marketing program is getting personal and business exposure. This is easily accomplished by seeking out speaking opportunities with potential client groups. Many professional organizations are constantly looking for free meeting and dinner speakers. This is an opportunity to distribute business cards and identify potential clients. It also provides potential clients with the opportunity to evaluate you and your business.

Writing guest articles for local newspapers is another method of getting introduced to the public. Consideration should be given to providing articles to the smaller neighborhood newspapers. Most cities have a weekly "business journal" and welcome business-related articles. The business journals frequently produce a book of lists that will identify various business groups, along with some identifying information on each business.

Writing articles for professional publications is an effective marketing tool. This gives the public an opportunity to evaluate your professional and business knowledge; however, this activity should not be restricted to professional journals pertaining to your area of expertise. This is similar to "preaching to the choir," and your clients will normally come from noninvestigative sources. For example, consider authoring an article relating to the Employee Polygraph Protection Act of 1988 for a HR or business publication. Such an article will provide advice to potential clients and demonstrate that you are aware of restrictions placed on your investigative activities.

HOW DO I DEVELOP A CLIENT BASE?

The best method for initially developing a client base is working with "the good old boy" network, both within and outside the investigation arena. Investigators who do pro bono work will eventually get clients through this activity. Pro bono work frequently becomes the subject of local media attention, and this is free advertising. It may be to your advantage to develop a subcontractor relationship with a larger firm but never succumb to "stealing" the firm's clients.

Some individuals have been successful in contacting large corporations or law firms and working as a contractor at reduced rates to develop a reputation within the community. Although you may work as an investigator for one party in litigation, your adversary will form an opinion of your professional expertise that may lead to work for you, either through the adversary's firm or via referral to another firm.

Essential to obtaining repeat business from a client is the manner in which you treat your client. Business firms and attorneys normally have a very heavy appointment schedule, and it is a cardinal sin to not keep an appointment or to be late for an appointment. Time is money to your clients, and they will drop you as an investigative resource if your apathy or carelessness costs them productive time.

It is also imperative that you keep your commitments and perform tasks or provide reports on an agreed-upon basis and time frame. When meeting with a client, it is normally best to work at a highly professional level. It is not time for gossip or discussion of the latest sporting events. Again, time is money.

HOW DO I ESTABLISH A FEE SCHEDULE?

This is the most difficult part of starting a business. To be competitive, your fee schedule cannot be too extreme or out of alignment with your competition. As a start-up business, if you set your fees too high, you will lose business to the more-established firms that work at a more affordable rate. If you set your fees too low, potential clients may wonder about your work quality and professional abilities. An individual who purports to have many years of experience should not set a fee schedule that is appropriate for an apprentice investigator. Your fee schedule should consider the influences of your level of expertise, the complexity of the case, your actual time and expense costs, and a realization of what the client feels is an appropriate return on his investment. As conditions and circumstances change, it may be necessary to adjust your fee schedule to meet changing situations.

In some cases it may be advantageous to work on a fixed fee basis. However, experience has shown that it is preferable to work on a time and expense basis. Situations change frequently and dramatically, and this causes problems in the fixed fee situation.

HOW DO I IDENTIFY AND WORK WITH COMPETENT SUBCONTRACTORS?

One of the better methods of identifying competent subcontractors is to seek referrals from your contemporaries. It is strongly suggested that you require the potential subcontractor to provide you with a résumé of his or her qualifications and experiences. A list of at least five clients for whom the subcontractor has worked in an investigative capacity should also be provided. Contact with the references should include queries about the type of work performed, the quality and detail of the investigative effort, report writing skills, and additional references. An identified number of years of verifiable experience should be a minimum standard for utilization as a subcontractor. Even though the individual is a subcontractor, you should make your choice based on whether or not you would hire the individual as an employee.

To ensure that there are no problems with the IRS, it is important to identify the appropriate interaction between the contractor and subcontractor. A general rule is that the employer, as the payer, has the right to control or direct only the results of the work done by an independent contractor and not the means and methods of accomplishing the results.

It is wise to have a written agreement with the subcontractor that defines your requirements and expectations for all activities conducted on your behalf. This agreement can cover more than one assignment. Instructions for a specific assignment should be conveyed to the subcontractor in a letter of instruction.

WHERE SHOULD I LOCATE MY OFFICE?

There are several options for an office location with advantages and disadvantages to each. Many start-up businesses have their initial office in the owner's residence. Because the residence mortgage or rental costs are the personal responsibility of the occupant, establishing a home office does not increase these costs. One advantage of the home office is the ability to work in an informal environment at any time of the day. The major disadvantages include conflicts and interference with family activities, a tendency to work excessive hours because of the ease of addressing business requirements, and lack of appropriate meeting space.

It is not wise to meet a client in your residence because the informal nature of the meeting place may have an adverse effect on your professional image and family activities. One solution to this problem is to identify facilities with free or inexpensive meeting rooms. Many public libraries have areas that can be reserved for meeting with clients. Many executive suite management offices have conference rooms that can be rented at a reasonable cost.

Locating your office in a city center area can be an expensive proposition. Although there may be a degree of prestige in having your office in a commercial building, the normal rental costs are based on a square footage basis and require a multiyear lease. It is important to remember that you will also be obligated to pay proportional costs of common areas within the building. If the building has a large lobby or atrium area, these additional costs can be substantial. Additionally, there is normally the cost of parking for you and any employees. There also may be a parking problem for your clients when they visit your office. City center parking lots and garages are normally expensive and metered parking is limited.

A third alternative is utilizing the services of an executive suite facility. This provides you with office space and an address that is identifiable with your business. These businesses usually provide telephone services and will answer the telephone with your business name. They may also provide receptionist services, conference rooms with audio-visual capability, and clerical services.

HOW SHOULD I DOCUMENT MY INVESTIGATIVE ACTIVITIES?

It is important to remember that your records may be subject to a court subpoena and critique by the court. Your files must be complete and accurate and have a professional appearance. The routine that you follow to document your activities should be precise and followed conscientiously and consistently in all cases.

Your primary case records should consist of a case log that, as a minimum, identifies the case number, subject and/or client, date of receipt, and type of matter. Secondarily, a case name log is a necessary cross-reference to identify the relevant case file. An activity file is an important document for each case file that briefly identifies your investigative activities to date. The activity file also provides a means of documenting time and expenses for that case. Using the activity file in this manner allows you to expeditiously report your costs to date if you receive a call from a client. If you have to respond to the client with "I will have to figure it out and call you back," it indicates to the client that you are disorganized when it comes to time and money issues. This may cause your client to wonder if you also conduct your investigative activities in a disorganized manner.

As with all important documents, your investigative files should be backed up periodically to another media. When the matter is completed, the computer files should be copied to a diskette, CD/DVD, or USB flash drive and be placed in a secured storage area along with your paper files. Your case files should be retained for at least five years or longer if the matter is still in litigation or under appeal. Any physical or documentary evidence should be stored under rigidly controlled circumstances in the event that it is required for court at a later date.

There are numerous case management software programs on the market to assist in documentation of investigative activities and control of time and expense costs. At agreed upon times, investigative progress should be verbally reported to the client, with a final written report upon conclusion of investigative activities. Periodic written or draft reports may put you in a position to defend your actions against claims that you allowed the client to shape your report if the situation changes dramatically during the course of your investigation.

HOW DO I INVOICE MY CLIENT FOR MY SERVICES?

The actions that you take to receive payment for your services should be discussed in detail with your client prior to the initiation of any investigative activity. When dealing with an attorney, it must be understood by all parties that the attorney and the law firm are your clients, and they are therefore responsible for paying you for your services. Your agreement should never be that you will invoice the attorney's client for your services. The attorney chose to do business with his client and they had a mutual agreement on fees, normally including an advance retainer fee. You did not choose to do business with the attorney's client, and therefore the attorney, and not the attorney's client, is responsible for paying your invoice.

In most situations, regardless of the client, it is wise to demand an up-front payment sufficient to cover the first 25 percent of your anticipated time and expense costs. After the initial retainer, the client should be invoiced at least on a monthly basis. The invoice should demand payment upon receipt of the invoice. If payment is not received by a stated date, no further investigative activity should be conducted until all invoices are paid in full and another retainer fee is received. At this point, all future investigative activity should require prepayment against a future invoice. Under no circumstances should you agree to work under a contingent fee agreement.

In the rare event that an attorney does not pay your invoice as agreed, it is prudent to send the attorney a return receipt letter by certified mail demanding payment within a stated number of days or the matter will be referred to the state bar association or other state regulatory agency for assistance in receiving payment. If it is necessary to address the nonpayment with the regulatory authority, they should be provided via certified mail with copies of any correspondence, contracts or letters of agreement, your payment demand letters and actions, and invoices. Normally, the attorney will pay your invoice in an expeditious manner.

If your client is reluctant to execute a contract for your services, the client should be sent a return receipt letter by certified mail that summarizes your understanding of the services requested, the agreed-upon fee schedule, and expected payment. The last paragraph of the letter should state that the client must notify you in writing of the disputed points within a stated time frame. Unless a notice of disagreement or dispute is received by a stated date, the letter will serve in lieu of a contract.

SUMMARY

Starting a private investigation business requires skills not normally found in other investigative environments. A detailed analysis of your abilities, market influences, and client development is necessary to be a successful businessperson. Realistic, and not idealistic, insight is a major requirement. Success takes time but is attainable in the longer term.

Chapter 3

TRANSITIONING FROM LAW ENFORCEMENT TO A CAREER AS A PRIVATE INVESTIGATOR

DALE J. SEYMOUR

If you are considering transferring from a law enforcement career into the field of private investigations, look before you leap. It is often difficult or impossible to return to a position that you abandoned to seek greener pastures. There are two ways to make the transition from a law enforcement career to being a private investigator. The easiest and obviously most secure way is to wait until reaching your retirement eligibility date before you make the transition. The other is to change careers prior to retirement. You should check with your HR advisor and see if there is a period of time during which you can return to your job or receive preferential treatment for other job openings in either case. Many law enforcement careers offer retirement packages after twenty years or more of service that include a pension and continued health benefits for the rest of your life, a deal too lucrative to pass up if you are anywhere near reaching that milestone. If you are unhappy at work, feel there is little chance for advancement or new challenges, and have a long way to go, then you should leave when a better opportunity comes along or create one for yourself. Time can pass quickly, so if it is only a matter of several years before you can retire and collect a pension, by all means stay where you are, make the most of a difficult situation, and prepare to embark on a new career. Some law enforcement organizations allow their personnel to work part-time as investigators with written permission, so if that opportunity presents itself to you be sure to take it and test the waters, but always with the requisite permission obtained first.

How can you prepare for a successful career as a private investigator while working at your chosen law enforcement profession? There are some basic questions you must ask yourself before you decide. Am I disciplined enough to work independently without the team concept? Do I have sufficient business skills to run a business? By believing in yourself, learning whatever you can about being self-employed, speaking with reputable private investigators to learn the nuances to succeed in the private sector, and networking whenever possible to expand your contact base, you will have a better idea if such a career change is right for you. Never forget for whom you are currently working and always go the extra mile while at work. Be willing to expend your time in furtherance of a worthwhile objective without being a clock-watcher more concerned with overtime pay than with the successful outcome of a case and keep an open mind in all investigations. Learn to minimize your mistakes by seeking and heeding sound advice from others. Develop a friendly working relationship with prosecutors and defense attorneys rather than giving them "attitude." They will not want to work with you as a private investigator if their experiences with you while you were on the job were not pleasant and professional. Your reputation may precede you and will be your best form of advertising. Develop the ability to relate to people from all different walks of life and be empathetic to their situations. It is far easier to get a person to consent to an interview, tell you the truth, or even confess when you convey a caring and responsible interest in someone's situation. Sincerity and hard work are far more effective than many tactics depicted on television. Read *How to Win Friends and Influence People* by Dale Carnegie for starters.

The most important overall skill to possess as a private investigator is the ability to conduct an in-depth interview and then write a detailed objective report of your findings. These reports and memoranda of interviews may someday be the key documents in some form of litigation. Information in your head has little value to clients compared to what they can read and easily retrieve via a printed report or an e-mail version saved on their computer. Become accustomed to printing and then reading your final report to eliminate mistakes that "spell-check" misses and to ensure factually and grammatically correct easy-to-read detailed reports.

Have you developed special skills that are in various levels of demand in the private sector? Here is a partial list: financial fraud investigations, polygraph examiner, accident reconstruction, facility security assessments, questioned document examiner, fingerprint expert, database researcher, surveillance and computer forensics examiner. Other skills such as supervising an investigative unit will assist you when transitioning to a career job in many industries such as insurance and banking.

Never underestimate the value of your training and years of experience as an investigator. You should also be proud of your integrity, ability to work under stressful and rapidly changing situations on important matters, and your ability to work long hours. Most private investigators usually work normal business hours, but interviews or surveillance on nights and weekends sometimes arise. You must be flexible and work when and where your business demands it.

Be prepared to learn new skills and understand that you must continually strive to improve your performance. Join reputable professional organizations such as INTELLENET, ASIS International or the Association of Certified Fraud Examiners and gain the benefit of a worldwide network of associates, many with invaluable special skills. If possible, join before you leave your present job so that you will have their collective knowledge and experience to draw upon. Learn about their certification programs and become certified. Attend the seminars and annual conferences they provide. Such events are costly and in most cases you will be paying the bill, rather than your former government employer. However, paying for your continuing education is a worthwhile investment. Join the professional organizations that are right for you. Most states have an organization for licensed private investigators. Join it, attend their meetings, and network with others. Offer to help others in your field.

If you want to make yourself marketable to the corporate security community then you should learn about facility access control, closed-circuit television (CCTV) systems, managing a security guard force, and overseeing a background investigation program, among other things.

When you begin your business, you may wish to consider working as a contract investigator for a large investigative firm while you are developing your own clients. Are there any firms near you and do you know anyone who works there? If you have been working in the same area for many years, it is reasonable to conclude that your present location is where you have established your reputation and contact base. Hence, you should "bloom where you are planted." If not, consider relocating if it is feasible and suits your family plans. If you are collecting a decent pension and your financial house is in order, you may be able to work on a part-time basis from a home office. That way, you eliminate a lot of overhead and commuting. If you intend to form a working partnership with others and develop a larger full-time business, renting suitable office space is necessary.

Be sure to learn of the licensing requirements in the states where you wish to practice before you make the transition. Most require qualifying experience, a background check, and references prior to being licensed as well as being bonded and insured. Some require passing an initial examination and continuing to obtain education credits in order to renew your license. Are you aware of the tax consequences of being self-employed? One of the best ways to learn about transitioning from a law enforcement career to the business of private investigations is to talk to those retirees who have successfully made the transition. If you do not personally know such a person, surely one of your law enforcement friends does. Do not rely on a phone call to seek information. Meet with experienced persons in the field and let them tell you about their experiences. Do not forget to pick up the tab for their lunch or dinner and become accustomed to saving your receipts for the appropriate business expense deductions.

If you decide to leave your career in law enforcement for the private sector, there are many things you must do in order to become and stay successful. Of primary importance is your self-development. To achieve success in this continuing process, that helping hand you are looking for is at the end of your own arm. You must develop a reputation for integrity, reliability, fairness, resourcefulness, and delivering high-quality services and reports. You will gain more business from referrals from happy clients, especially attorneys, than from anything else. Learn to underpromise and overdeliver. Learn to view each case with an open mind, think creatively and review all available information or evidence, whether it hurts or supports your client's case or not. Remember this quote from the fictional detective Sherlock Holmes:

"The temptation to form premature theories upon insufficient data is the bane of our profession."

Never forget where you came from and the respect you had for your law enforcement colleagues while working with them. Regardless of the beliefs of some of them, you are not going to "the dark side" when working for a defense attorney in a criminal case. You will be working to gain accurate and complete information of what your client is accused of doing, just as in your previous career, but usually with a lot more time available to you. Law enforcement gets it right in the great majority of cases. Maintain your respect for your former colleagues but realize that even the best of them can and do make mistakes, and you might be asked to review their work to ensure accuracy and compliance with the law and their guidelines. On the other hand, you might be surprised to learn that not all clients tell their defense attorney the truth about their situation. This makes defense of their case more difficult and costly, and more challenging for you.

Even though you will become a "private" investigator your work product, in most cases, will belong to the attorney who has retained you. In that regard, you must understand your obligation to keep that information confidential. You cannot share it or trade it with anyone, especially if that person is a member of the law enforcement community and you need information from them. Having contacts in the law enforcement community and the courts is a great benefit, but you cannot ask those contacts to obtain information for you that you are not entitled to receive anymore. If you ask for and are given such things as criminal history, motor vehicle department information, and active case reports from restricted databases or files, you could expose your friends who provide them, as well as yourself, with work sanctions and/or prosecution. Instead, you must use what is legally available to you from public records, private vendors, and subscription websites.

You must realize that you will be going into two new careers. The obvious one is the transition from a government investigator to a private investigator. Of equal importance, if self-employed, is the realization that you must now learn how to manage your own business. Most small businesses fail within the first several years for one of two reasons: undercapitalization or lack of experience in owning and operating that business. Let us begin with your start-up costs, or part of your business investment, which should be moderate at best unless you want to lease and furnish a nice office. You may need, among other things, a good desktop computer, scanner, fax machine, photocopier, digital camera, camcorder, filing cabinets, desk and office chair, a laptop computer and portable printer, a separate office and fax phone line, business cards, and letterhead stationery. You need to consider how you want to receive your business mail: at your office address or at a private postal facility such as UPS or Mailboxes, Etc. Obviously you will want to resolve this prior to procuring business cards and stationery. Consider using a computer program like QuickBooks to help you keep track of the business finances. You will also need a federal tax ID number and a state tax ID number, and a separate business checking account.

You may wish to have your attorney establish an LLC for your business. You should purchase professional liability insurance, whether it is required or not in your state. Remember that you will be exposed to being sued, even if you are careful, and the government will not be there to defend your actions. Some state licensing fees are expensive, and some states also require bonding. Speak with an accountant about your new tax responsibilities. You will be required to pay estimated quarterly taxes to both the IRS and your state government, and you may also be liable to pay quarterly state sales taxes if your investigative services are subject to sales tax in your state. You must maintain clear and concise books and records to document your income and expenses. You may now wish to have an accountant prepare your tax returns to allow for the proper credit for depreciation and all legitimate expenses. Understand that part of the capitalization process is having enough cash to pay your normal living expenses while you wait for your business to turn a profit. Collecting a pension and working from your home when you start is a big advantage. As your business becomes more established, or if you want to initially form a partnership, then you should consider leasing professional office space.

Do not forget the continual expenses of professional organization dues and meeting costs, seminars, and networking events. You may wish to join civic organizations such as Rotary International and your local chamber of commerce to promote your business, meet new friends, and do something good for your community. Such costs can usually be considered valid business expenses deductible from your tax return, but that does not mean that the money you spent will be refunded to you. It only decreases your tax liability. Many people who have had a successful career in law enforcement have the ability to start a private investigation business, but not all of them succeed because they fail to plan for their business costs and developing new business.

I am proud to have had a long and successful career in law enforcement and consider my transition to the private sector a success. I join many of my colleagues who are contributors to this book in encouraging you to consider a career as a private investigator. We did it, and so can you!

Chapter 4

BUT, I'M NOT EX-LAW ENFORCEMENT OR MILITARY: CAN I DO THIS?

GREGORY J. CALDWELL

By now you have read the first chapters and been treated to some very pragmatic and valuable advice regarding your transition from a former law enforcement or military career to the private sector. There is much more to come in later chapters. To that end, this may be the best book you will ever purchase because not only have most of the contributing authors successfully and similarly transitioned but also, they have, over the years, mentored many others in that regard.

Although the remainder of this book addresses the more practical and specific "how to" of private investigations, one question has not been addressed yet. How does someone who does not have a former career in federal, municipal, or military law enforcement break into the private investigations business?

In private investigations, there are a variety of first steps that may be taken on the path to achieve that goal. Not unlike some other careers, it could be argued that one's experiential background will have more to do with success as a private investigator than one's educational background will. Think about that for a moment. The totality of your life experiences to this point may have more bearing on your success as a private investigator than your formal education will.

As an example, to become a practicing attorney essentially requires two college degrees: a Bachelor's and Juris Doctor and the ability to pass a bar exam. Collectively, however, they will not guarantee that the bearer will be anything other than a mediocre lawyer. Instinctively, we know that. Great and even good attorneys bring other intangible yet important attributes with them to the law. So it is with private investigations.

ARE YOU AN INVESTIGATOR?

Although this may seem counterintuitive, it is not. It may be the most misunderstood lesson of all.

A degree in criminal justice, tenure being an ex-cop, certifications from various organizations, having a $100,000 annual marketing budget will all help, but none will make you a good private investigator. So, where to start?

If you are entering this field without a past career in law enforcement, this then is your chapter. Let us get the obvious out of the way.

As a private investigator, your new "thing" is your time and knowledge. Time is not an issue—you have plenty of it—more than 10,000 minutes every week, some of which you could be billing a client for if you have the knowledge someone needs. Simple, right?

Knowledge, however, is subjectively defined and obtained from myriad sources. The two obvious ones are past work and educational experience. No one will deny education is a wonderful thing. Graduation from an institution of higher learning will always serve you well. Formal education has also evolved.

Forty years ago a criminal justice degree was almost always an associate or two-year program. Thirty years ago, they became bachelor's programs, and since 9/11 they have branched into hundreds of specialties, most lumped under homeland security, law enforcement, firefighting, or related protective services. The purpose here is not to suggest one approach or program over another or to disparage any. Simply said, an appropriate degree will help you in this career choice. Appropriate, however, is also subjective; it could mean a degree in journalism, accounting, behavioral science, business administration, emergency management, information technology, communications, or even fine art. There are no restrictions; any degree will benefit and smooth the path for you.

What we are focused on here, however, is experience. If you have no previous law enforcement experience, cynics would suggest you have no experience investigating anything, regardless of your degree. Succinct, perhaps, but generally without merit.

Say you were someone who grew up in a family that owned restaurants. By high school and beyond, you would have probably experienced every facet of the business. If your parents were smart, you would have washed dishes, mopped floors, bussed tables, waited tables, tended bar, did kitchen prep, prepared menus, counted cash drawers, purchased and been responsible for inventory, and made payroll for the other employees. If you were that lucky, you became, by osmosis and hands-on experience, an expert in the hospitality industry. You probably learned how to calculate losses and project profits and how to set goals and, when the latter was not achieved, to go back and find out why. Were your projections off? Were sales up, but profits down? What does that suggest? Were you missing inventory, such as food, liquor, or tableware? In learning to manage the business what you had to do was become a pretty good investigator if you were to survive and prosper. If answers were not obvious, you dug in and around until you found them.

Likewise for a reporter, at least reporters in the old days who did not just print someone's press release as a news story. These reporters would interview a subject (or relevant witness) for a story and if that interviewee said something that did not ring true, it meant the reporter must spend more time running down the truth from other sources. Certainly it was more work and more difficult, but it was required for the complete story to be presented. Was the person just mistaken or was he deliberately misleading the reporter, and if so, why?

As it is for a bookkeeper whose balance sheet does not balance. She checks her calculations and if the error is not hers, she sets about to find what caused this irregularity, ultimately discovering embezzlement. Similarly, the home buyer wonders one day what type of tree is growing in his yard and ends up an arborist, or the soldier who by happenstance and fate learns incredible self-reliance and preservation.

You absorb yourself in the issue; you study it; you research it; and, if you are tenacious, intuitive, and know your subject, you ultimately reach a conclusion. In short, you investigate. To some extent, everyone has done these investigations throughout their lives. That they are still employed (or alive in some cases) is a testament to the success of their investigational skills and subsequent decisions. So, if you picked up this book because you were wondering about your own intuitiveness, put it down and look in the mirror. Congratulations. You are already an investigator. Now we will hone some of those skills you already possess.

The lucky person who mopped floors in the restaurant example earlier has a natural investigations career assisting other restaurant owners in uncovering the source of their losses. Perhaps he or she starts a business called Texas Restaurant and Club Surveillance Company, joins the Texas Restaurant Association, and markets these specialized services to nightclubs and fast food and fancy restaurants, as well as hotels. Do you think he or she will have any problem speaking the language of the business to his potential clients? Of course not!

Intrigued with her findings, the bookkeeper continues her education and as a result of her developed skills in ferreting out the cause of accounting anomalies, refines those skills further and becomes a forensic accountant. She speaks fluent accounting and understands business; these are wonderfully marketable skills.

The point is to not fear the investigation but do make certain you have a marketable skill and the requisite knowledge for which someone else will pay money. Just wanting and wishing to be a private investigator is not enough.

Many years ago a private investigator was asked how he got into the business. He replied, "I was in business suffering some losses and tried to hire a Private Investigator to look into the problem. During our first meeting, I found I had to teach him all about the business world. He did not have an understanding of EBITA [earnings before interest, taxes, and amortization], profit and loss statements, working capital, or triple net leases. I just figured his job wasn't that hard; I had the knowl edge he needed to investigate business problems, just not the time to do it. So I quit my job and started my own company specializing in investigating business losses. That was thirty years ago."

This is an appropriate time to address a sensitive issue that can sometimes be the white polar bear standing in the corner of the room wherever private investigators gather.

People entering private investigations with backgrounds in law enforcement will admittedly have experience the lay person will not. They have, to some extent, become familiar with interviews, information research, and reports and have an understanding of the human element, crime, surveillance, and motives. How they apply these experiences in the private sector, however, does not always translate well. Being an ex-cop is no guarantee of success as a private investigator, and, in many cases, if the experience and skills are not adequately adapted to the private sector, the transition is doomed. Those who do adapt, however, soar as long as other proficiencies are added, as thoroughly addressed throughout this book.

So, just as it is undeniable those transitioning from the public sector will arrive with experience you do not possess, it is equally irrefutable you need to obtain training in these areas–and quickly. We will touch on a few shortly.

FIRST THINGS FIRST: LICENSING

There are currently five states that do not require private investigators to be licensed (Colorado, Idaho, Mississippi, South Dakota, and Wyoming). As someone entering the field without a law enforcement background, you will be at only a slight disadvantage unless you live in one of those five states. In order to enjoy your career as a private investigator without fear of criminal or civil penalties–or develop the wrath of licensed investigators–you should take care of this part first. Jimmie Mesis, Editor of *PI Magazine*®, has one of the most up-to-date sites providing links to each state's licensing requirements (www.pi magazine.com/private_investigator_licence_requirements.html). I would also suggest subscribing to the magazine because it always is educational.

The states requiring licenses call for anywhere from months to years of documented investigations experience in order to get a license. (Author's Note: Contrary to earlier pontificating in the opening paragraphs of this chapter, your life's experience at investigating your own issues will not, sadly, qualify you for a license.)

Each of these states, however, has some form of intern or apprentice Program whereby you can easily obtain a license and begin to work with a licensed firm, alongside and under the tutelage of an experienced private investigator. When you interview with such a firm, ask for the curriculum: how and how often he or she intends to train you and what types of cases the firm handles? Many states prohibit you from working for more than one firm at a time, which is an unfortunate and sometimes illogical reality. Therefore, make certain you are with a company that will keep you busy learning, not standing around emptying ashtrays or watering petunias. When you hook up with the right firm, you will learn firsthand, and without a substantial investment, whether this business is truly your career path. Do not expect to make much money during this internship, but the lessons you learn about the nuts and bolts of this business will be invaluable when you open your own agency.

INTERVIEWS AND INTERROGATIONS

The lack of ability to get someone to talk to you about anything will doom you from the start. The ability to conduct successful interviews is paramount to the activities of a private investigator. An understanding that there is absolutely no legal or otherwise compelling reason for a witness, suspect, or subject to willingly talk to a private investigator means one must have a highly developed sense of communication. Investigators certainly must know when to push, when to back off, when to listen, and when to ask questions, but to do so they must know how to relate to the person with whom they are attempting to talk or the interview will go nowhere. They must be aware of legal boundaries as well as human behavior. Threatening a witness rarely works except on television. In real life you will either be ignored, get your backside kicked, or end up in jail.

People must *want* to talk to you where you find them and as you find them; thus your presentation to them has to be part sales, part friend, part protector, and part coconspirator–as necessary. If allowed, people love to talk. Therefore, of all the education, degrees, certifications, or experiences you have, there is one essential skill to perfect in this business: spend the money for serious courses in interviewing and interrogation. This is not the place to distinguish between the two terms; suffice it to say there are many very good courses out there worth every penny if you are serious about this career. The Reid Technique® of Interviewing and Interrogation is widely known and highly respected. Wicklander-Zulawski is yet another. Regardless, the more you know about interviewing techniques and understanding nonverbal communication, or kinesics, the better you will be in your field regardless of specialty. Do not shortchange yourself in this training. You may be naturally glib and gifted at gab. It is not the same thing. There will be times you will only get one opportunity to interview a potentially critical witness to your client's case. Get the training; you will never regret it.

REPORTS (DO I HAVE TO?)

An equally critical area is the ability to prepare and write an intelligent and comprehensive report about the case that you have just investigated. A well-written report details what you did during the investigation. It is also the written justification for what you invoiced the client. Without it, you will not get referrals, you will not get repeat business and you may not even get paid. All of your now highly tuned skills will be for naught but for this significant requirement.

I was one of about eight advisory board members on the curriculum committee of a four year criminal justice degree program years ago. We were asked, "What skills would you like to see our students leave here with?" In other words, "Were you to hire one of the college's criminal justice graduates, what training should they have to help you in your business?"

The answers were varied and depended on whether the board member was from a corrections institution, a police or sheriff department, a federal law enforcement agency, or private sector business. To a person, however, the number one answer was *report writing.*

The department chair, Dr. Walt Copley, politely answered, "Alas, by the time the students get to us, those writing habits—whether atrocious or exceptional—are too deeply ingrained for us to have any effectual change." He was politely telling the board that these graduate students would be either very good or perfectly horrible at report writing and there was little the college or the hiring agency could do about it.

Again, this is not a forum to promote programs or correct deficiencies in our educational system but do understand this point. If you can write adequately, using proper grammar and spelling, you already know it and you are already ahead of many others in the business.

If you cannot write but recognize it, you will also be okay. You just need to do what you are already doing, such as reading this book. Recognizing shortcomings and addressing them is a huge step. Study the successful private investigators who have authored chapters here-in; go to work for one in your city; find a mentor and copy what he or she does when it comes to reports. Do not write a report that raises more questions than it answers. Be succinct. Do not proffer opinions unless requested and so identified. Get a proofreader and use a Spell Checker and dictionary. This list goes on. Believe this, however: How far you go in your new career will depend on the readability, accuracy, and professionalism of your reports.

Lastly, if you cannot write and do not believe in its importance to this business, you might want to practice saying, "Would you like fries with that?"

ASSOCIATIONS AND THEIR DAMNED ACRONYMS

This part cannot be overemphasized: Because you are coming to this dance without a law enforcement background, you absolutely need to become a member of and be active in appropriate private investigation groups. There are reasons galore but consider that you will immediately have a peer group to whom you can turn with questions about how to best approach a case. You will be able to ask (for instance) "what are the legal aspects of interviewing a minor without a parent present" or "can I use a GPS locater unit on a client's car in this state?" You are naturally going to have legal and procedural questions as you grow in the business. The members of these groups are a wealth of experience and information and are almost always willing to share with someone who is asking the question for the right reasons–to learn how to do the business the correct way.

Each state has at least one professional association for private investigators; some states have more than one (Florida, for instance, has four). Find one in your state, join it, and attend meetings. You will meet some unbelievably talented private investigators who might turn out to be your next, best mentor. They also offer annual educational programs, and if your state requires continuing education units (CEUs) to maintain your license, these will be important and are generally very affordable.

There are also some international professional organizations (including INTELLENET) and some political action committees and then there are the professional certifying organizations, such as ASIS

International (Certified Protection Professional [CPP®], Professional Certified Investigator [PCI®], Physical Security Professional [PSP®]), the Association of Certified Fraud Examiners (CFE), and the National Association of Legal Investigators (Certified Legal Investigator [CLI]), to name just a few. As you find your feet, that is, as you settle into an area of case work you enjoy, you should avail yourself of an appropriate certification. There is argument on both sides as to whether any certification actually increases your earning potential, but all who have gone through the testing to achieve a certification agree that the education received while studying for it was invaluable.

One last, but no less important, thought on this point. There is strong anecdotal evidence suggesting that private investigators that "step over the line" and get into legal difficulties are generally those who never availed themselves of professional organizations. In ignoring this brotherhood and sisterhood of fellow investigators, they missed having peers to whom they could turn with questions. They missed the educational seminars put on by these groups, which exist for that very reason, to keep private investigators operating in an informed, legal, and ethical manner. There is a Chinese proverb, that reads, "A single conversation with a wise man is better than ten years of study." You have much to learn. Learn from those who have been there and done that.

IT MAY BE FUN, BUT IT'S STILL A BUSINESS

This topic will undoubtedly be addressed numerous times and in many ways throughout this wonderful book, but perhaps a few additional words are in order. Remember time and knowledge? What follows are some very important lessons. First, you may charge a fair rate for your time, supported by your knowledge. You may not, however, charge anything for your time while you are gaining the knowledge with which you can solve someone's case unless specifically agreed to by the client. Notice the difference here. It was not said you cannot charge for gathering information, just not for gaining the knowledge to solve the case. Here are some examples.

Suppose you get your first workers' compensation assignment. It is an authorization for thirty-six hours of surveillance to see if the claimant is actually hurt or working off the clock for someone else while collecting disability compensation. Simple, right? Except you have never done surveillance before. You sit on the subject's home for three days, but he never comes outside. You get ready to submit an invoice for thirty-six hours of surveillance with no video evidence of anything untoward, having dutifully logged every fifteen-minute increment you sat watching the house. Then you read in the newspaper the subject was on his honeymoon in another state for those three days.

Imagine the same scenario, but the subject comes out of his house, gets in a car, and leaves. You follow but lose him in three blocks. For what exactly are you going to charge your client?

You are hired to investigate the theft of proprietary information involving some technology now being manufactured and sold by a company started by some of your client's ex-employees. In order to adequately investigate, you must educate yourself on the technology, which includes meeting for hours with the client's physicists and having them attempt to explain it to you. You then spend hours reading technical books on the topic. Is this billable time?

Regardless of your previous life, there is much to learn about the "business" of being a private investigator. After establishing your hourly rates, you must carefully consider what to charge your client for every minute legitimately spent on his case. There will be time for which you could have invoiced the client, but because it was spent learning from a mistake or figuring out a better way to gather the information, you eat it.

You submit a five-page typed case report that took you more than five hours to write, but you charge your client one hour. You do so because it is not his fault you type with two fingers at a blazing fifteen words per minute. You also do it because in five years when you have three investigators working for you as a result of treating your clients fairly, you will also have someone who does transcription for you and you will bill that time out at $25 per hour!

You must change the way you think about time. Your world now revolves around six-minute increments. Two of those equals two-tenths of an hour and is generally the acceptable minimum time charge to pick up a phone, dial a number, and get voice mail. A client is not going to look favorably, however, if there are twenty of those charges on an invoice.

Time is indeed your "thing." If you protect it, control it carefully, document it judiciously, and invoice for it fairly this can be a lucrative business. As a neophyte you have many lessons to learn. There are flat fee billings, retainers, different rates for surveillance, investigations, and testifying. This book is a great beginning.

The private investigator who earlier explained how he got into this business concluded his comments by saying, "This is the most rewarding business I can imagine. I've helped people where others could not; I've put bad guys away with my investigations; I've reunited loved-ones separated for many years; I've helped save entire corporations by discovering, and helping to solve their problems. I've met some of the most interesting people in all walks of life and made lifelong friends. And in so doing, I've developed an incredible knowledge of the law."

How many people can say all of those things about their career? This is a very fulfilling, rewarding business on which you are about to embark. I believe all the contributors to this book would agree with this wish: Best of luck!

> To find a career to which you are adapted by nature, and then to work hard at it, is about as near to a formula for success and happiness as the world provides. One of the fortunate aspects of this formula is that, granted the right career has been found, the hard work takes care of itself. Then hard work is not hard work at all. Mark Sullivan

Chapter 5

DEVELOPING MARKETS AND PARTNERSHIPS FOR PROFITS

THOMAS MILES

We live in a very complex society these days. Major advancements in technology and our constant population growth steadily spawn more and more business ventures. In turn, consumers are confronted with a massive array of choices in selecting someone to satisfy fundamental needs for services or goods. Investigators are routinely engaged to provide a unique service in acquiring and reporting information, but that does not mean you will not have to worry about competition. Consumers are always selective in choosing something, even a special service. Therefore, your perpetual goal as an investigator can be simply stated: to be *perceived* as the best choice available in your locality and to be creative and innovative in expanding your business operations. Start with the basics.

Investigators, perhaps more so than other service providers, must always project an appropriate image in every aspect of their activities. Remember that your clients are people needing help with personal or professional problems, and they need reassurances from the moment they first contact or meet with you. Accordingly, you must perform in both word and conduct as someone who is empathetic, knowledgeable, and very trustworthy. In short, an investigator's image is of paramount importance.

The following list depicts rudimentary items for acquiring clients and keeping them. As time passes, a periodic review of each subject

51

should occur for legal and social reasons. To manage your general affairs, these points are important. To develop new markets and grow your business as an investigator, however, these matters are crucial for success.

LICENSE REQUIREMENTS

State laws for investigators vary considerably; some are quite simple, but several states have complex standards, procedures, and qualifications. As a minimum, even if you are working from your home, be sure that you are in complete compliance with all laws.

PHONE SYSTEMS

Prospective clients may call at any time, day or night. Install a dedicated phone to take calls 24/7, and be sure it is answered in a standard mode. If no one is available, ensure that your line has a brief recording that invites callers to leave a message. Consider paying a professional–a "voice over" artist or local radio announcer–to make your recording.

Also, obtain a reliable cell phone and use it responsibly. If you are away from your office, have all calls forwarded to your cell phone.

WEBSITES

Although a website is not absolutely necessary for success, it is highly recommended. Ask for design help from inexpensive but reliable sources such as print shops or students who are majoring in computer technology at a local college. Designing a website can be a very daunting process, but some factors must be perfect: grammar, spelling, and punctuation.

Study the sites of competitors, then design and write your material to be much better.

BUSINESS CARDS

Plan carefully for your business cards, and use a professional printer for advice, design reviews, and production. Your cards should include your company name, and your name and contact information: mail address, office or cell numbers, and e-mail address. The inclusion of a striking logo or motto would also be a nice touch.

STATIONERY

As with business cards, use a professional printer to help in selecting top quality paper for personalized letters and envelopes. If possible, your stationery should match the colors of your business cards or at least blend well with them in similar tones. Written reports will be a separate and less costly expense. Your case reports can be submitted on good quality paper, bought in reams, with moderate brightness and twenty-pound weight or slightly higher.

CHECKING ACCOUNTS

You must have a business checking account; it is unwise and very unprofessional to use one checking account for both personal affairs and business transactions. Your business financial activities must be maintained separately, especially for accounting reasons and tax purposes. Establish a good relationship with your banker and solicit assistance. For example, checks for most new accounts will be initially printed with low numbers. This is a routine procedure in the banking industry, but it is not a legal requirement. Ask your banker to print your original business checks by starting them with a high number in the original series. Otherwise, you will be perceived as a beginner—and inexperienced.

DRESS FOR SUCCESS

Regrettably, for many years movies and television programs have depicted private investigators in an unsavory light with respect to sartorial features. There may well be a time when an investigator needs to dress casually to blend with surroundings. However, remember that your success is primarily a matter of how you are perceived by others, and first impressions will linger indefinitely. Never meet a prospective client, much less an established one, without always being well-groomed and neatly attired. Always! You must constantly project and maintain yourself as a professional person, someone who is deserving of the trust and confidence your clients require and that you want to convey.

NETWORKING

First, assess your competition. Scan the Yellow Pages phone directory, closely study the ads for other investigators, and select those with whom you might want to affiliate. If respectable local or statewide organizations exist, join them and get involved with their meetings. Use the Internet in the same manner, but avoid obvious scams by companies promising to list your business for a fee. Instead, spend your money wisely by placing your own ads in selected local publications.

Finally, there is a special feature about networking that you should commit to memory and never forget. It applies to every type of investigator: governmental or private; civil or criminal; local, national, or worldwide. *The capabilities, reputations, and successes of all truly professional investigators are not vested purely in who they are, what they know, and what they can do. Instead, those factors must be continually inclusive of others—investigators or not—who they are, what they know, and what they can do.* That is the benefit of networking, and strict adherence to this contention will virtually guarantee your success. Regardless of case locations or circumstances, you should strive to never have to tell prospective clients that you are limited and incapable of providing help. Ethics and legalities mandate, however, that you can only do so if you have sources and contacts—acquired by continuous networking—that can, indeed, be of service.

PAMPHLETS AND BROCHURES

Perform a realistic evaluation of your personal skills and interests and decide what you do best or would prefer to do as an investigator. Background checks, insurance claims, missing persons, civil or criminal case work, surveillance, photography, electronics or debug sweeps, security surveys, and so on; the list of opportunities for private investigators is virtually endless. Once you have compiled an accurate roster of your capabilities, even if it entails the skills of affiliates, put them in writing with your credentials. Next, draft up a pamphlet and obtain design or format help in having it printed professionally. A business card is nice, but a pamphlet is wonderful. If someone calls, for example, tactfully ask for a mailing address and offer to send them a business pamphlet with a polite reassurance that you will not impose on them later with follow-up calls. Your prospective clients will have the reinforcement of something to anticipate for reading, and they will appreciate this simple but effective gesture. Years ago, a gentleman named Lee Iacocca caused a surge in sales of Chrysler automobiles by saying, "If you can find a better car, buy it." That's the point—you are avoiding arrogance but implying that you are very good.

MARKETS AND PARTNERSHIPS

Once you have established your practice as an investigator, hopefully by using all or at least some of the guidelines previously discussed, shift your energy and actions to what will be an everlasting objective: to expand your business with clients and colleagues. An old military premise for success in war is that the best defense is offense. The concept of winning, even in business ventures, is vested in aggressive action. Do not wait for clients to come to you. Go out and find clients! Be aggressive and creative. Networking, advertising, mailing pamphlets, and so on are commonplace, but you will have to do much more to succeed in coping with competitors. Consider some proven suggestions given in what follows.

SECURITY SEMINARS

Essentially, investigators provide a unique service in many ways, mainly in obtaining and reporting information. A savvy investigator, however, should consider a different premise: *the presentation of information.* Everyone is concerned about crime, but most people are oblivious to actions that can significantly reduce their vulnerability to crime and help guard against becoming a victim. This facet of human nature is an opportunity.

The Internet has an abundance of websites, blogs, and references that give countless discussions and sound advice on enhancing one's safety and security. Also, your local police department will likely have a website with a portion dedicated to public safety, including criminal statistics and tips on how to avoid crime. Additionally, police agencies usually have informative brochures and handouts addressing security issues for people: personal protection measures for individuals, homes, the workplace, and even travel.

Using an assortment of good references, compile a list of the most helpful information you can muster. Next, prepare an outline containing the primary concerns people have on crime in your particular locality and what they can do about it. Finally, assemble a list of audiences—social organizations, civic groups, churches, businesses, and so on—and either draft up an appealing flyer for direct mailings or make personal calls to promote your offer for presenting security seminars. If you anticipate expenses such as handouts or literature on your investigative business, you might specify a minor fee. If possible, consider appearing with no charge or obligation as a purely humanitarian gesture. In turn, your responses will probably be much higher; everyone likes receiving free items.

Your costs are generally tax deductible for advertising, you will gain priceless exposure, and you will be amply compensated if just one member of any audience engages you for any type of case activity. Prospective targets for security seminars are numerous: home-owner associations, gated communities, apartment complexes, college sororities, civic groups, social clubs, and so on *ad infinitum.* The local chapters of national organizations are often in need of guest speakers, especially those with topics of such universal interest.

LIBRARIES

A growing trend in libraries nationwide is to rent conference rooms for business meetings or social clubs. This activity might be an ideal mode for presenting seminars to any small civic or social groups that are devoid of meeting facilities. Additionally, many libraries also host certain displays or discussion programs having general public appeal, merely to entice visitors and new patrons. Rental rates vary by time usage and room sizes, but they might be worthy of consideration for an investigator intent on addressing small selective functions in a very convenient location. However, it would be prudent to first contact the head librarian in a selected community and offer a free public presentation on crime and crime avoidance techniques in exchange for usage of a meeting room at no charge. This serves library goals of enticing visitors, acquiring patrons, and serving the community—all at no cost to a civic-minded investigator. Properly stated, it is a win-win scenario. It is potentially beneficial for everyone, and investigators only need to make a proposal.

SPECIAL LETTERS

For various reasons, attorneys and law firms are commonly in need of investigators for their clients. Whether civil or criminal in nature, litigation is rampant nationwide. Other needs (e.g., witness locations, background investigations, asset searches, and estate settlement research) are also prevalent concerns for attorneys. Some investigators choose to distribute mass mailings to law firms. That action is often perceived with disdain by members of the bar, however, theirs is a close-knit profession, selective in operations, and usually having a biased opinion of investigators, thanks to movies and television. As stated earlier, your goal is to be perceived as something special: the best investigator available. Act accordingly and limit any correspondence to the best in the legal profession. Mailings to all attorneys in your vicinity will soon be noted, and it is an action denoting desperation for case work. There is an alternative approach.

Make a habit of continually reviewing newspaper articles or legal publications that cite an attorney or law firm that has earned an award or some special merit. Mail something to these people, stressing that you are also selective—and good—in your own endeavors. In short, avoid the expense of mass mailings and the ensuing regards. Instead, approach only the largest and most prominent attorneys, and candidly declare your selectivity with your matching skills and resources. As stressed before, networking is the crucial factor.

RADIO SPOTS

In the broadcasting industry, radio stations are listed or known by one or more types of programming: sports and weather; classical, jazz, or country music; public service, and so on. Check your local radio stations and find one in the MOR category. MOR is an old radio term, still in use, meaning "middle of the road" or one with general interests. Contact a particular station, especially an MOR type, and offer the general manager or program manager the weekly provision of a recorded commentary having brief but good security tips or advice on combating crime. Ask for nothing other than the mention of your name or company.

Radio stations are receptive to new ideas, especially public service announcements (PSAs). You get a free ad and the station gains listener appreciations. Again, it is a win-win proposition, but you will never know unless you ask. Do so in person, of course, and remember to dress and act in a very professional manner.

NEWSPAPER ARTICLES

Newspaper editors routinely welcome articles by guest writers, if the subject contents have good public appeal. Personal security, privacy, safety, and tips on crime avoidance are paramount interests for everyone. Contact local newspapers, starting with one having the largest circulation, and submit an informative but succinct article (about 750 words) with suggestions and sound advice. Be sure to ask for a byline —your name—plus the fact that you are a local professional investigator. If you are a good writer and have many helpful points, you might even propose a weekly article for a negotiated fee. You should not expect to get rich; a weekly article in a local newspaper normally generates no more than about $15 to $50 in income for each submission. Still, you can benefit in many ways such as exposure, recognition, and respect—and probably some case assignments, too. If you are not proficient as a writer, seek assistance from someone who is. English majors at nearby colleges or regional freelance writers, for example, can edit your articles in advance for reasonable rates.

LAW ENFORCEMENT

Private investigators frequently know or learn about unusual criminal activities, things not taught at law enforcement academies or known by the most seasoned police officers.

Contact local police officials and establish a friendly rapport with them to enlighten them with helpful information, to share your knowledge, and to pledge your sincere support in community crime problems. Tactfully offer to be an unpaid guest speaker for in-house police training classes. You might elicit referrals from police officers, provided conflict of interest is avoided, but your self-esteem and skills will be notably enhanced.

LOCKSMITH SHOPS

Touch base with locksmiths in your community and ask them to accept your business cards or company pamphlets as referral items for prospective clients. While there, ask many questions, too. At a minimum, you will become a better investigator, one who is more well-informed than most others. Professional locksmiths are endowed with unique knowledge and skills, and they can be valuable sources for general information–topics for articles or seminars plus mutual business referrals. As usual, affiliate with the best.

ALARM COMPANIES

Sales and installations of home or business alarm systems are prominent in society, and you can profit, too. Visit the offices of the largest and most reputable alarm companies in your vicinity to learn, to share information, and to establish mutual reference grounds for any future and respective business interests. Learn about the many features, advantages, and shortcomings of different alarm systems; expand your knowledge and resources.

FUNERAL HOMES

Your initial reaction to this topic might be a very profound question: why? The answer is easily explained. Insurance industry statistics indicate that a yearly average of 28 percent of life insurance policies–those with death benefits payable to someone–go unclaimed each year in America. The primary reason is that beneficiaries are totally unaware that a life insurance policy exists. By law, companies having a life insurance policy on someone are not required to notify policy beneficiaries upon the death of insured persons. Instead, the insurance beneficiaries are responsible for filing a claim for receipt of any payments.

Many people have life insurance policies, paid-up or active, that are lost, misplaced, or forgotten. That fact understood, it is not surprising that so many life insurance policies go unclaimed year after year, and it gets better or worse, according to your perspective.

We live in a very mobile society; people change jobs, marry and relocate, lose contact with family and friends, and so on. In doing so, based on the complexity of social affairs, many people unintentionally leave behind unclaimed funds or property to which they have a legal entitlement. Unclaimed money can exist in several forms: bank account balances, utility refunds, stock dividends, mortgage refunds, payroll checks, savings bonds, and especially the inheritances from unclaimed life insurance policies. Unclaimed property is also diversified, such as land tracts, stock certificates, safety deposit boxes, clothing or jewelry, and so on. The federal government has rigid laws and procedures regarding unclaimed money or property falling under its jurisdiction, and the same is true for each state. Laws of each state will vary, of course, but the basic process itself is simple.

Following a specified waiting period, unclaimed property is held in storage, whether at federal level or within a particular state. However, unclaimed money will be deposited in either the treasury of the federal government or the treasury of a given state, according to jurisdictional determinations. The total amount of unclaimed money held by the federal government and in the treasury departments of all fifty states fluctuates with daily matters of incoming deposits and claims. Still, the combined total figure is astounding: roughly $200 billion! That is where investigators can help, especially with research.

Some funeral homes are small family-owned enterprises, but larger ones are often owned by major corporations. Study the funeral homes in your area, and approach the small ones for a better likelihood of success with a unique but potentially rewarding proposal.

Using the information just provided about unclaimed money and property, contact a funeral home owner or director and offer your investigative services to perform in-depth research for families of the decedents. Funeral arrangements, for example, are governed by a blend of desires and budgets stated by surviving relatives during consultations with a member of a funeral home's staff. These are sad affairs, of course, but funeral homes are still business facilities striving to maximize profits. In that context, consultations for any funeral services will necessarily include the availability of various options and prices. In conferring with the family of a decedent, funeral staff personnel want to sell as much as they can, albeit with tact and sympathy. Suggest *your* services as yet another option, one that might well be of much interest to surviving relatives of the deceased party. Caution is advised in setting a fee for your assistance as an investigator, however, and you would need to discuss various options with interested families at a later date.

For a flat rate, you could conduct specific investigative research within various states. If potential discoveries appear to be prolific, you might offer your services for a percentage of recoveries. Naturally, before considering this market idea, you must become familiar with everything pertinent to the location and recovery of unclaimed money and property. It is not a difficult task; Internet sources and intense study will soon make you an expert.

ASSISTED LIVING FACILITIES

Nursing homes are for ill or elderly people who are unable to live alone because they are incapable of taking care of themselves. In contrast, assisted living facilities (ALF) offer a caring environment for aging or ill residents who have limited mobility but are still functioning with mental awareness and emotional stability. Comparable to an apartment complex in structural design, a typical ALF is closely supervised by staff personnel managing many different amenities: dining rooms, small libraries, game rooms, and so on. Additionally, because competition for resident occupancy is quite high, ALF managers routinely plan and offer a variety of entertainment activities such as craft classes, board games, special parties, or a dance with live music. Relatives and friends of the residents are encouraged to visit and participate, and ALF managers are continually receptive to new ideas. Here is one.

Select an ALF in your area that seems appropriate, meet with the management, and offer to be an unpaid guest speaker for the families and friends of the residents. Topics could encompass many of those used in a security seminar, but stress the prudent act of preparing for the ultimate demise of loved ones. Your presentation should be slanted to cover two separate but related conditions: the welfare of all attendees who are already burdened by obvious personal concerns, and what steps to take when someone passes.

Comments in this chapter about establishing your business as an investigator should be deemed essential. Suggestions for marketing, however, are not all inclusive. Like other business ventures, success is limited only by your imagination.

Chapter 6

MARKETING YOUR BUSINESS*

MICHAEL J. WEST AND DIANA L. GARREN

Michael

When I first started out with the idea of opening my own agency, I thought I knew something about business. I was so mistaken. Little did I realize the nuances involved in so many aspects of the business and how many hours I would be working every day.

Diana

What Michael just said is so true and indicative of entrepreneurs. Many people open their own agency because they love the work they do and are skilled in investigations. They feel they have what it takes to make a business work. They also want to be their own boss and call their own shots. What many do not realize is that to be successful when they open their own agency, they must transition from being a private investigator into a business person who provides investigative services.

Conducting investigations and building and operating a viable business are two different things and require different skill sets and knowledge. To be able to conduct investigations and run a successful business takes much more time than just conducting investigations. To

---

(Editor's Note: The information in this chapter outlines the efforts Mr. West made to market his private investigation company into the highly successful business that it is today. The commentaries of Ms. Garren substantiate and further explain the strategies used by Mr. West.)

have a successful agency they must be 100 percent committed and willing to put in twelve to sixteen hours a day, five to six days a week, and sometimes seven days a week. They must be prepared to do whatever it takes to get it done. Without doing so, they will shortly learn that what they have really done was buy themselves a job, and probably one of the lowest paid jobs they ever had.

Michael

Marketing your business is plain and simple. It is an *attitude*.

First, let me give you a perspective of what I thought marketing was. When I first convinced myself that I was going to work for myself instead of drawing a paycheck every month I decided to learn from other people. I told myself that I should listen to other people who have done this before and are a lot smarter than I am. This was an opportunity to do what I always wanted to do, but I'd need to take the advice of others for a change. My plan was to find someone who had been successful in the business and follow his or her lead. I found someone who would help me get started. I ultimately found that he was exceedingly helpful and knew what he was talking about. Without his help I would never have gotten started on the right foot. Now, mind you, he did not have all the answers, and I now do some things differently than I did at first, but I am truly grateful to him.

My first rendition of things necessary to start out in the business was so very far off base that I now laugh at some of the things I did. To explain further, when I hired the consultant, he asked me to send him copies of all of my advertising and promotional items. He wanted business cards, letterhead, envelopes, brochures, giveaways, and anything else that is used to advertise or promote the business. I did just that, and a week later he called me for my hour-long consultation. Over the years, I have concluded it was the best money I had ever spent. By the end of the telephone conversation I felt dejected, rejected, and completely out of touch with what I wanted to do.

My goals from the very beginning were to be a cut above other investigators. I realized that there were many investigators who were very good, but they did not know how to position themselves. It was my intent to use that attitude to my advantage.

During our hour-long consultation I realized how unprofessional and unrealistic my approach was. For example, my initial logo was an outline of the state of Arkansas with the proverbial "spy in the trench coat" superimposed over it. In retrospect I cannot believe I did that. Nevertheless, it was what it was.

I had also provided him with a promotional writing pen that I used as a giveaway. Now that I think back, I had provided a really cheap pen that no one would want to use, much less keep. He took a look at my brochures and recommended that I obtain a professional design and get over the concept of printing my own brochures on my office printer. He also gave me a couple of sage words of advice that I am really glad I listened to.

When we started our conversation, and remember he had all of my advertising material already, he asked me where my office was located. I advised him that I intended to work out of my house and that was why I had the Mailboxes Etc. "PMB" mailbox address. He asked me to identify the most recognized building in the town I live. I told him, and he responded that as of the next morning I was going to have an office in that building. He did not care how much it cost, he did not care what I had to do, but, I was to get an office in that building. He recommended that I find an executive suite or virtual office area so that a real person would answer the telephones and greet clients. I took his advice I found an office the next day, and I have been there since.

Diana

Michael was very smart in reaching out to others who had knowledge based on experience and success and even smarter to follow the advice he was given. Your business image and reputation is one of the most valuable assets you own. It can make or break your business. How your market perceives you and your business will dictate the level of success you achieve.

The number one thing that has been shown to undermine the credibility of a business is inconsistencies. Look what happened to Toyota in 2010. They will spend billions trying to win back their reputation of being a "reliable" car manufacturer and to gain the public's trust back. Consistency is key! With everything you do, strive for consistency. Be consistent in the look, feel, message, and quality of your materials, communications, and work product. As Warren Buffett says, "It takes 20 years to build a reputation and five minutes to ruin it. If you think about that, you'll do things differently."

Before developing or revising your sales and marketing material be sure to properly identify your market–not everyone is your market–then build your business image and brand to align with the market you want to capture. Private investigators often think and/or want to look like "PIs." For instance, Michael's first logo was the "spy in the trench coat." This is the image television created for the private investigator, however, it is not the image attorneys, insurance adjustors, and business professionals look for when hiring a private investigator. They are looking for professionalism when hiring a private investigator. They are not looking for the spy in the back alley. They do not care how you do what you do. They care about the results of your work.

Attorneys care about winning their cases. They want a private investigator who can not only conduct a thorough investigation but also provide them a concise, well-written report and be credible to their client and on the witness stand.

Now, if your market is the general public, they might be drawn to the "spy in the trench coat" or "the bounty hunter" image. The image you choose for your agency should not be based on what you think or what you like. It should be based on what your market wants.

Another common mistake made on a regular basis is the text in brochures and on websites. When people are new in business, they have a tendency to create a brochure and/or website that tells all about them and the services they provide.

First, people do not buy services, they buy benefits. You might be asking what the difference is. A service is just that, a service. It focuses on what you provide. A benefit is what the prospect will receive from the service you provide. It should evoke a positive emotion and create a desire within the prospect to want what you provide. It has to be about them. People are tuned into the WIIFM station ("what's in it for me"). So it is important to talk about what is in it for them instead of what you do. For example, the service could be a background check. The benefit would be to decrease employee turnover and increase profit margin.

Second, prospective clients do not care about who you are until they know you can provide something they need.

Third, prospective clients do not care about your past accolades. They want to know what you can do for them today.

To create effective marketing pieces, the focus needs to be not on you and your business but on your client market, their needs, and how you can fulfill those needs. This takes knowing and understanding your market.

Michael talked about marketing being an attitude. Part of marketing is an attitude. Marketing is not a cut and dry issue. It is very complex. There are many ways to market. Shotgun marketing is always a waste of time and money. Effective marketing should be planned and executed with a specific message to a specific demographic. The real attitude should come into play concerning your overall business image, in other words how you are perceived by your clients and your market.

Just about everything in life is about presentation. When Michael was giving away cheap pens, printing his brochure and probably business cards off his computer, it sent the message loud and clear to everyone he came in contact with that he was either struggling or cheap. Guess what, people do not want to do business with struggling or cheap people. This does not give them a sense of security and confidence. People want to hire successful people. They want to feel confident in those they hire and know that the job will be done properly and professionally.

Michael

The second bit of sage advice my consultant gave me was after he asked me what the prevailing rates were for my competition. I told him what I had been able to find out, and he advised me that as of that moment my rates were 10 percent above the highest competitor rate I could find. No matter what they raised their rates to I was to make mine higher. Clients perceived that higher rates meant higher quality. I did it, it is true, and I have maintained that philosophy since day one.

I recently had a University of Arkansas study completed that validated that I was the highest. If I have heard it once, I have heard it a hundred times. Clients have remarked they feel that "you get what you pay for." This is also why I go "above and beyond" when providing customer service. I answer the phone twenty-four hours a day. When they call, I respond. This is why I cringe when I hear about people "low balling" or undercutting prices. You are only hurting yourself. As a matter of fact, I took all of his suggestions and reduced them to a single-line entry on a piece of paper. I still have them today as a guideline. I am confident that without his guidance I would probably have failed the first year. It was not that I was any better or worse than my competition, but as you will learn in this chapter most of your successes are a result of perceptions that are held by your clients.

Diana

What Michael is saying is true. If you are seen as expensive but worth the price because of excellent work product and great customer service, then people will pay the price. If you are seen as cheap, then people will pay you very little. The problems with being cheap and getting paid very little are twofold. The problem that directly affects you is that you have actually priced yourself right out of business. Now that you own an agency, there are operating costs and overhead that must be paid. It is no longer "just getting paid" for the investigative work. The second problem is when you low ball your price, you have hurt not only yourself but also your industry. Speaking of your industry, one thing that is keeping your industry from becoming a profession is low-ball pricing and the poor business image many agencies have.

According to the most recent Bureau of Labor Statistics[1] the "median annual wages of salaried private detectives and investigators were $41,760 in May 2008. The middle 50 percent earned between $30,870 and $59,060. The lowest 10 percent earned less than $23,500, and the highest 10 percent earned more than $76,640."

Percentile	10	25	50 (Median)	75	90
Hourly Wage	$11.30	$14.84	$20.08	$28.40	$36.85
Annual Wage	$23,500	$30,870	$41,760	$59,060	$76,640

When you look at these numbers you learn that 50 percent of investigators only make between $30,870 and $59,060. Now, this money has to cover home and business operating expenses. Worse yet, the lowest 10 percent earn less than $23,500. Imagine splitting this pie between home and business expenses. These low numbers are creat-

---

1. http://www.bls.gov/oes/current/oes339021.htm

ed and maintained because many in the investigative industry are low balling price. Until the majority of investigators know their value and charge what they are worth, these numbers are not going to increase. Would you not like to be in the highest 10 percent and beyond where you are making $76,640 or more?

When you have cheap pricing it will not be long before you no longer like what you do. When you do not get paid what you are worth, it creates bad feelings and ultimately bad relationships. In the end, cheap pricing hurts all involved.

Now, as far as having someone answer the phone, this is critical. If clients are looking to hire a private investigator, and they cannot reach you, or their first impression is not a professional one, do you think you will get the work? Probably not. After interviewing more than 500 attorneys, 96 percent of them said that when looking for a private investigator, they first ask for referrals from colleagues; once they have some names, they go to the Internet to learn about the agencies' credentials and to see how professional they appear. If the website is not professional, they go no further. If the website is professional, they then call the agency. If nobody answers the phone, they move on to the next name on the list. Why? They want someone who is accessible and reliable. An unanswered phone does not meet what they are looking for.

Perception Creates Reality®. However you are perceived by your clients and your market will create the reality for your agency. Perception may not be the reality, but in the eyes of your clients and your market their perception is their reality. Agencies who fail to manage their business image will ultimately struggle and often fail. You are actually choosing how your agency is being perceived every day by everything you do or not do. The question is, are you making the right choices?

Michael

I tell you all this because I want you to have benefit of my perspective when I first started out. I had previously had some experience in the private sector, but for most of my life I have been a badge carrier who worked for somebody else and drew a monthly paycheck. I had no real entrepreneurial experience even though I thought I did. I had no clue.

I sought out ideas and applied them. You can find some wonderful ideas and suggestions by listening to other successful people. You can find some great ideas by reading about other successful businesses. I like some of the ideas and suggestions in the Guerilla Marketing books.

Diana

Even though Michael was given good advice and followed it, it is important to point out that not all advice given or read fits all business models. There are many things that apply to all businesses, but not everything. For instance, if you provide surveillance and the general public is your main market you will want to spend money on advertising in the yellow pages and on search engine optimization (SEO). These are the avenues the general public utilizes to find private investigators. However, 96 percent of the time attorneys hire private investigators through referrals. Attorneys will resort to searching the Internet if they need a private investigator outside their local area. To know if the advice you read and hear applies to your business, you must know your business model and your market. You must also take into account that there is a great difference between marketing a product that everyone uses and a service that people do not have an everyday need for.

Michael

I did well the first two years and actually exceeded the goals I had lined out in my business plan, which brings me to my next point. I cannot overemphasize the need for you to have a good, thorough, lengthy, detailed, solid, realistic, and concise business plan. I purchased a software program that I used to develop the business plan. It ended up being much longer than I thought it would be and because it was my first attempt I did not know if I was including too much information or the wrong information. I took it up to the local university where they have a small business development center and asked them to review my business plan. I was actually surprised when they called me back informing me that my business plan was one of the most thorough they had seen and they wanted to use it as a model for their classes. Since that point I have used the small business development center quite frequently to feel out different marketing plans and ideas, and I have even taught a few classes there.

After I started teaching at the university, I fell back into an old, comfortable pattern of years ago when I used to teach at law enforcement academies. I had been told that one of the best ways to meet new people who were interested in learning about a topic was to teach the topic. It turned out to be true. I have met a number of people who became clients and I have met a number of people whom I used as contacts as a result of this experience.

Diana

Michael used some key words when speaking about a business plan: thorough, detailed, solid, realistic, and concise. Your business plan becomes your foundation. Would you build a house without a foundation? Why try to build a business without a foundation? Many entrepreneurs do not take the time to plan. However, success truly is in the planning. If you were going to take a vacation, would you decide on the destination and find a place to stay, a way to get there, and some activities to do once you were there? If you would do this for a vacation, why would you not do it for a business that is going to provide your livelihood?

Often, the first thing an entrepreneur does is decide on a name for the business. This is mistake number one. How can you realistically name your business if you do not know your market or the long-range vision for your business? Another common mistake made is using some part of your name in the name of your business. Why? You are training people to buy you. The problem with this comes into play when you want to expand. Then you will have to spend great time, effort, and money getting people to accept that those you hire will do as good a job as you do. Yes, this strokes the ego but is not a healthy plan of action if you want to grow your business.

Once you have taken the time to write a good business plan, do not put it in a filing cabinet never to be seen again. You need to turn that business plan into a *working plan* that has short- and long-term goals, strategies, and deadlines to achieve those goals, and most importantly you must execute those strategies. Once you execute your plan, you must keep it on course; evaluate, measure, and monitor your plan on a regular basis and make adjustments as needed. Efforts without strategy bring little return. Strategy without execution is delusion.

Over the last twenty-seven years working with businesses, one thing has not changed. For those who do make it past five years in business, most will remain in the start-up phase well into their twentieth year of business and until they close. They never grow. The two most common reasons for this are (1) that they are actually afraid of success and (2) the reason they are afraid of success is that they do not have the infrastructure to support the success. All successful businesses have an infrastructure to support growth. This is where it takes the investigator to become the business person to create what is needed for real success. What does a foundation and infrastructure have to do with marketing? What happens if you market and bring in many new clients but cannot handle them due to your lack of infrastructure? Marketing before infrastructure is putting the cart before the horse and can destroy your entire business.

Michael

This brings into play another concept that I think is important in marketing your business. That concept is in the word "networking." Everything you do, every person you meet, every activity you are involved in could be considered networking, and it is business development. I have found that networking is exceedingly important and should be high on your priority list. You will not always see the benefit right away. As a matter of fact, you will rarely see the benefit of networking by way of a direct or immediate increase in business. The benefit of networking is that, if done properly, the new person that you just met becomes an advocate and an advertiser of your business. Those with military experience will think it as a "force multiplier." There are many different activities you can become involved in that help you with networking.

Some ideas might include

- giving talks at a local school
- joining local civic clubs
- participating in your Chamber of Commerce
- participating in organizations in the local area
- getting on the board of directors of organizations

I will give you some practical examples of what I did with each one of these and maybe some thoughts as far as how they benefited me. One of the things you must remember is that everything you do is networking and marketing, and you need to keep that in mind all of the time. One of the services I provide is pre-employment background investigations. One day I was with my wife when she had an appointment with a neurosurgeon. The doctor came into the room and was talking to my wife about a test result. At the conclusion of the conversation I simply asked him if he had an office manager. He replied that he did and asked why. I complimented him on the size of his office staff and noted that I had seen new faces recently. I wanted to know if they did background investigations on all employees, particularly with all the turnover. He replied he had intended to do so but had not started doing it yet. He called the office manager in and before I left I had a new client and three background investigations to do. My point is that you need to think of every occasion where you meet someone as a potential new client. You never know unless you ask.

Diana

Many opportunities are missed because one is afraid to ask. As Michael said, you have to ask. One of the main reasons people do not ask is fear of rejection. So, if this is true for you, please make the word next a part of your vocabulary. Do not take the rejection personally. You have to understand that whoever tells you no, is not rejecting you. They just do not have a need for your service. This is okay. Think of every no as a sign that you are getting closer to a yes. Say to yourself, next and thank you for getting me closer to my yes.

Michael

I use group memberships as a focal point and a reason for meeting new prospects. Your local chamber of commerce is an excellent opportunity to do this. The first organization I joined when I opened my agency was the chamber of commerce. I became involved in what is called a "leads group." A leads group is composed of twenty to fifty individuals, each of whom represents one business in one market area. They get together every two to three weeks, usually for an hour. Each member gives a thirty-second "elevator" presentation about his or her business. Ultimately the other members of the group come to know the business, and they become advocates for your business. If they ever hear someone say "I wish I knew a good private investigator," they immediately think of you, thereby becoming that force multiplier I mentioned earlier.

Over a period of the six years my business has been exposed to literally hundreds of people on a personal level. I've had a number of new cases and new clients who came out of referrals from the leads groups. Another activity through the chamber of commerce would be what is called "business after hours." This is a networking event that is open to not only business owners but also employees. It is a social event where people meet other people, talk about their business and often gain referrals. We always walk out with thirty to fifty business cards of other attendees. Another local event through the chamber of commerce is referred to as "speed networking." A takeoff on a popular theme of speed dating, business owners give a short thirty to forty-five-second presentation of their business and then move on to the next person doing that same presentation again. This is your exposure to twenty or thirty people whom you might not have met before. There are several other functions at the chamber of commerce that you can take advantage of, including breakfasts, luncheons, training, business groups, and any other sponsored program. I strongly urge you to participate in these activities. Getting to know one new person may make the difference in working today or not working today.

Diana

Marketing has many different arms. Networking is just one of the marketing arms, and it does work. However, you need the right elevator speech that delivers the right message about your agency. This message must be about benefits and not services. You have to be good at follow-up and relationship building to make this work for you. You also need to make sure you are networking in the right arena and right geographical area that aligns with your market and your business model. If you only want to reach people in your local area, then what Michael has done will be effective for you. However, if you have a business model that is regional, national, or international, what Michael has done will not be beneficial to you. You want to look for the organizations that reach into the area you want to serve geographically and that comprises your target market. For instance, if your target market is attorneys, the most beneficial place for you to network would be events put on by the bar association and other legal organizations. If your target market is regional, national, or international, you need to be networking in those arenas.

Michael

Another way to maximize exposure through networking is membership or participation in various groups. I have talked to local Lions, Rotary, and Kiwanis clubs. I have spoken at chamber of commerce functions, including newcomer's orientation, business development meetings, small business advisory groups, and seminars. I also found that a good way to maximize your exposure is to join one of the civic groups. I became an active member in the local Civitan group. Participating in local community service projects is a great way to build a positive reputation and do something good for the community at the same time. This gives me exposure to city officials, mayors, and civic leaders as well as a voice to speak from when I talked to the local chamber of commerce. If you always keep in your mind that everyone you talk to is a potential client, you will find many opportunities to engage a new client.

Diana

Speaking is a wonderful vehicle to give you access, visibility, and credibility. However, you need to be sure you are speaking to your market. It was said before and it is being said again, not everyone is your market. If you try to speak to everyone, you actually speak to nobody.

The most effective way of becoming a leader in your industry is to become a subject matter expert. You achieve this by choosing one thing you know best and specializing in it. Then build on this and strive to be the very best at this one thing. This will make you the "go to" person and very sought after.

Once you do this, you want to increase your success by marketing to one or two niche markets. This will allow you to have a direct, succinct, powerful message that speaks right to your market. This will increase your referrals and revenue and decrease your marketing expenditures and time.

You might be thinking, if you do this, you will miss a lot of business. This is true to a point. However, this will provide you the work you know and love and will in time provide you more business than if you stayed a generalist. Why? You will have separated yourself from most and put yourself in a different league. This means you will have far less competition and be able to charge a much higher rate for being an expert.

Michael

Another approach that I have used as far as maximizing contact and advertising is to publish articles. Although you do not have to be a writer in order to publish an article, it helps if you have something positive to say about a topic. For instance I have written articles such as *Finding and Hiring a Private Investigator, Turning "F's" into "A's" When Hiring a Private Investigator, Hiring and Utilizing a Private Investigator In Your Law Practice.* These can be in print form or for websites. Many websites welcome articles and will post them for free. I published an article in the Association of Certified Fraud Examiners magazine based on one of my actual cases, and then I have published quarterly newsletters that are available online to clients. Although it is hard to quantify any particular new client that has come in as a direct result of the articles, knowing that you have written them results in clients' feeling more comfortable and secure with your credibility, background, and work products.

Diana

Writing articles is a good way to become a subject matter expert in your area of investigations and gain positive exposure. People want to hire people in whom they have confidence. Another thing you can do is put out press releases about new employees, new services, and successful cases worked that are known and that were won. This is called public relations.

PR is very beneficial in positioning your company. Again, be sure the PR and articles are published in magazines, newspapers, and such that your market reads. This will add to your credibility and visibility. Be sure to also put these articles and press releases on your website. They will assist "spiders" in locating your website and give you a higher ranking on the search engines.

Michael

You can also get articles written about you. Local magazines and newspapers always love to write profiles of local businesses. Find one and let them know you are available. People love reading about private investigators because we are mysteries to most people. Yes, there is a time for discretion and a low profile. On the other hand, I look at this as a business and I cannot grow if I am locked up in a room.

Diana

Michael just hit on a key for success: visibility. You must be visible to get business. Not until you are known and established will business find you. You have to be like the tiger and be on the hunt to find business. Hopefully by now you can see that you are a business owner. As a business owner, you have much more to learn and do along with your investigations. What we have covered so far is only the tip of the iceberg.

Michael

Another area to help you establish credibility and/or abilities in the community is by taking advantage of television and radio. I have been advertising on radio two times a week over the past year and a half. People tell me that they have heard my ads on the radio, so that makes me think people are listening.

Insofar as television is concerned I have used two different approaches. I have acted as a consultant to one of the local television stations. They called me and interviewed me about privacy issues after a large quantity of boxes were found apparently abandoned behind an attorney's office. The story and my interview were shown on television. On another occasion, the television station came to me for a seven-minute segment, and we talked about global positioning systems (GPS) and how they could be used to protect children. (In particular, we were speaking about one of the Amber Alert GPS devices.) Using radio and television is a positive means of marketing your business and lends credibility to what you do.

I have also used television stations as a method to put out a plea for assistance when we have a difficult case, such as a missing child. Not only do they get that message across but also it is publicity for you. People watch the news, and when they see you being interviewed you have instant credibility.

Another sure way of getting your name out to current or potential clients is to attend related conferences as a vendor. I attend a local bar association annual conference, a conference for self-insured associations, defense attorney groups, trial lawyer conferences, paralegal conferences, and any other I can get into as a vendor. Participants in these conferences are always looking for free giveaways, such as pens, writing pads, notepads, brochures, letter openers, and other trinkets they can collect and take home. I always maintain a significant supply of pens and letter openers for these events. I recommend that when you look for items like pens or other giveaway items you look for high quality. This is all about how your prospective client perceives you, so do not skimp on the cost. You can have pens laser engraved with your name and a short message. I found that better quality items make a difference in the reaction of the person receiving the item. For instance, earlier I mentioned that I had obtained some very cheap pens that did not speak well of my quality control. Since then I only obtain metal pens with good ink refills and then have my business name engraved on them. Usually when I am a vendor at a conference I also provide some type of door prize for those stopping by my booth and leaving a business card. The last couple of conferences I have been to, I gave away wine, cheese and cracker baskets. You may or may not be able to do this in your jurisdiction but I find it is a great tool for tracking people. I give away one of these baskets every day of the conference. With a decent wine included, these baskets only run $17 to $18 each. The recipients are appreciative, and it is a good way to get your name in front of the group. They announce the winners when the full sessions are in progress. That way the entire participating group hears your name and knows that you have done something special.

While we are on the topic of giveaways or gifts, I acknowledge referrals from clients by sending them a small token of thanks. I found a really nice gift on the Internet; the company will send via FedEx some really good cookies with your name on a card. The clients usually receive these three or four days after they are ordered, while the referral is still fresh in their minds. When a secretary or paralegal calls you specifically to say thank you for the cookies, to me your name is now at the forefront of their mind. Guess who they will call next time they have a referral?

Diana

Referrals are one of the best ways to obtain business. It is a proven fact that someone who is referred is more likely to refer you to others. Make it a practice to ask for a referral from everyone you speak with, and you will quickly build your business.

Michael

I also encourage Christmas cards and gifts. These do not have to be expensive, but they should be something practical. Books that reflect an individual's interests are always good, and you can usually find them at a reasonable cost if you use something like eBay or Amazon .com. One year I purchased a quantity of wine glasses. I or one of my employees hand carried them to the individuals and made sure there was enough for the attorney and all the staff. Another really super tool that I have used is to go to a local printer and have mouse pads made. These are not ordinary mouse pads, but they are actually notepads with twenty or twenty-five pages bound together. They are just like a mouse pad, but you can write on them and they are large enough to tear off and put inside a file. Close to the end of the year I always have clients asking me when I am going to bring around the mouse pads because there is a calendar on them. They are not cheap, but they get attention and keep my company name in front of my clients.

I always try to send some sort of birthday acknowledgment—a birthday card or an e-mail—to those clients whose birthdays I know. A little research on the Internet or in your state's listing of attorneys will help provide this information.

I often scan the local newspaper for news articles involving existing or potential clients, clip out the article, stick in a short handwritten note, and drop it in the mail. The note says something such as "Saw you in the news" or "Saw this in the paper and thought it might be of interest to you." Many people know that the articles have been written about them, but they did not see them or get a copy of the newspaper. Sending it to them lets them know that you are looking out for them.

Diana

What Michael is doing is very powerful. He is doing many things that keep him in the forefront of his clients' minds, and that makes him stand out from the rest. He is building relationships, which evokes loyalty. He is saying "thank you," something that is not said enough. He is making his clients feel valued and cared about. No matter what, we are all human, and we all want to be valued and acknowledged. This will never change. Michael is keeping his name in front of his clients. This is critical. Why? Other investigators are knocking on your client's door. If you are out of sight and out of mind, and others are persistent, they will steal some, if not all, of your business. It is always cheaper to keep a client than to replace one.

Another good way to keep your name in front of your clients is through electronic newsletters. It is critical to keep the content in the newsletter relevant and something that will benefit the recipient. They cannot just be advertising for your business. Electronic newsletters also provide a vehicle to be shared with colleagues and friends. They can be shared with a click of the mouse. Like anything else, you must be consistent in sending these. When you are, people look forward to receiving them.

Michael

Handwritten notes are a big priority of mine, and they have been a long-standing policy in my agency. My employees know how important it is to send a hand-written note. When we go to an event (for instance one of the Chamber of Commerce Business After Hours events) my employees carry a notepad, a stack of envelopes, stamps, and a blue pen. At the end of the night they write out a handwritten, very short note that says "Enjoyed meeting you tonight. If I can refer any business your way I will." They sign it and we do not stick a business card in with the note. We don't try to sell them anything at this point. We just tell them we appreciate meeting them and we do. This is about them and we want them to understand that we're not trying to solicit anything but we do appreciate the opportunity to meet them. Those letters are required to go out either in that night's mail (I drop them off at a post office box on the way home) or no later than next morning's mail. I have had countless people that I didn't remember who came up to me later and complement us about taking the time to send them a handwritten note. I don't think this can be overemphasized. It has impact and it gets attention.

Diana

Oh yes, the personal touch. With technology moving at the speed of light, many have forgotten how nice it is to receive a handwritten note. What does this say? It says the person who sent it cared enough to personalize something to them. It makes them feel special. Once again, it makes you stand out from the rest. It is the possible start of a relationship, not a sales pitch. That is why you should not include a business card. Something you can use is to print up a card that is the same size of your envelope. On this card have your picture and company information, your main marketing message, and room to write your handwritten message. This allows them to have a picture of you that will help them remember you and associate you with your business.

Michael

When any of us go to one of the chamber of commerce events or any other kind of event, we carry business cards, but we do not go with the purpose or intent of passing out business cards. Our interest is in getting business cards. People are generally so focused on collecting cards and trying to sell their own services that they forget the purpose is to find out information about the other person, not pass out information about themselves. There have been times when a new employee would go to a conference and come back and report that he or she passed out twenty-five business cards but only received a few. Again, the purpose is not to pass them out but to receive them. It is okay if they do not pass out any at all. That person will eventually receive plenty of contact from us. As a matter of fact, I have it planned so that over a period of time every person that might be a potential customer or client receives nineteen different contact messages from us. Those messages might be an e-mail, telephone call, letter, postcard, or something else, but reinforcing your name and your existence to them will pay dividends and allow you to be in control of the contact instead of waiting for someone to remember and/or contact you.

Diana

Michael is doing everything right when it comes to networking. He is keeping the focus off himself and on the people he meets. He gives them the opportunity to do what they love to do best, which is talk about themselves. By doing this he has put himself in the driver's seat in many ways.

1. By learning about them he learns how he might be able to help them. This works to his advantage when he corresponds with them. Now his correspondence can be focused on what is important to them instead of a laundry list of what he does. This increases his probability of business.
2. By having a follow-up procedure in place and executing this procedure he puts his name in front of prospective clients nineteen times. This helps build his brand and keeps his name in the forefront if and when a need arises for them or anyone in their circle of influence who might have a need. Statistically, it takes a minimum of seven contacts for someone to buy from you. Michael exceeds this, which is very beneficial for him.
3. This separates him from the rest and makes a lasting impression.

Michael practices what we have all heard many times: we have two ears and one mouth; therefore we should listen more than we speak. If you are going to take the time out of your schedule to show up at the events, you need to be sure to listen more than you talk, gather as much information as possible, and follow-up.

Michael

When you attend conferences, such as legal conferences or anything like that, you need to step up your advertising a notch. Bring your brochures and newsletters, bring giveaways too, but also provide a high-quality professionally developed display. Get one that projects a good image of your business. I use one that is approximately eight feet by eight feet, and it can either sit on a table behind me at a conference or sit on the floor. It has high-resolution graphics and a well-thought-out message and design that speak directly to my markets needs and how they will benefit. The images on this display are very carefully selected so they evoke the right emotion. These displays have a lot of white space and they portray your business in the most professional manner. Do not use hand-printed or hand-designed flip charts or poster boards. This is one area where you do not want to skimp on cost. Find a good graphic designer, content writer and quality display. There are several very good quality displays available on the Internet for a reasonable cost. I actually have two different displays that I interchange depending on the audience.

Diana

Remember that ***Perception Creates Reality***®. A first impression is a lasting impression. You only have one opportunity to make a first impression. Keep in mind that having consistency and professionalism in all you do is critical to your success. If you are going to spend money on a booth, then you need to spend money on what you display at that booth. Displays are not cheap, so you want to be sure you do it right the first time. Your booth will create an overall perception of your entire organization. If it is well-done and professional, then the prospect will believe your agency is professional and that your work product is done well and packaged well. If your display is amateurish, then the prospect will think your business is amateurish and that your work product will be the same way.

Years ago I saw an ad in the Yellow Pages for "Elite Rug Cleaning." I thought, Elite . . . that sounds good. They will probably do a good job. I will add them to my list for next week when I call around for pricing. Over the weekend I had to go to Lowe's for some supplies and in the parking lot I saw an Elite Rug Cleaning van. The van was beaten up and dirty. Not so elite. When I got home, I removed them from my list. What they claimed and what I saw were inconsistent, and their presentation–their van–painted the real picture for me. Michael is positioned as "Arkansas' Premier Investigator," and every piece of his marketing material, displays, giveaways, and such are of a high quality that supports this title. Your words, actions, work product, and materials need to be consistent and speak the same message in both words and appearance.

Michael talked about evoking emotion. All great sales, marketing, networking, and advertising pieces evoke emotion. This is what they are supposed to do. This emotion is created through pictures that speak a thousand words and through words that create a picture and evoke emotion. When creating a display, there needs to be a lot of white space, pictures, and a focused and powerful message that speaks directly to the prospect and paints a positive picture of the end result that will be achieved if they hire you.

EXAMPLE: One of the best taglines belongs to Walmart: "Save Money. Live Better." This creates a picture of more money in your pocket to live a better life. It creates an emotion and desire to have that. Then consumers think that if they shop at Walmart they can achieve this. Now, if you add a picture of someone in a lounge chair at the beach, the thought of this happening and your having enough money to go to the beach increases and so does the urge to shop at Walmart, where you can save money and live better. The picture enhanced the emotion and desire.

When creating a display, there needs to be a message that evokes a desire of want or need in the prospect or you have wasted your money. A laundry list of services does not evoke emotion or create a desire within a prospect. Remember people buy benefits, not services.

Michael

Another means of advertising and getting your name out in front of people is to work with groups such as the Innocence Projects or Legal Aid. They are always looking for people who will assist them. Often they cannot afford to pay for services, but I believe the publicity is well worth the investment. I do not do much for them because they are very conscious about asking people to do things for free, but there are some good programs, and I encourage participation.

I find that it does not hurt to occasionally do things for free or to promote goodwill. I had been trying to get a director of the regional chamber of commerce to write a testimonial for me. He said they wanted to, but it was policy to not write letters of recommendation. One afternoon one of the fine folks at the chamber (I prefer to call her and think of her as a friend) called me and related that her car had been involved in an accident while parked at the chamber. Someone had driven over the curb and crashed into her car. It was almost a total loss but a witness had observed the accident and written down a license plate number. The local police had been called and even with the number they misidentified the culprit's vehicle. Within five minutes after calling us, we had the name and address of the offender, and a few minutes later we had a picture of the driver. Witnesses confirmed he was the one driving. The end result was that her car was repaired and working again. The charge for her was $0.01. The result was a really great, full-page letter in the chamber newsletter telling everyone how fantastic we were and how efficient we were. I could not have bought that letter, and I certainly could not have bought the good will we received. Priceless!

Diana

Testimonials are one of the best things you can obtain from a client. People only believe 10 percent of what you say about yourself or your business and 90 percent of what others say about you. In order to gain these precious testimonials, you have to ask for them. The old saying of ask and thou shall receive is very true. When you ask for them, ask that they write them on their letterhead. It is critical to show proof that the person you said wrote the testimonial actually wrote it. Letterhead usually proves this.

Michael

I also recommend speaking to groups anytime you have the opportunity. I was once able to get the attention of a local radio station owner. He invited me to participate in a weeklong public service spot for which I, the attorney general (now governor), the director of the state police, and the director of a statewide civic organization did a series of interviews on the radio. As it turned out, we did these for three years in a row. Great PR. Additionally, I volunteer to make presentations to school groups or to attorney's groups and teach classes, particularly about what private investigators can do for them. I recently gave presentations to the paralegal associations and legal assistance associations and talked about the many things that private investigators can do for them and their business. At one of these conferences I received four new assignments from two different attendees. Those jobs paid for my time to attend that conference, plus my name is out in front of prospective client.

I do not know about your particular state laws, but I was prompted to see if I could get continuing legal education (CLE) accreditation for one course I developed. It seemed a worthwhile effort if future groups could get credit for legal education by attending one of my presentations. I was able to obtain CLE-equivalent hours for a legal assist's group. We decided to expand on that, and through the State Board of Continuing Legal Education I was able to eventually obtain approval for one hour of CLE credit for those attending one of my presentations. I have received laudatory responses to this, particularly when people realize how difficult or unusual it is to get this kind of approval. I believe this will be a definite plus for future engagements and marketing and I will try to maximize it as a tool to get in front of more attorneys.

Diana

Education-based marketing is one of the most powerful marketing tools. It also takes more time and effort, but it does pay off. When you get accredited for CLE, CEU, or any other designation, it does many things for your business.

1. It instantly gives you more credibility in the marketplace.
2. It provides you an additional marketing tool.
3. It makes you a subject matter expert, who can charge a higher rate.
4. It makes you the "go to" person.
5. It separates you from the rest.
6. It opens more doors.

As you can see, marketing your business can be a full-time job. If done properly, it will pay high dividends.

Michael

One area that I have not discussed as of yet relates to websites, and actually this is an area of particular interest. First, I need to give you some background on my thought process. I like to design websites as a hobby. I've probably developed many dozens of websites over the years for various clients. I developed and modified my original website. I have recreated my websites, again and again. I think I did a good job with them, but there was a point when I thought that I needed to rebrand my company image and redesign my website. I was on a short vacation with my family and had plenty of time to just search around for the right company. When I started looking for a good website developer, I found literally thousands of people who did website design. Many of them were very good. Many of them were exceptionally good. It was a daunting task for me to try to find someone who understood the nuances of my business and what I wanted to portray. I did not want this to be any old website; I already had one. I did not want an average website; I already had one. I wanted something that stood out above the rest. When I really got to looking around and calling different designers, I started running into problems. I recall calling one web designer who really had a nice-looking portfolio, and I asked him about the content information that would be displayed, the message that would be displayed. This response was "you tell me what you want the content to be and I will put it there." This is when it hit me.

I did not need a website designer. What I needed was a "content designer." I needed someone who would take my message and get it across to the reader. Although I know some people will argue with me when I say that there are a million great web designers out there but very few quality content designers. This is what I needed. I called and I called and I called, but I did not have very much luck finding someone who even understood the concept of content design. I finally found one and I am so happy that I did. This lady has been a godsend to me. She is is so ingrained in my business that we talk several days a week, and I almost want to say on a daily basis. We have expanded our relationship to where we are writing coaches for each other. We share some of the funny stories that we run across, and we share ideas. This is precisely what they mean when they say that you immerse yourself with your client. She certainly has with me, and I refer business to her because I know what she has done for me. She is not cheap, and I do not expect her to be. I am not looking for cheap. I am looking for quality.

This is what I do. This is my livelihood, and I want to portray the best image I possibly can. Once we started on the project, we found there was a great deal that needed to be done. Not only was it necessary for me to redesign the content of my website, but we also both felt that a complete rebranding with a new identity for my business and my website was in order. We started on October 2008 and the new website was launched in December 2008. It is still an ongoing process, however. We are always adding new things as my business evolves, and I gain new testimonials that I now actively seek from clients. I used to hope they would send one. Now, I ask for one.

I know some people will say they cannot afford to spend the money. I am telling you that you cannot afford not to spend the money. Suck it up and get on with it. It takes money to make money and rather than sit there and whine about not drawing any customers I chose to take charge of my future. I have never regretted a minute of the entire project. It absolutely, positively has made a difference, and some of the things that we are doing have put me out ahead of the competition.

Now, my competition emulates what I do rather than being in front of me. I honestly do not mind their following in my footsteps; that simply means I am out in front of them. I use that same thought process in writing this chapter. Many of my counterparts hesitate to give up this kind of information and speak bluntly about what they have done to increase their business, but I feel differently. I prefer to see private investigators being thought of as professionals. Professionals take care of each other. By testing concepts, failing on some, and trying harder on those that we can win we have an opportunity to meet and possibly even exceed our goals. I am always looking for more, and I will always look for more, but that takes work and if you are willing to put out the work and the time then you can achieve it.

Diana

As Michael said, content and the organization of the content are critical to achieve results from your website. You also need a call to action, ease to the end user, and pathways to get them to where you want them to go. Web designers do what they say they do: they design websites. Design is important. Design without content, however, equals nothing. Web designers rely on you to provide the content. You are an investigator, however, not a marketing person. It behooves you to hire someone to handle your website from start to finish, someone who has a marketing background and who knows your market. As Michael says, you get what you pay for, and having quality material will bring business in your door. You have three seconds to capture a prospect's attention and get them to stay on your site. To do this, you have to be able to wow him or her and speak to their need. Does your website do this? If not, it is not doing you any good. Your business is your livelihood, and you need to invest in those things that will foster growth and bring in revenue.

Michael

As you might detect, I have finally gotten it through my head that in order to be successful you have to build and present a proper business image of yourself and your business—business image that is a positive perception of you and your company—to your market. Without it you are just another average investigator trying to make a living. People should perceive you as a professional sought after for your experience and expertise. You need to do all you can to ensure they have a *true perception* of the value you bring to them.

Diana

The Better Business Bureau says that "Image can mean everything. Having a strong corporate image cannot be overemphasized."

Business image is the public's perception of an organization, whether that perception is intended or not. A good business image does not just happen; it needs to be cultivated and managed. You must play to your strengths and manage your weaknesses. The more you pay attention to your business image, the less you have to convince people to do business with you. They will want to do business with you because they can trust you.

To be seen as a professional and be a leader in your industry, you must break the old stereotype that television created. Your success is counting on this.

How others perceive you and your agency will determine

- Your level of success
- Your credibility
- If people will do business with you
- If people will continue to do business with you
- If people will refer others to you

The benefits of achieving a professional and consistent business image are as follows:

- Increase in *ideal* clients
- Client retention
- Abundance of referrals
- Reduced marketing cost
- Reduced marketing and sales effort
- Reduced marketing and sales time
- Increased profitability
- Employee retention
- Market confidence
- Cutting edge in the market place
- One solid and consistent marketing message
- Credibility and longevity in the marketplace

Do not leave the future of your business to chance. Take time to work on your business and not just in your business. Do not let your business lose its edge. Invest in your business, and it will provide your financial future.

Remember you need to be a business owner first, investigator second. You are a business person who provides investigative services, not an investigator who happens to be in business.

The U.S. Department of Labor Bureau of Labor Statistics states that the employment of private detectives and investigators is expected to grow 18 percent over the decade of 2006 to 2016, and keen competition is expected.

These statistics are proof of *survival of the fittest.* Only 80 percent of new businesses survive the first two years. One in twenty-five businesses survive ten years or more. *Each person's destiny is what he or she makes it. Do the work. Become a business owner first, investigator second and create your destiny.*

Michael

I have changed my attitude since I started on my own. Clients do not care and do not want to know how many schools you have been to, what your education is, how many years you have been a cop, how many cases you have handled. They want to know what you can do for them. They want to know that they are getting value by hiring you. They want to know you will do the right thing and that is in the results.

Chapter 7

DEVELOPING A NICHE BUSINESS

JAMES P. CARINO

Survival as a private investigator in the coming years may well depend on one's ability to adapt to the impact of legislation and consumer demands. Post 9/11 was by all accounts to usher in an era of new business opportunities for the security and investigation professional, and it has, but not generally for the entrepreneur private investigator operating as a sole proprietor or small business person.

At the turn of the new millennium the private investigator already had to cope with the negative impact on the so-called Vail letter, the Federal Trade Commission (FTC) policy that made it mandatory to obtain prior approval from the subject or an employed person to investigate the allegation of which he or she is suspected if the outcome could put his job in jeopardy. The requirement also involved giving the subject an unredacted copy of the investigative report. The restriction fortunately was overturned in 2004 with a revision to the Fair Credit Report Act (FCRA). Additionally, many businesses diverted dollars previously allocated for company investigations to ensure that Y2K (the generally accepted term to describe January 1, 2000) did not cause computer crashes nationwide and worldwide. The mild recession earlier in the twenty-first century also had a negative impact on many regarding billable time. As a result, many investigators are not in a strong business position to cope with the economy that set in before the end of the first decade of this new century.

The plight of the small business private investigator actually, in my professional judgment, started in the early 1970s with new stronger legislation through passage of the Freedom of Information and Right to Privacy Acts by Congress. Although it had little impact that time it began to set the table for the future. Legislation following the Rebecca Schaeffer and Amy Boyer killings put private investigators in a negative national spotlight, leading to legislation limiting access to some public records. The Gramm-Leach-Bliley Act addressed the problem of private investigators pretexting techniques and eliminated such practices against banks. Protection against identity theft legislation by closing down other databases is an ever-increasing threat to the private investigator. Fortunately, exemptions for the private investigator are always possible with national and state private investigator associations becoming increasingly involved to protect the investigative tools, methods, and methodology we use to assist our client base, including the public. The paradox of course is that as public law enforcement continues to get overloaded with major significant threats to national security and public safety, the private investigator is increasingly involved in many cases previously in the sole domain of public law enforcement. At the same time, contravening forces are passing or demanding legislation with the effect of limiting private investigator access to pertinent information. As such, the public loses—and so does the private investigator.

The preceding is intended to be an overview of many, but not all, of the acts and events that have contributed to creating both the dilemmas and the opportunities facing private investigators today. It is not intended, however, to be a detailed primer summarizing or highlighting the entire spectrum of activity that has affected the private investigator profession and will continue to affect private investigators in the future.

This chapter will examine business pursuits that a private investigator can undertake that are either or both recession proof or legislation proof—a niche so to speak to enhance business survival. All business plans should include such niche development for long-range business growth. It is not an all-inclusive list but does address many of the more significant areas of opportunity. Simply, it may be time to reexamine your current billable time model with a new approach toward "diversifying" your business. Selecting the niche to pursue should be based on the education, training, experience, and/or interests such as hobbies, prior nonsecurity or noninvestigative work experience, unique opportunities or special talents, and specialized interests for future studies.

HOW TO START

Any investigator or security professional who claims he or she is an expert in all facets of investigations and security is a person to avoid. These fields of endeavor have become so complex and so extensive that no one can possibly be perfect in all areas of both fields. Simply, there is not a field of study or an employment that does not have a place in this career field. That does not, however, connote that one can automatically qualify in either the investigative or the security career field simply by any type of employment or education. Rather, either can give guidance or direction on what aspect of one of the fields to pursue in the quest to develop a recession or legislative proof niche.

This chapter does not address, however, how to enter into the field. That is left for other authors to develop. Suffice to note, this chapter assumes you are already a private investigator. This chapter also does not address either how to conduct the investigation in any of the niches or fully develop how to market those services. Networking is the name of the game and the key to success. One must have professional colleagues who possess the skills and specialized expertise you do not have if you are to be able to offer a full range of services to clients. Networking fills not only the specialized skills needs but also the geographical needs. Your state-issued license only gives you authority in your own state. Some states offer reciprocity, and a declining number of states (four as of this writing) have no private detective acts, ergo no minimum standards or investigative restrictions. As such, anyone, including convicted felons, can conduct investigations for the public and other clients. A word of caution here; be cognizant of the risk exposure in using an unlicensed private investigator to assist you. Trust, but verify is the credo here. Networking may well hold your key to survival as a business entity.

Networking within the profession is best accomplished by joining professional associations. This is not only the best way but probably the only way to keep abreast of current legislation. It also is, of course, the time-tested method to develop a network of colleagues for mutual benefits. For maximum success, as a minimum, one should join one's state private investigator association and at least one of the national or international associations. Once you overcome the unfounded paranoia that a fellow private investigator will steal your clients, you will find that close professional relationships are a key to survival. Referrals, both from and to you, and assistance are commonplace. There are times when fellow private investigators will require another's help to meet suspense dates or supplement manpower requirements, such as for surveillance. A fellow private investigator's niche can also be of benefit to you to assist in a local or functional basis.

Another major advantage of association memberships is the LIST-SERV® that each utilizes. Used as a major business sharing/referral tool, such e-mail-based mailing lists also offer the opportunity to raise questions on business and operational matters, enabling members to get solutions from fellow members and assist in problem solving. This tool, in itself, can be worth the price of membership.

Membership in associations, however, is not enough for niche business development. Attendance at seminars, conferences, workshops and so on is necessary to keep current with new tools, techniques, methods, methodology, and tradecraft, as well as legislation. Further, it is through these that networking is accomplished. Attendance is also required to qualify for and remain current with the various certifications such as PCI®, CPP®, PSP®, CFE, and CLI, to name a few. As recently pointed out in an article on arson investigations in the May 2010 issue of *PI Magazine,* a basic understanding of fire cause and origin will make one more desirable as an arson expert in the conduct of arson investigations. As noted later, most experts will not conduct certain investigative leads when retained as an expert.

ATTORNEYS

This potential client group is perhaps the most difficult to market. A contact made through a personal visit will at best generate a polite thank you for your time and material. Unless it is a good "keeper," any document finds its way to the circular file. More often than not, the attorney may (1) already have a private investigator on staff or available, (2) use his paralegal for local investigations and internet searching, or (3) call another attorney for a referral. In short, direct marketing to an attorney is difficult at best and improbable for success. Thus, your primary focus needs to be a technique that captures the attorney's attention.

Through personal experience and interfacing with other investigators, several approaches have met with success in the past. Perhaps the best of all is to arrange for a speaking engagement at attorneys' association meetings. Your subject should be one suggested by the group's program chair because he or she will know the group's interests. Make sure you have capability and credibility on the subject matter, however. Prepare as a handout a keeper document that contains your name and related contact information. Lawyers are pack rats. They will not necessarily save a business card or company brochure but will file a document for future retrieval that has potential future applicability.

Determine if the attorney or law firm utilizes expert witnesses, especially in civil suits. Every litigated matter has the potential for four hires: those serving as expert witnesses for either plaintiff or defense and investigators for both sides. If there are multiple defendants, there is a need for more of both. Most, if not all, experts will not conduct any investigative leads in order to refute a challenge by the opposing attorney that he or she only reported information favorable to support a preconceived opinion. Professionally befriending a security expert or positioning yourself to be in the expert's network can be your segway into a law firm.

If the attorneys use a paralegal, ask who conducts the investigative leads outside the local operating area. This, as in all client services, is where membership in a national or international investigative association is an important and essential networking tool.

Many investigations in general, regardless of the client, are suggestive of investigative leads to address under due diligence. The law firms with paralegals will conduct some due diligence depending on the paralegals' training and experience. In civil litigation cases, the normal leads, such as courthouse records checks, background checks of the parties involved, credit and financial histories, vehicle or driver records, are available through database services that attorneys can subscribe to. Civil litigation access can also involve the need for crime scene sketches, checks of city ordinances, interviews of witnesses, canvas of the neighborhood, obtaining crime statistics for prior years, and a host of other leads the attorney may desire prior to taking depositions. Two important points to keep in mind in working with attorneys is that due diligence is needed by both sides and regardless of legislative restrictions. Attorneys can obtain subpoenas and court orders where record checks have been legislatively closed to investigators.

Another area of investigative interest is that of video. With increasing frequency law enforcement is obtaining the videos when pertinent to their investigation, thus preserving it for use in a civil suit. More often than not a civil suit will result from a criminal act. The O.J. Simpson case is perhaps the best-known scenario to illustrate that point. With regard to videos, it is important to act immediately because many commercial, retail, and corporate establishments do not routinely retain videos, tape or digital, more than thirty days. Some locations have been known to tape over the next day, often "accidentally" in order to not have them available as evidence.

Many private investigators will tape interviews and prepare statements for the interviewee's signature from their notes and the taped interview. In those cases, permission to tape the interview is essential with the interviewee acknowledging at the onset and conclusion that the interview was taped with his or her permission.

Photos and videotaping of the incident site are also tools for the private investigator and also frequently beyond the capability of paralegals in many investigations conducted for attorneys. These are two capabilities that all private investigators should possess. Simply, the physical setting where a crime occurred can change by passage of time or by "design." For a plaintiff, it may be important to document the setting as soon as possible after the incident to preserve the scene.

Conducting investigations for attorneys is both legislative and recession proof.

BACKGROUND INVESTIGATION

Background checks were historically a fertile area for one- or two-person private investigator operations. The recent influx of companies offering "full backgrounds" for low prices, however, has made this a less financially lucrative and a competitive area for the small private investigation firm. Many states do not require a private investigator license to conduct background checks, referring to this type investigation as preemployment screening. Further, more and more entities are establishing employee screening, including software programs, for offer to corporate America.

More attractive is the specialized custom-designed background checks for top executives and administrators for which sophisticated, in-depth, specially designed investigations are needed. These scopes are normally beyond the reach of at least some of the "packaged" backgrounds offered by the "new breed" of background investigation (BI) firms with their low fixed price offerings.

Constantly changing privacy protection legislation being passed by states also poses additional challenges for sole proprietor or small firms. Unless one remains current with new laws and rules at both the federal and the state levels, the risk of noncompliance is high. Background investigations are not a particularly complicated type of investigation, but anyone involved should ensure their E & O insurance covers the conduct of background investigations. One should also ensure that the client has received approval from legal counsel regarding the scope and policies. Release forms are required for the conduct of many checks and must be FCRA compliant. If leads are to be conducted in international areas, check with that country's rules and permissible purposes. Complete knowledge of the European privacy protection laws is suggested prior to making any commitments or financial quotes before client interface. It is illegal in many countries to even request a criminal records check from an official law enforcement agency. Costs for criminal checks, where legal, are much higher in the international area than the United States. The conduct of background investigations for the U.S. government is a separate issue and normally not an arena for the new investigator to pursue. Most who employ private sector private investigators will usually consider experienced federal or military special agents with prior top security clearances. There are, of course, exceptions, but such are seemingly very limited. This particular area, although certainly a recession- and legislative-proof niche is not a lucrative field for the less-experienced private investigator.

INSURANCE INVESTIGATORS

The scope of this opportunity includes all types of insurance with perhaps the most common involving workers' compensation and now, increasingly, mortgage fraud. When an insurance policy is written the potential for fraud exists, and the need for investigation is essential. To combat fraudulent claims, many insurance companies have established special investigation units referred to as SIUs. A false claim submitted against an insurance company is, pure and simple, fraud.

Many insurance companies require investigators to possess experience in financial and fraud investigations to qualify for retention as a subcontractor. The CFE certification is highly useful and should be considered. Familiarity with video equipment and surveillance is also a prerequisite required by many insurance companies because many insurance investigators require surveillance as part of the investigation.

INTEGRITY SHOPPING

Some states require a private investigator license to conduct "integrity shopping," but many do not, so competition can arise from noninvestigators. Integrity shoppers can also be found in some city Yellow Pages of telephone directories. Many nonprivate investigator firms will hire housewives, students, friends, and neighbors at a low hourly pay rate to conduct these shopping trips. One key in this initiative is to offer services extant from the primary objective, which exceeds the capability and competence of a nonprivate investigator integrity shopper. To illustrate, in conducting an integrity shopping service for a parking garage company, bar, department store, or other commercial or retail outlet, in addition to the normal checks regarding appearance, honesty, politeness, money handling and processing, also offer other observations appropriate to the location such as injury and accident hazards, lighting outages, security personnel observed, and vulnerabilities exploitable by the criminal element (unlocked doors and open windows, parked vehicles open and unlocked, merchandise out of place, nonfunctioning security equipment, etc.). Integrity shopping requires the operative to meet the appearance of standards required of the task to blend in as a customer or client. As such, race, color, creed, national origin, and sex have the same standards in undercover operations and need to be considered in any integrity shopping project. Care is needed to monitor any new legislation regarding acting under pretext because this initiative could be made illegal if overly restrictive laws are is passed without containing an exemption for licensed private investigators.

SECURITY SURVEYS AND RISK ASSESSMENTS

A security survey and risk assessment is an objective critical on-site examination and analysis of risk exposure to a business, industrial facility, institution, building, and residential complex–any structure that produces, manufactures, and provides a service that houses equipment, property, or people. It is related to but a separate discipline from investigations. A private investigator license is not required nor is any other credential mandated. However, possessing either the ASIS International CPP credential (demonstrated competency in security management) or the PSP credential (for those who conduct threat surveys and design security systems) is a valuable tool for marketability in this security arena. Academic courses in security or attendance at seminars that offer security and security-related courses are suggested for those wanting to pursue this niche. Virtually all security textbooks or private security publications provide excellent guidance and instructions for those wanting to pursue the self-taught approach. My personal favorite is *Introduction to Private Security* by Karen Hess and Henry Wrobleski. A copy of the *Protection of Assets Manual* is also an important reference to process.

Pursuance of security training, as opposed to private investigations training, and the conduct of security surveys, and threat and risk assessments is an important step to eventually qualify as an expert in premises liability and negligent security cases. An expert can be defined as a person whose education, training, and experience can provide the court with an assessment, opinion, or judgment within the area of his or her competence that is not considered known or available to the general public.

LEGISLATIVE AND RECESSION PROOF NICHES

The preceding merely scratches the surface of investigative and security opportunities protected from legislation no matter how severe and restrictive. Each of us can identify other avenues open for exploitation based on individual skills, experience, interests, and hobbies. Your imagination, ingenuity, creativity, and inspiration can come into play. For example, an interest in genealogy–in tracing one's family heritage–can lead to finding missing heirs; fluency at the S-4, R-4, or higher level in a foreign language, especially the less commonly spoken languages, can lead to interpreter or translator assistance and marketability; a background as a CPA or auditor can be a segue into financial and fraud investigations; an engineering or architectural degree can open many doors in the security systems design field; most types of employment experience can be exploited in the undercover or integrity shopping niches.

The development and delivery of training and training programs for business, industry, commercial, and retail environments can also open doors for business opportunities. These can include employee protection travel programs, protection of proprietary information, home security, and certain situations that can be related to preparation of training manuals and other corporate policies and procedures guidelines. Again, where are your skills and interest and what can you develop and market?

As investigators, we are selling our experience, talents, skills, and knowledge. Accepting speaking engagements at association meetings and civic groups, whether for a fee, honorarium or *pro bono* is believed by many to be the best tool for business development. It is certainly less costly than mailing company brochures and so on, which carry a high probability of ending up in the recipient's waste basket. Studies indicate 1 to $1\frac{1}{2}$ percent responses to mailings–not a particularly effective return on investment. Other studies indicate it takes about six contacts (personal visit, mail, radio, television, newspaper or magazine advertisement, etc.) before product, service, or name recognition by a client can be expected. A speaking engagement addresses many of those in one "contact" and if a relevant handout is prepared rather than (or in addition to) a business card or company brochure, recall is further enhanced. For example, a presentation to a small businessmen's group on the need to conduct employee backgrounds along with an FCRA-approval release form as a handout led to two contracts; another presentation to a group of defense attorneys and a prepared checklist for attorneys' use to evaluate the defensibility of clients led to an estimated 100 expert witness civil litigation engagements over a six-year period.

Pro bono and low pay assignments involving criminal defense for the indigent is not only good experience but also good public relations. It also is a niche area safe from legislative extinction.

Some pitfalls to avoid in the judgment of many is focusing solely on providing services for only one client. It may suffice well for a movie plot or fictional thriller and can be tempting, especially if it is in a niche field. However, the loss of the contract can put you out of business. The longer you have a single client, the more difficult to recover if the contract is lost. Your contact and networking base can erode, and your skills and knowledge of other types of investigations can become obsolete. This single client should be interpreted to include a single line of business; for example, undercover, should sweeping legislation make investigating under pretext illegal for everyone, as well as all types of pretext investigations with no exceptions.

There are several other niche fields that have not been included in addressing niche fields: those in the specialized skills matrix such as computer forensics, questioned documents, handwriting analysis, fingerprint examination, polygraph, technical security counter measures (TSCM). These all by definition fit that of a niche, but all require highly specialized training and are basically beyond the reach of many private investigators absent an investment in educational and training time to master those trades and financial expenditures for equipment.

In summary and conclusion, know your exploitable skills and be aware of your limitations. Maximize what you do best and minimize the risk of damage to your reputation by not accepting assignments you are not qualified to handle. It could be advantageous to refer those to others to generate return favors. Finally, make sure you have that legislative- and recession-proof niche for business survival.

Chapter 8

PROFESSIONALISM AND ETHICS–
WALKING IN THE MINEFIELD

WILLIAM F. BLAKE

The life of a real-life private investigator is unlike that portrayed on the television screen. Many of the television private investigators would be in jail if they worked in the real-world environment. The world of the real life investigator revolves around two key words: professionalism and ethics. A tiny step over the line of expected conduct can be disastrous, both for the individual and for the business. Unfortunately, many people believe that the television investigator is always an ethical and competent person–how well we know that is not correct!

The question of ethical conduct presents the same dangers as a minefield in a military conflict–step in the wrong place and your world explodes around you. The television private investigator has the luxury of working under the concepts of literary license and fiction; otherwise, they could not solve a murder or robbery in an hour. Those of us who are professional private investigators have to keep a wary eye on everything we do to ensure that our actions are within legal and ethical guidelines. The legal guidelines can be easily researched and understood. The ethical guidelines are not as obvious.

According to *Webster's II New College Dictionary,* ethics is a principle of right or good behavior, a system of moral principle or values, the study of the general nature of morals and specific moral choices an individual makes in relating to others, and the rules or standards of conduct that govern the conduct of a profession.

Your personal ethics and professional business conduct are your most valuable assets. Professionalism is the embodiment of ethical conduct. You are responsible not only for your personal activities but also the activities of those who are employed by you. Although you may not personally violate ethical standards, you will be "tarred with the same brush" if you allow an employee or subcontractor to commit an illegal or improper action.

WHAT IS PROFESSIONAL BUSINESS CONDUCT?

Among the many attributes of the investigator's professional reputation are his personal appearance and the appearance of his office. Personal appearance includes the style and type of clothing worn, personal cleanliness, and that of your clothing—even your hair style and length.

A cluttered, noisy, and disorganized office is not a confidence builder for potential clients. Additional attributes of professionalism include the language you use. Is it proper English or does it consist of sarcasm, regional idioms, and vulgarity? The words spoken to an individual clearly affect the reaction to your statements. "I want to talk to you" is an authoritarian statement implying one-way communication in the same manner you might speak to an errant child. "I want to talk with you" is less threatening and implies two-way communication seeking input and information.

The language you use and the manner in which you speak to others is a key ingredient in soliciting cooperation. The use of regional speech or dialect may not be understood by individuals from other geographical areas. In the southern part of the United States, the word "peckerwood" is frequently used to describe a person of lesser intelligence, integrity, or family status. At the least, this is an insult to the individual being discussed and confusing to the non-Southerner.

Another example of unprofessional conduct is displaying the accoutrements of a law enforcement officer and of police jargon, such as "perp," when describing someone who may have committed an illegal act. We are not police officers and need to use language clearly understood by the public. We frequently use the word subject, which implies that an individual is guilty of some illegal or improper act. The findings of criminal activity and impropriety are within the venue of the courts and our clients, not the investigator.

It is very unprofessional and dangerous to make a derogatory statement about any person or organization, including law enforcement agencies and other private investigators. If you do so, it will eventually become known by the person or organization. This will ruin your reputation and interfere with your ability to interact with these people or organizations. How would you respond if you made a statement that Joe Jones was a crooked cop and the individual to whom you made this statement replies that Jones is his son-in-law? Here you are—right in the middle of a minefield.

Is Joe sitting with his feet on his desk and reading *Soldier of Fortune* magazine? Is Suzy, the receptionist, chewing gum and filing her nails at the front desk? Over the years, the customs of our society with respect to our interaction with others has declined. One area of concern is the way the younger generations speak to those who are of a much earlier generation. The formerly common habit of shaking hands is not as frequent today. I personally dislike being addressed as "you guys" when I'm in a public area with my family. It is a direct disrespectful inference that my wife is a guy. Some individuals today do not bother to stand up when talking to a person standing beside their desk. Is there an appropriate degree of respect shown to visitors to your office? Remember, you and your business are only as good as the personal and professional conduct and activities of your poorest employee.

One of the quickest ways to be labeled as a nonprofessional is by failing to keep commitments, not being on time for appointments, or failing to return telephone calls or respond to e-mails. Remember that to the business person, "time is money," and failing to recognize this will have a negative impact on your business and personal reputation.

Another common failure in projecting a professional image is the naming of your business and your company slogan. Your business name and slogan are indicators of your business acumen and attitudes. You may consider yourself a very aggressive investigator and think that "mad dog" describes your aggressiveness. The result may be quite the contrary. A mad dog is frequently considered a crazy and foolish person; a reputation of this type will not get you business. Other names to avoid would be similar to "Texas Gumshoe" which sounds like it comes from old-time detective magazines or movies; "007

Investigations," also known as James Bond and Associates, complete with all the movie gimmicks and gadgets; or "Peye069," which could be interpreted as pertaining to a sex act.

An area of professionalism and ethical conduct concerns the content and quality of your written report. Your client did not observe you acquire the information and must rely on your written report of your actions. It is extremely important to ensure that your report is comprehensive, unbiased, nonjudgmental, and a thorough and impartial representation of the facts. Hearsay and unsubstantiated information should not be included in the report unless the information is identified as such. The appearance of your report is another indicator of professionalism. Is your report on ordinary twenty-pound copy paper or is it on twenty-four-pound linen paper? Does your report contain typing errors or obvious corrections? Is your report organized in a logical sequence to facilitate understanding? Remember, appearance is important.

POTENTIAL ETHICAL MINEFIELDS

Ethical dilemmas come in many formats, some obvious and some more subtle, but the resulting actions should always be to *"avoid evil and the appearance of evil."*

The following scenarios represent problems that could arise in your business activities. For each of the following, answers to three questions are important:

1. Is there an ethical issue and, if so, what is it?
2. What could have been done to prevent such a situation?
3. How would you handle the ethical issue(s)?

A. You have been retained by Joe Smith, a small business man in Denver, Colorado, who has agreed to pay your hourly rate and reasonable and necessary expenses. Joe wants to meet you in Las Vegas, Nevada, and you decide to stay in the Presidential Suite of the Desert Hotel and Casino.

The ethical question is whether the use of the Presidential Suite can be considered "reasonable and necessary." As a small business man, your client probably would not use the suite for his own purposes because of the cost. A question to be considered is "Why does Joe want to meet me in Las Vegas instead of at his business location in Denver?" This type of problem can be eliminated by setting a clear standard for the type and cost of hotel facilities to be utilized when in a travel status. A good criterion is to refer to the U.S. government per diem rates.

B. Your client has agreed to meet with you in a distant city and pay your travel, hotel, rental car, and other reasonable expenses. The day of your meeting is extremely hot and your rental car will be too hot and not cool off quick enough, so you take a taxi to the meeting location and charge the taxi fare to your client.

> This is obviously an expense that should not be charged to your client. If you choose to use transportation other than the authorized rental vehicle, it should be a personal expense and not one chargeable to the client. If charged to the client, it would actually be a duplicate transportation cost.

C. You receive a telephone call from Bill Smith, a member of the board of directors of the Ajax Corporation, one of your better clients. Smith asks you to conduct a surveillance of Mary Jones to determine how, where, and with whom she spends her nonworking hours. He tells you Ms. Jones is not married and that you should bill the Ajax Corporation but send the invoice to Smith's residence address. He also asks you not to discuss the matter with any other corporate employees.

> An obvious question is the real intent of Mr. Smith's request: is it a personal or a business request? If it is a business request, why does he want you to send your invoice to his residence address? I would ask him to submit his detailed request to you on company letterhead stationery. I would also ask him the purpose of the request, ostensibly to be better prepared to complete your investigation. Be careful, this could land you in court at a later date, either as a defendant or as a plaintiff's witness against Mr. Smith.

D. You are working as an investigator for a plaintiff's attorney who has initiated civil litigation against the Acme Corporation, the defendant. You receive a telephone call from an attorney representing the Acme Corporation against the plaintiff. The Acme attorney states he would like to meet you for dinner at an exclusive club to discuss the allegations of the plaintiff.

> You should be very suspicious of any request from an opposing attorney to meet without all attorneys being present. This could easily be an attempt to mitigate your investigative action by paying for an expensive meal at an exclusive club. This could also be a violation of the attorney's code of ethics. Never discuss anything with an opposing attorney without permission of all attorneys involved in the matter.

E. You have been contacted by the HR manager of the Alpha Corporation, who tells you that Bill Richards is a troublemaker within the company because he is trying to unionize the employees. The HR manager asks you to get any information possible to discredit Richards.

> This is a situation where you should be very wary of the true intent of the request. Interfering with unionizing a business is a violation of federal law. It appears that the HR Manager wants to use you to gather information and pass the responsibility for illegal conduct to you at a later date. You should refuse such a request because of the potential law violation.

F. During the course of another investigation for the Ajax Corporation, you determine that Sally Doe, the accounts payable manager of a subordinate company of Ajax is the owner of an auto parts store where the Ajax Corporation buys large quantities of auto parts during the year.

> The question here is whether you notify the Ajax Corporation of possible improper actions and/or financial benefits accruing to Ms. Doe. If you have been employed by Ajax to review the activities of all corporate units for improper activities or conflict of interest, being aware of this information would obligate you to communicate it to the corporate headquarters for appropriate action. Another question would be how you became aware of this information? Was it received directly from a corporate headquarters employee or from inquiries at

the subordinate levels? Even if you were not tasked to review the operations of subordinate units, the fact that you got the information from a headquarters employee during the course of your tasked inquiries would make it appropriate to report the information to your headquarters contact.

G. You are being paid for personal vehicle travel at a given rate per mile. As you are leaving for work, your wife asks you to drop her off at the local mall where they are having a "fabulous" sale.

> The question here is does the side trip to the mall increase the mileage charge to your client? If you decide to charge your client for the "diversion mileage," it would be a fraudulent charge. If you did not deviate from your normal travel route, there would be no problem as there should be no additional mileage charges.

H. You are on an extended trip for your client to another city. It is Saturday, and you want something to read to help pass the time. You go to the local news store and purchase the *Washington Post, Boston Globe, New York Times,* and the *Seattle Times* at a total cost of $10.00 and charge the expense to your client.

> This would be a questionable and probably unethical charge to your client unless you can demonstrate an investigative need to obtain information from national newspapers. This is probably a personal expense. Any action or expense that you would not take at your residence or office location should not be charged to the client because you are out of town.

I. You have assigned a single investigative task to a private investigator in Detroit, Michigan. He is to contact the Peace Officers Standards and Training Division of the Michigan State Police in East Lansing, Michigan and determine if an individual, currently assigned to a U.S. Army unit on the east coast, was a former certified police officer in Michigan. You subsequently receive an invoice for eight hours of travel time from Detroit to East Lansing and return as well as four investigative hours for contacting a local U.S. Army Criminal Investigation Command (CID) unit to review the subject's military records.

There are several problems in this situation. You assigned a single task to the Detroit investigator and he, without permission, performed additional tasks. The trip from Detroit to East Lansing is obviously inflated. Prior to assigning tasks to another investigator, you should determine the approximate costs as a part of normal case financial management. The one-way mileage from Detroit to East Lansing is approximately ninety miles with a travel time via Interstate highway of 1.5 hours. This is an overcharge of approximately four hours. The trip to visit his friend at the local U.S. Army CID office was a sham. Military personnel records would not be at, or accessible from, a CID office in Michigan, particularly when the individual was assigned to an east coast unit. In all, this was an inflated invoice for about four hours of alleged investigative effort.

J. You are on an extended business trip for which your client is paying your expenses. You are tired of watching television as your only entertainment and decide to go to the hotel bar for a "couple of drinks." While in the bar, you order a couple of bottles of vintage wine that sell for $75.00 a bottle that you share with a young lady you met in the bar.

This is obviously an unethical and improper expense without prior approval of your client. Even if the event were related to your investigation, the cost of the wine is exorbitant, when a less-expensive bottle of wine would serve the purpose. This appears to be a case of questionable actions on the part of the investigator.

K. You are conducting an investigation in Nevada and are observed by one of your hometown neighbors entering the Mustang Ranch outside of Podunk, Nevada.

Based on the preceding information, it cannot be determined if this is ethical or unethical conduct. If the investigator went to the Mustang Ranch for a legitimate investigative reason, there is no problem. If the investigator went to the brothel, Mustang Ranch, for personal reasons, it is a goldmine for criticism. Investigators must avoid evil and the appearance of evil.

SUMMARY

If you are a truly professional private investigator, you will inherently have a good code of ethics. Without ethics, you will never be a professional investigator. Your personal ethics and professional business conduct are your most valuable assets. Professionalism is the embodiment of ethical conduct. Not only are you responsible for your personal activities but those who are employed by you. Although you may not personally violate ethical standards, you will be "tarred with the same brush" if you allow an employee or subcontractor to commit an illegal or improper action.

Chapter 9

FINANCIAL DISPUTE PREVENTION AND RESOLUTION

WILLIAM F. BLAKE

Financial disputes occasionally arise between the private investigator and the client as in any business endeavor. These disputes may result in unnecessary frustration, animosity, loss and distrust. For only a minimum effort, these problems can be prevented. If agreement cannot be achieved, both parties may become involved in expensive and time-consuming litigation.

INTERACTION WITH CLIENTS

One of the business faults of the private investigator is to get into a situation where there is a conflict of common expectations with the client. This is best prevented through the utilization of written documentation that specifically and clearly outlines the expectations of all parties, including the business and investigations to be under taken. Annex 1 at the end of this chapter is a sample Private Investigator Retention Contract. As with all legal documents, the contract should be reviewed by an attorney for legal sufficiency in the investigator's jurisdiction.

When interacting with law firms it is important to unequivocally inform the law firm that they, not their client, are responsible for all payments. The law firm accepted the client's work based on, among other things, an evaluation of the client's ability to pay for services rendered. The investigator did the same when agreeing to perform services for the law firm.

If a dispute arises with an attorney or law firm, there is an alternative to litigation. Each state has an entity that monitors the activities of attorneys and can be a facilitator in resolving disputes without litigation. If an appeal is made to the state board, the letter should outline the areas in dispute and be accompanied by copies of all relevant documents and letters.

On occasion, a client may not desire to execute a written contract for some reason. This does not eliminate the need and desire for a written understanding of expectations. In lieu of a formal contract, it is possible to arrive at virtually the same contractual obligation through the use of a letter of agreement. This letter of agreement is prepared by the investigator and forwarded via U.S. Postal Service Certified Mail with a return receipt to provide evidence that the client has received the document. Annex 2 of this chapter provides a sample letter.

INTERACTION WITH SUBCONTRACTORS AND NONEMPLOYEES

Unfortunately, there are occasions when disputes arise between the investigator and others with whom he or she has subcontracted work. Again, these disputes can be eliminated or reduced with proper documentation that enumerates expectations and responsibilities.

When there is a probability of working with the same subcontractor on multiple occasions, it may reduce the administrative workload by using a primary contract and subsequent letters of instruction for each assignment. Annex 3 shows a sample Subcontractor Agreement. Annex 4 provides a sample Letter of Instruction.

Another method of defining expectations and responsibilities is to use a modified Letter of Agreement similar to that seen in Annex 2. The Letter of Agreement is the most efficient method of documenting interaction with subcontractors on a one-time basis.

Regardless of the subcontractor documentation used, there should be a confidentiality agreement and a detailed report of daily activity to justify the fees and expenses. A statement that incorporates all investigative hours and expenses into one listing is not adequate to justify the subcontractor costs to the client.

The daily activity report should list investigative efforts by date, investigative time, and expense detail. Expenses in excess of $25 should be substantiated with a receipt that specifically details the expense item and costs.

SUMMARY

Disputes are always costly to everyone involved. With little effort misunderstandings can be avoided through the use of various forms of documented agreement on expectations and responsibilities. The cost of disputes is excessive compared to the minimal actions necessary to prevent adversarial actions that reduce or eliminate the probability of future investigative actions.

ANNEX 1

Private Investigator Retention Contract

1. **Parties.** This contract is made between (Investigator or Agency, Address ("Investigator") and the Firm of (Name and Address) ("Client") regarding the matter of _____.

2. **Retention.** The parties agree that Investigator will only become retained by Client once this contract has been mutually executed and Client has paid the initial nonrefundable retainer specified in paragraph 4.b. Investigator has no duties to Client until such time.

3. **Investigator's Fees and Expenses.** The parties agree that the fee for all time Investigator spends on the case will be compensated at a rate of $_____. It is agreed that this specifically includes (but is not limited to) investigating, research, conferences, consultations with Client, reviewing documents, organizing documents, analysis, testing, responding to requests, report writing, testifying, reading and signing transcripts, local portal-to-portal travel, waiting time, preparing exhibits, preparing demonstrative aids, and preparation time for testifying at deposition, trial, hearing, arbitration or other venues. Investigator's time will be tracked and invoiced to the nearest one fourth of an hour. In lieu of the above hourly rate, duties that reasonably require overnight travel will be billed at the flat rate of $1000/day on site. In any and all events, Client will be responsible for all reasonable out-of-pocket expenses including, but not limited to travel, hotel costs, testing, research, copying, storage of evidence or documents, and so on.

4. **Payment Terms**
   a. All payments are to be made to (Agency Name and Address) Investigator's Taxpayer ID # is _____.
   b. The *nonrefundable* retention retainer amount is $1500.00. Investigator will invoice against this retainer. This nonrefundable retainer amount is the minimum fee due Investigator and is earned upon receipt.
   c. Investigator agrees to invoice client no less frequently than monthly.
   d. All invoices will be paid within 30 days.
   e. Overdue invoices will accrue interest at a rate of 1.5% per month.
   f. Fees for any time Investigator is asked to reserve for testifying (at trial, hearing, deposition, arbitration or other venue) and preparation for said testimony must be paid in advance and in full five (5) business days prior to the time reserved for the scheduled testimony. Investigator is under no contractual obligation to reserve the time or to appear to testify and provide opinions unless Investigator has received

this payment in full five (5) business days prior to the time reserved for the schedule testimony.

g. Client is responsible for collecting any and all testifying fees owed by other lawyers or parties. In the event Investigator's testifying fees are reduced by court order, Client shall still pay Investigator, Investigator's full fee specified in paragraph 3.

h. Investigator will invoice Client upon completion of Investigator's report(s). All fees must be paid in full before a report is released to Client, other parties or anyone else. Investigator is under no duty to release a report until Investigator has been paid in full for all work performed to date.

i. Investigator will invoice Client before scheduled testimony for any outstanding fees and expenses for work performed to date. All such fees must be paid in full before Investigator testifies. Investigator is under no contractual duty to appear to testify and provide opinions until Investigator has been paid in full for all outstanding services performed and expenses incurred on behalf of Client.

5. **Fees for Late Notice Cancellation or Rescheduling of Testimony**

a. Client understands that Investigator will suffer damages from late notice cancellation or rescheduling of Investigator's testimony and that since the precise amount of these damages would be difficult to determine, Investigator shall instead be entitled to the cancellation and rescheduling fees specified in paragraphs 5.c and 5.d.

b. The fees specified in paragraph 4.f are 100% refundable to Client in the event Investigator's scheduled testimony is cancelled or rescheduled with notice to Investigator of three (3) or more business days.

c. In the event Investigator's scheduled testimony is cancelled or rescheduled with one (1) or two (2) business days' notice, Investigator may retain a cancellation fee of 50% of the amount from paragraph 4.f. The remaining amount will, at Client's option, be applied to future testimony or refunded to Client.

d. In the event of same-day cancellation or rescheduling of Investigator's testimony or if Investigator's testimony is completed in less time than was reserved pursuant to paragraph 4.f, Investigator may retain 100% of the amount specified in paragraph 4.f.

e. In the event of any cancellation or rescheduling of testimony, Client shall be responsible for all nonrefundable out-of-pocket travel expenses incurred by Investigator such as airline tickets and hotel rooms.

6. **Duties of Client.** The Client's duties specifically include, but are not limited to,

a. Abiding by the applicable rules of professional conduct for attorneys.

   b. Making *all* payments as specified in paragraphs 4 and 5 under the terms specified in paragraphs 4 and 5.

   c. Providing Investigator with copies of or access to *all* nonprivileged, arguably relevant documents, evidence, and other materials in the underlying matter.

   c. Notifying Investigator of all parties and attorneys in the case so that Investigator can check for conflict of interest.

   e. When circumstances reasonably allow, providing Investigator with prompt notice of any *Daubert* motions, *Frye* motions, motions in limine, or other pretrial motions made by other parties or persons to restrict, exclude, or in any way limit Investigator's testimony or Investigator's participation in the underlying legal matter.

   f. Obtaining Investigator's advance approval (for accuracy) of the relevant portions of any and all answers to interrogatories, motions, Investigator designations or other documents that summarize Investigator's qualifications, methodology, opinion(s), and/or anticipated testimony.

   g. Being available as reasonably requested to meet with Investigator prior to anticipated testimony.

   h. Promptly notifying Investigator of when and where Investigator may be requested to appear to testify.

   i. Promptly notifying Investigator of any issues related to paragraph 8.b of which Client is or becomes aware.

   j. Promptly notifying Investigator of the settlement or final adjudication of the underlying legal matter.

7. Duties of Investigator. The Investigator's duties are

   a. To truthfully represent Investigator's credentials.

   b. To obtain all information and documentation only from legal sources utilizing only legally accepted methods.

   c. To cease work on the underlying legal matter and promptly inform Client whenever Investigator has accrued unpaid fees and expenses totaling more than $1000.00. In this event, Investigator shall not perform further work on the underlying matter until approval is given by Client.

   d. Subject to paragraph 7.d, to prepare a written report if Client requests one.

   e. Subject to paragraph 7.d, and to circumstances beyond the Investigator's control, to meet all reasonable deadlines requested by Client.

   f. To retain and preserve (during this engagement) all evidence provided to Investigator from the underlying matter unless Client gives written permission for destructive testing or the like.

g. To be available on reasonable notice to testify.

h. To be available on reasonable notice to consult with Client. Investigator's cellular telephone number is _____.

j. To work exclusively with Client in the underlying matter unless the parties mutually agree in writing otherwise. Investigator is authorized without consultation with Client to engage in similar or related activities in matters not directly or indirectly pertaining to the underlying legal matter.

k. Upon receipt from Client of the list of attorneys and parties specified in paragraph 6.d, to within 30 days check for conflict of interest with due care and within the same 30-day period to notify Client of any conflict of interest discovered that preclude Investigator's further involvement in the underlying legal matter.

8. **Investigator's Right of Withdrawal From Case.** Investigator shall have the absolute right to withdraw, without any liability, from the case if Client violates any of the duties specified in paragraph 6 above or if

a. Investigator discovers a conflict of interest that precludes Investigator's further involvement in the underlying legal matter.

b. Investigator discovers that because of legal restrictions Investigator's involvement or testimony in the case could reasonably be deemed to be practicing Investigator's profession without a license.

9. **Withdrawal.** Notice of withdrawal under paragraph 8 shall be in writing from Investigator to Client. In the event of withdrawal, the parties agree that Client remains fully liable for all accrued but unpaid fees, expenses, and interest.

10. **Termination.** This contract shall be terminated upon written notice to Investigator from Client at any time, by Investigator's withdrawal pursuant to paragraph 8, at such time as Client is no longer involved in the underlying matter, or upon the settlement or final adjudication of the underlying legal matter. In the event of termination, Client is still responsible for all sums owed Investigator.

11. **Document/Evidence Retention.** Investigator shall have no duty to retain any documents, reports, evidence, transcripts, exhibits, e-mail messages, electronic files, or other materials from the underlying matter for more than thirty (30) days following the termination of this agreement. Investigator shall return (at Client's expense) all records and evidence in the underlying matter to Client if a written request to do so is received by Investigator within the thirty (30) days following the termination of this agreement.

12. **Airline Flights.** All airline flights taken by Investigator shall be direct,

nonstop, coach class where possible. All airline travel in excess of four (4) hours flying time shall be business class where possible.

13. **Disputes.** Any controversy, claim, or dispute arising out of or relating to this Contract, shall be resolved through binding arbitration conducted in accordance with the rules of the American Arbitration Association in the state in which the Investigator is domiciled. The law of the state in which the Investigator is domiciled will be the governing law. The arbitration award will be enforceable in any state or federal court. In any arbitration or court proceeding, the prevailing party shall be entitled to recover reasonable attorney's fees and costs. In addition, Client shall be responsible for payment of attorney's fees and expenses associated with the Investigator's efforts to collect monies owed under the terms of this Contract.

14. **Miscellaneous.** Each party agrees that it may not assign its interest, rights, or duties under this Contract to any other person or entity without the other party's prior approval. (Investigator is under no duty to work for successor firms on the underlying matter.) The performance of this contract by either party is subject to acts of God, death, disability, government authority, disaster, or other emergencies, any of which make it illegal or impossible to carry out the agreement. It is provided that this contract may be terminated for any one or more of such reasons by written notice from one party to the other without liability. If either party agrees to waive its right to enforce any term of this contract, it does not waive its right to enforce any other terms of this contract. This written contract represents the entire understanding between the Investigator and Client. The individual signing this contract on behalf of Client represents and warrants that he/she is duly authorized to bind Client.

15. **Additional Provisions (check all those that apply)**

    a. ❑ **Investigator Unavailable.** Notwithstanding paragraph 7, Investigator is unavailable to perform obligations under this contract during the following time frame(s):

    _____

    _____

    _____

    b. ❑ **Business Class Flights.** Notwithstanding paragraph 12, all flights taken by Investigator longer than four (4) hours shall be by business class or first class if business class is unavailable.

    c. ❑ **Scope of Work.** Client is requesting an inquiry in the follow area(s):

    _____

    _____

    _____

INVESTIGATOR, by

CLIENT, by

_____

_____

Signature

Signature

_____

_____

Print Name

Print   Name

_____

_____

Date: _____

Date: _____

ANNEX 2

Letter of Agreement

(Business Letterhead)

To: Certified Mail Number _____

Re: (Case Name, My File Number _____)

Dear Client:

The following is my understanding of our discussion on (Date) concerning this matter:

1. To accomplish our mutual goals, (Business Name) agrees to undertake the following tasks as follows:
   a. (Conduct an inquiry to determine the facts and situation surrounding the assaults of [Mr. Jones on Date]).
      (1) (Interview Mr. Jones, Mr. Smith, and other identified witnesses)
      (2) (Obtain documentation of Mr. Jones' injuries)
      (3) (Request Mr. Jones to provide medical information from individuals who provided medical care at the time of, and subsequent to, the date of injury)
      (4) (Develop any relevant information obtained during the inquiry)
   b. (Provide you with a written report of the information developed during this inquiry)
   c. (Provide you with weekly verbal progress reports and a final report not later than _____)
   d. (Obtain all information from legal sources via legally permissible activities)
   e. I certify that I have all the insurance and licenses required by law.
   f. (Client Name) will be invoiced no less frequently than monthly
2. To accomplish our mutual goals, (Client name) agrees to the following tasks and obligations as follows:
   a. A nonrefundable *retention* retainer amount of ($ Amount) will be paid to (Business Name) in the amount of ($_____) before any tasks will be performed relating to this matter.
   b. All invoices will be paid to, and received by, (Business Name) within thirty (30) days of the date of the invoice.
   c. Overdue invoices will accrue interest at a rate of 1.5% per month.

     d. In the event that litigation is required to obtain payment of previously provided invoices, the nonprevailing party will be responsible for all attorney fees and related expenses of the prevailing party.

3. (Business Name) will be paid at an hourly rate of ($_____) for investigative and administrative activity related to this matter.

4. (Client Name) will be responsible for all reasonable expenses incurred by (Business Name) relating to this matter. Any anticipated expenditure by (Business Name) in excess of ($___) will require advance authorization by (Client Name).

5. Local area travel mileage will be paid at the rate of (____) in accordance with the Internal Revenue Service authorized rate. The local area is defined as _____.

6. Out-of-area expense will be paid in accordance with the official U.S. Government per diem rate for the area to which travel is performed.

7. Out-of-the-area investigative time in excess of eight (8) hours will be at a daily rate of ($_____) plus reasonable expenses.

8. Receipts will be required for all expenditure in excess of $25.00 dollars. When a receipt cannot be obtained, an affidavit of expenditure will be provided. The reason for lack of a receipt will be stated in the affidavit.

9. No investigative activity in excess of that outlined above will be undertaken by (Business Name) without the prior authorization of (Client Name).

    If you disagree with my understanding of our discussion, please notify (Business Name) in writing within ten (10) days or I will consider this a valid agreement between (Business Name) and (Client Name).

Sincerely,

Name
(Position Title)

ANNEX 3

Subcontractor Agreement

THIS SUBCONTRACTOR AGREEMENT made this _____ day of _____, 20___, by and between (Business Name and address), a (State) corporation (hereinafter "Contractor"), and (hereinafter "Subcontractor") _____, and _____ (hereinafter "Subcontractor's Principal").

WHEREAS, the Contractor is engaged in the business of offering private investigation and litigation support services to its customers; and

WHEREAS, Subcontractor is also engaged in the same field; and

WHEREAS, Contractor has previously entered into an agreement with various attorneys (hereinafter "Attorneys"), identified by Contractor to Subcontractor in the Letter of Instructions for each investigative or litigation support matter, to provide private investigation and/or litigation support services to Attorneys (hereinafter defined as the "Main Contract"); and

WHEREAS, Contractor wishes to obtain the services of Subcontractor to assist it, as an independent contractor, in performing the above-referenced services; and

WHEREAS, Contractor's execution and performance of this Agreement will also materially benefit Subcontractor's Principal; and

WHEREAS, the parties have entered into an agreement under which Contractor will obtain the services of Subcontractor pursuant to the terms and conditions set forth in this Agreement;

NOW, THEREFORE, in mutual consideration of the covenants passing by and between the parties as set forth herein, and $10.00 and other valuable considerations paid, the receipt of which is acknowledged, the parties hereby agree as follows:

1. At the request of Contractor, Subcontractor will provide private investigation and/or litigation support services as may be required by Contractor, in Contractor's sole discretion, from time to time in order for Contractor to fulfill its obligations under the Main Contract. The terms of the Main Contract are hereby expressly incorporated herein and Subcontractor shall perform all obligations under this contract in conformity with the terms of the Main Contract. To the extent any of the terms of the Main Contract and this Agreement conflict, the terms of this Agreement shall control.

2. Prior to undertaking said services, Subcontractor will be entitled to review the request made to determine whether or not the services as requested are of a nature and type of services typically offered to be per-

formed by Subcontractor. In the event said services are not in the scope of the services typically performed by Subcontractor, Subcontractor will not be required to perform said services.

3. Subcontractor shall perform all services hereunder pursuant to the terms of this Agreement and the Main Contract and in accordance with all applicable federal, state, and local laws and regulations. All information obtained by Subcontractor in the course of performing its obligations hereunder will be obtained only through legal sources.

4. As part of the services to be performed by Subcontractor hereunder, Subcontractor shall prepare written reports summarizing all investigative and/or litigation support activities engaged in by Subcontractor.

5. Subcontractor acknowledges that the services performed by Subcontractor hereunder are intended to be used by Attorneys in their representation, as attorneys, of their clients. As such, Subcontractor agrees that any communications made to Subcontractor by Contractor, Attorneys, their clients, or any third party in the course of Subcontractor's performance of any of its obligations hereunder shall be deemed privileged communications which shall not be divulged to any third parties whatsoever. Subcontractor further agrees that any information, data, documents, recordings, video recordings, or computerized data which comes into the hands of Subcontractor during the course of this Agreement shall be deemed the property and work product of Attorneys and shall also not be divulged to any third parties whatsoever. The provisions of this paragraph shall survive the termination of this Agreement.

6. Upon termination of this Agreement Subcontractor shall turn over to Contractor and/or Attorneys the originals and all copies of any and all documents, tape recordings, video recordings, all computerized data or any other information or data, whatsoever and any copies or duplications thereof obtained by or prepared by Subcontractor during the term of this Agreement or which are in any way related to the services performed by Subcontractor under this Agreement. Also, upon termination of this Agreement, Subcontractor shall execute a certification certifying to Contractor and Attorneys that neither Subcontractor nor any of its representatives, agents, or employees have retained any such documents, recordings, or information or any copies thereof.

7. The parties agree that in the event Subcontractor shall disclose any information it may obtain in the course of this Agreement to any third party or shall fail to turn over any data or other information referred to in paragraph 6 hereof to Contractor or Attorneys upon the termination of this Agreement, that Contractor, Attorneys, and/or Attorneys' Client shall be entitled to seek appropriate equitable remedies from a court of compe-

tent jurisdiction, including any injunction prohibiting Subcontractor from violating the provision of the Agreement, and that Subcontractor will not advance as a defense in any such action that Contractor, Attorneys, or Attorneys' Client have an appropriate remedy at law therefore.

8. Subcontractor shall be responsible for the supervision, management, and control of all of its employees and representatives engaged in the performance of any portion of Subcontractor's obligations under this Agreement. Subcontractor acknowledges that it and its employees and representatives are independent contractors and not employees or servants of Contractor and that Contractor has no authority to manage, control, or direct the operations of Subcontractor or its employees or representatives in the performance of this Agreement.

9. Subcontractor warrants to Contractor that Subcontractor and all of its employees, representatives, and agents who will be performing any services under this Agreement shall at all times hold valid business and other licenses as required by any jurisdiction in which services are to be performed under this Agreement.

10. During the term of this Agreement, Subcontractor agrees to maintain in full force and effect liability and workers' compensation insurance issued by a carrier acceptable to Contractor insuring Subcontractor, its agents, representatives and employees, and Contractor against all claims of liability which arise out of Subcontractor's actions undertaken during the period of this Agreement, including any claims, in a minimum amount of $1,000,000. Subcontractor shall provide Contractor with evidence of such insurance prior to commencement of any activity on behalf of the Contractor. Subcontractor and/or his agents will not carry firearms while performing duties for the Contractor.

11. Subcontractor and Subcontractor's Principal agree that the provisions of this Agreement shall be of material benefit to both Subcontractor and Subcontractor's Principal. Therefore, in material consideration of the promises made by Contractor herein, Subcontractor and Subcontractor's Principal hereby agree as follows:

    a. Subcontractor or Subcontractor's Principal agree to indemnify and hold Contractor harmless from and against any and all claims, actions, judgments, damages, liens or costs, including reasonable attorney's fees incurred by Subcontractor in defending against same or in enforcing the provisions of this paragraph arising out of any actions or services undertaken or performed by Subcontractor or its agents, representatives or employees at any time during the terms of this Agreement.

    b. Subcontractor and Subcontractor's Principal agree to indemnify and hold Contractor harmless from and against any and all claims, actions, judgments, damages, liens or costs, including reasonable attorney's fees incurred by Subcontractor in defending against same or in enforcing the provisions of this paragraph arising out of Subcontractor's relationship with any of its employees, agents, or representatives, including, but not limited to, any claims for payment of fringe benefits, payroll, or other employee related taxes.

   c. Subcontractor and Subcontractor's Principal hereby agree to indemnify and hold Contractor harmless from and against any all claims, actions, judgments, damages, liens or costs incurred by Contractor, including reasonable attorney's fees incurred in defending against same or in enforcing the provisions of this paragraph, arising out of any untrue warranties made by Subcontractor in this Agreement, or as a result of any breach of any provision of this Agreement by Subcontractor.

12. Subcontractor shall be solely responsible for the payment of all appropriate payroll and other taxes, as well as the salaries of its employees, representatives, or agents.

13. This Agreement shall be terminable at will by either party. Contractor shall be entitled to withhold the payment of any funds owed to Subcontractor at the conclusion of this Agreement until such time as Subcontractor has returned all documents, records, recordings, video recordings, data, or other information received by or prepared by Subcontractor during the terms of this Agreement and all copies and duplicates thereof and has executed the certification set forth in paragraph 6 above.

14. In consideration of Subcontractor's full performance of its obligations set forth in this Agreement, Contractor shall pay Subcontractor at the manhour rate stated in the separate Letter of Instructions for services performed by the representative or employees of Subcontractor in performance of the investigative and/or litigation support services undertaken by Subcontractor under this Agreement. Subcontractor shall not undertake any services under this Agreement until instructed to do so in writing by Contractor. At the time Contractor notifies Subcontractor to undertake such activities, Contractor will notify Subcontractor in writing the total amount of hours Subcontractor is authorized to spend in the performance of said services. Any hourly services performed by Subcontractor or its agents, representatives or employees in excess of those expressly approved in writing prior to their being undertaken by Subcontractor shall not be chargeable to Contractor.

15. In addition to the compensation set forth in paragraph 13 hereof, Subcontractor shall be entitled to be reimbursed for all documented expenses incurred by Subcontractor, its agents, representatives, or employees in the performance of any services as set forth under this Agreement, sub-

ject to the following:

a. Subcontractor shall be responsible for providing to its representatives, agents, and employees, at its sole expense, all supplies and equipment, including, but not limited to, motor vehicles, recorders, videotaping equipment, or cameras necessary to fulfill Subcontractor's obligations under this Agreement. Subcontractor shall also be responsible, at its sole expense, for making all necessary repairs and maintenance to said equipment.

b. Contractor shall pay to Subcontractor a mileage allowance of ___ cents per mile for all motor vehicle travel undertaken by Subcontractor, its employees, representatives, and agents in performance of its obligations under this Agreement. Subcontractor shall not incur more than ___ miles in vehicle travel without the express written consent of Contractor. Contractor will have no obligation to reimburse Subcontractor for any mileage claimed in excess of said ___ miles unless Subcontractor shall have obtained the written consent to exceed said mileage allowance from the Contractor prior to incurring same.

c. Contractor shall reimburse Subcontractor for all verifiable nonmotor vehicle expenses incurred by Subcontractor in the performance of any services set forth in this Agreement. Notwithstanding the foregoing, however, prior to incurring any such expenses over $_____, Subcontractor shall present Contractor with a written summary of all of its anticipated expenses which summary must be approved in writing by Contractor prior to Subcontractor incurring same. Contractor shall have no obligation to reimburse Subcontractor for any expenses not approved in writing by Contractor as set forth herein prior to Subcontractor incurring same. Contractor shall further not be responsible for reimbursement to Subcontractor for any expenses claimed by Subcontractor which Contractor cannot independently verify.

16. Subcontractor shall not assign any of its rights, duties, or obligations under this Agreement without the express written consent of Contractor.

17. This Agreement sets forth the entire understanding and agreement of the parties and supersedes all prior oral or written agreements among the parties hereto relating to subject matter contained herein and merges all prior and contemporaneous discussions among them. No party hereto shall be bound by any definition, condition, representation, warranty, covenant, or provision other than as expressly stated in this Agreement or as hereafter set forth in a writ that has been executed by such party or by a duly authorized representative of such party.

18. All notices required by this Agreement or as may arise during the term of this Agreement may be relayed to the parties by personal delivery,

telegram, or private courier or by certified or registered mail, postage prepaid, return receipt requested addressed to the party to whom intended at the following address:

a. If to Contractor:

(Contractor name and mailing address)

b. If to Subcontractor:

19. The validity, instruction and enforceability of this Agreement shall be governed in all aspects by the laws of the State of _____, without regard to its conflict of laws rule.

20. The parties hereto expressly agree that it is not the intention of the parties hereto to violate any public policy, statutory or common law rules, regulations, treaties, or decisions of any government or agency thereof. If any provision of this Agreement is judicially or administratively interpreted or construed as being in violation of any such provision, such articles, sections, sentences, words, clauses or combinations thereof shall be inoperative in such jurisdiction and the remainder of this agreement shall remain binding upon the parties hereto and in full force and effect.

21. This Agreement shall be binding upon and shall endure to the benefit of the parties hereto and their respective heirs, executors, administrators, personal representatives, successors and assigns.

THE PARTIES HERETO ACKNOWLEDGE THAT THEY HAVE READ THIS AGREEMENT AND UNDERSTAND ITS TERMS AND AGREE TO BE BOUND HEREBY;

AND IN WITNESS WHEREOF, the parties hereto have caused this Agreement to be executed as of this ___ day of _____, 20___.

"Contractor"
(Business Name).
By:_____
Name: _____
Title: _____

"SUBCONTRACTOR"
By: _____
Name: _____
Title: _____
"SUBCONTRACTOR'S PRINCIPAL"

By: _____
Name: _____

ANNEX 4

Subcontractor Letter of Instruction

(Business Letterhead)
(Date)

(Subcontractor Name and Address)

    Re: Letter of Instruction (Date)
    Sam Spade v. Dick Tracy
    Our File Number

Dear _____;

    This Letter of Instruction supplements the Subcontractor Agreement, dated _____ by and between (Business Name) and your firm, and the Subcontractor Agreement, dated _____, by and between (Business Name) and your firm.

    Per our conversation of _____, it is agreed that you will be compensated at the rate of $_____ per man hour and _____ per mile for motor vehicle mileage and actual expenses.

    Compensation is limited to ____ man-hours and ____ miles of motor vehicle travel. Actual expenses are limited to no more than $_____ for any one expenditure and $_____ in total expenditures. Authority to exceed these financial guidelines and the below outlined task limitations must be authorized by (Business Name) based on adequate justification.

    In accordance with the terms of the Subcontractor Agreement and this Letter of Instruction, please conduct the following activities:

1.
2.

You are reminded that the services to be provided by you may involve preparation of and access to privileged information intended to be protected under the attorney-client privilege and attorney work product rule. For the purposes of the attorney-client privilege and work product rule, you may not assign your duties under the Subcontractor Agreement.

    Please account for your investigative hours, mileage, and other expenses, rates, and computed charges on your separate invoice. Your invoice must be submitted upon completion of the requested service or at least once monthly.

To meet my client's needs, please provide me with an update of your investigative activity and results as of Friday of each week and a completed report of your investigative efforts by _____.

Sincerely,
(Name)
(Title)

Part II

BASIC INVESTIGATIVE SKILLS

Chapter 10

INTERVIEWS, INTERPRETERS, AND STATEMENTS

WILLIAM F. BLAKE

T he private investigator's principal stock in trade is the ability to
obtain information from various sources. This assumes the ability
to communicate with others. In a multicultural society such as the
United States, the English language ability of some residents poses a
problem. Also contributing to this problem are the limited linguistic
skills of many investigators. To circumvent these issues, it may be necessary to interject a third person into the quest for information. This
creates another problem to be addressed.

Because communication is a two-way exchange between the speaker and the listener, it is important to be accurate in the interpretation
of the speaker's words. When conducting the interview, it is important
to remember that the job of the investigator is to determine whether
an incident occurred and to identify a particular person as being the
responsible party. It is important to ensure that the focus of any interview is on the incident and not the alleged perpetrator. Being impartial requires that all individuals be considered innocent until there is
adequate proof that a specific individual is responsible.

The professional investigator must ensure that the words spoken
during an interview do not suggest to the person being interviewed
that a specific response is required; it may deliberately or mistakenly
indicate a particular individual is responsible for an incident. The
investigator must have many skills to be a highly skillful interviewer—
some are instinctive and some must be learned. To achieve the goal of

impartiality and professionalism, the investigator must have some unique attributes, among which are

- Observant of body language and locations
- Resourceful
- Patient
- People oriented
- Understanding of human nature
- Knowledgeable of the legal implications of his or her work
- A skilled communicator
- Receptive to different ideas and concepts; impartial and receptive to alternate ideas
- Possessed of a sense of confidence and well-being
- Dedicated to work
- Self-starter
- Skeptical
- Intuitive
- Energetic
- Good actor
- Capable of good judgment
- Logical
- Intelligent
- Imaginative
- Of good character
- Professional

PLANNING THE INTERVIEW

As with any part of an investigation, it is important to prepare for an interview. The manner in which you conduct the interview will be directly related to your success. If the investigator uses a rambling approach to obtain information, she or he sends a message to the person being interviewed that she or he is not prepared and can probably be easily misled by the interviewee. A structured approach sends a message of professionalism and competence.

The most essential preparation is a complete and thorough understanding of all available information concerning the matter under inquiry. The first few minutes of an interview with an individual sets the tone for the rest of the encounter. It is the investigator's responsibility to create a calm atmosphere in which the interviewee will feel relaxed and willing to communicate. This is especially important when the interviewee is a native of a country where investigators are not respected or use unconventional and frequently repressive interview techniques.

Cultural awareness is a key component of establishing a respectful rapport with the interviewee. Because of cultural background differences, there may be those who are afraid of anyone who appears to have "authority" over them. This may be caused by a uniformed officer, supervisor, or manager or the manner in which the interviewer speaks. Family and cultural loyalty is also an influence to be overcome. A few minutes of general conversation not related to the matter at issue may help to develop mutual rapport with the interviewee. Initially showing a conversational interest in the interviewee as a person is a considerable help in reducing the possible fears of the interviewee.

INTERVIEW METHODOLOGY

The interview format and methodology should be known by all interviewers and interpreters prior to the start of the interview. A second interviewer should be present during the interview of a person of the opposite sex to reduce the probability of a claim of impropriety on the part of the interviewer. There should be a prearranged signal between the interviewers for when it is desirable to change interviewers. There should also be a separate signal to be used between the interviewers and the interpreter when there is a need to talk out of the hearing of the interviewee. Caution should be exercised when selecting the interviewers. If the interviewers are significantly larger in stature than the interviewee, there is always the possibility that the interviewee may claim intimidation because of the size of the interviewers. Regardless of stature, an interviewer with a calm, nonconfrontational and respectful demeanor will achieve better results.

The physical setup of the interview room plays a significant part in reducing problems of perceived restraint of freedom for the interviewee. The ideal setup is with the interviewee in a position in which there is no actual or implied indication that the interviewee is not free to leave the interview at any time. The primary interviewer should be directly across the table from the interviewee to maintain eye contact. The room furniture should be limited to a table and chairs for the interviewee and the interview team. The walls should be free of all distractions such as pictures and related items. The interpreter should be seated where he or she is not directly facing the interviewee, although in a position to observe the facial expressions and body language of the interviewee. The use of audio and visual recording equipment is a matter of personal preference. However, it is wise to advise the interviewee that such equipment is being used.

As a private investigator you are not required to advise individuals of their Miranda rights unless you are conducting an interview under the direction and control of a law enforcement officer or prosecutor. Using an off-duty law enforcement officer who may be acting in a security officer or private investigator capacity can create problems. Prior to using such a person to conduct an interview, it is wise to obtain written legal advice concerning the interview tactics.

WEINGARTEN RIGHTS

There are additional legal requirements when the person being interviewed is a member of a labor union. Principal among these are the requirements of *NLRB v. J. Weingarten, Inc.*, 420 U.S. 251, which was decided by the United States Supreme Court concerning the rights of unionized workers. The pertinent parts of this decision are:

A. Weingarten rights apply only during investigatory interviews. An investigatory interview occurs when: (1) management *questions an employee* to obtain information; and (2) the employee *has a reasonable belief that discipline or other adverse consequences may result.* For example, an employee questioned about an accident would be justified in fearing that she might be blamed for it. An employee questioned about poor work would have a reasonable fear of disciplinary action if he should admit to making errors.

B. Under the Supreme Court's *Weingarten* decision, the following rules apply to investigatory interviews:
   1. The employee can request union representation before or at any time during the interview.
   2. When the employee asks for representation, the employer must choose from among three options:
      a. Grant the request and delay questioning until the union representative arrives;
      b. Deny the request and end the interview immediately; or
      c. Give the employee a choice of: (a) having the interview without representation or (b) ending the interview.
C. If the employer denies the request for union representation and continues the meeting, the employee can refuse to answer questions.
D. Employers sometimes assert that the only function of a union steward at an investigatory interview is to observe the discussion; in other words, to be a silent witness. This is incorrect. The steward must be allowed to advise and assist the employee in presenting the facts. When the steward arrives at the meeting:
   1. The supervisor or manager must inform the steward of the subject matter of the interview; in other words, the type of misconduct being investigated.
   2. The steward must be allowed to have a private meeting with the employee before questioning begins.
   3. The steward can speak during the interview, but cannot insist that the interview be ended.
   4. The steward can object to a confusing question and can request that the question be clarified so that the employee understands what is being asked.
   5. The steward can advise the employee not to answer questions that are abusive, misleading, badgering or harassing.
      When the questioning ends, the steward can provide information to justify the employee's conduct.
E. An employer does not have to inform an employee that he or she has a right to union representation.

QUESTIONS AND ANSWERS
REGARDING WEINGARTEN RIGHTS

Steward's Request

Q: If I see a worker being questioned in a supervisor's office, may I ask to be admitted?

A: Yes. A steward has a right to insist on admission to a meeting that appears to be a Weingarten interview. If the interview is investigatory, the employee must be allowed to indicate whether he or she desires the steward's presence.

Coercion

Q: An employee summoned to a meeting with her supervisor asked for her steward. The supervisor said, "You can request your steward, but if you do, I will have to bring in the plant manager and you know how temperamental she is. If we can keep it at this level, things will be better for you." Is this a Weingarten violation?

A: es. The supervisor is raising the specter of increased discipline to coerce an employee into abandoning her Weingarten rights.

Can The Employee Refuse To Go To Meeting?

Q: A supervisor told an employee to report to the personnel office for a "talk" about his attendance. The employee asked to see his steward, but the supervisor said no. Can the employee refuse to go the office without seeing his steward first?

A: No. Weingarten rights do not arise until an investigatory interview actually begins. The employee must make a request for representation to the person conducting the interview. An employee can only refuse to go to a meeting if a supervisor makes clear in advance that union representation will be denied at the interview.

Medical Examination

Q: Our employer requires medical examinations when workers return from medical leaves. Can an employee insist on a steward during the examination?

A: No. A run-of-the-mill medical examination is not an investigatory interview.

Lie Detector Test

Q: Do Weingarten rights apply to polygraph tests?
A: Yes. An employee has a right to union assistance during the pre-examination interview and the test itself.

Sobriety Test

Q: If management asks an employee if he will submit to a test for alcohol, does Weingarten apply?
A: The employee must be allowed to consult with a union representative to decide whether or not to take the test.

Locker Search

Q: If a guard orders an employee to open a locker, can the employee insist on a steward being present?
A: No. A locker search is not an investigatory interview.

Counseling Session

Q: An employee was given a written warning for poor attendance and was told she must participate in counseling with the HR department. Does she have a right to a union steward at the counseling sessions?
A: This depends. If notes from the sessions are kept in the employee's permanent record, or if other employees have been disciplined for what they said at counseling sessions, an employee's request for a steward would come under Weingarten. If management gives a firm assurance that the meetings will not be used for discipline and promises that the conversations will remain confidential, however, Weingarten rights would probably not apply.

Private Attorney

Q: Can a worker insist on a private attorney before answering questions at an investigatory interview?

A: No. Weingarten only guarantees the presence of a union representative.

Recording the Interview

Q: Can a supervisor tape-record an investigatory interview?
A: This depends. The Weingarten decision itself does not forbid an
employer from tape recording an investigatory interview. If this
represents a new policy on the part of the employer, however, the
steward can object on the ground that the union did not receive
prior notice and have an opportunity to bargain.

Questions About Others

Q: If a worker is summoned to a meeting and asked about the role of
other employees in illegal activities, can the worker insist on assistance from a union representative?
A: Yes. Although the employee may not be involved in wrongdoing,
he or she risks discipline by refusing to inform on others or admit-
ing that he or she was aware of illegal activities. Because what he
or she says at the meeting could get the employee into trouble, he
or she is entitled to union representation.

Obstruction

Q: The company is interviewing employees about drug use in the
plant. If the union representative tells the employees not to answer
questions, could management go after the union representative?
A: Yes. A union representative may not obstruct a legitimate investigation into employee misconduct. If management learns of such
orders, the representative could be disciplined.

WHAT ARE THE RIGHTS OF A NONUNION
EMPLOYEE IN A UNIONIZED BUSINESS?

For various reasons, it is not uncommon to have a mixture of union
and nonunion employees in the same business entity. Some individuals may choose to not be a member of the union. Others may be excluded from union membership because of their supervisory or man-

agement positions. These individuals do not have Weingarten rights.

As a matter of fairness and to preclude potential allegations of impropriety, nonunion employees should be allowed to have an observer of their choice present during the interview. The observer should not be allowed to participate in the interview in any manner. The observer is not an adviser to the interviewee, and both parties should be made aware of this restriction. The observer should be seated in a position where it is not possible for the interviewee and observer to exchange nonverbal cues.

At a later date, the circumstances of an interview may be called into question for the purpose of claiming intimidation of the interviewee. As a precaution, the circumstances of the interview should be documented. At a minimum, this documentation should include the start and ending times of the interview, the location of the interview room and the location of each person within the room, all persons present during the interview and the reason for their presence, how long each person was present in the interview room, any refreshments provided to the interviewee, and the times and length of each break in the interview process. If the interviewers have drinks or other refreshments, the interviewee should be provided with similar amenities.

INTERVIEWING MINORS AND THE ELDERLY

No interview should be conducted with a minor, normally less than eighteen years of age, without the knowledge and permission of a parent or guardian. When possible, this permission should be obtained in written format. A parent or guardian is normally allowed in the interview room as an observer and does not participate in the interview unless requested to do so by the interviewer.

Interviews with the elderly pose a different problem. Depending on the status of their mental acuity, they may resort to chatter and digress from the issues. For many of the elderly, the interview may be a temporary respite from loneliness that gives them an opportunity for interaction not normally available to them. On the other hand, the elderly may pay extraordinary attention to details of an incident because it is an exception to their daily routine.

DEVELOPING INTERVIEW QUESTIONS

The structure of the questions will control the quality and length of the interview. Your interviewing techniques will define the amount and accuracy of the information obtained from each interviewee. A question that solicits a yes or no answer should be used rarely. This type of question should only be used to determine if the interviewee has access to a greater variety of general information.

Each question should be based on the use of the six basic interrogatives of who, why, what, where, when, and how. The basic interrogatives should be applied to the interviewee's response to each question to obtain the maximum information. Every question should be structured to specifically obtain desired information but not to indicate the desired answer. The interviewer should be wary of leading questions and letting the interviewee ramble on. A leading question is one that implies the answer. For example, "John Smith was at the scene of the incident, wasn't he?" This type of question will result in a yes or no answer. A more proper question would be "Who was at the scene of the incident?"

WHAT IS THE BEST LOCATION FOR CONDUCTING AN INTERVIEW?

Whenever possible, the interviewer should normally conduct the interview in a location that provides a psychological advantage to the interviewer. The location may vary with the type of person being interviewed.

A minor witness interview can be conducted in an office or residence where there is no interference from office activities or family matters. The purpose of this type of interview is to meet the interviewee in an environment where he or she feels at ease. A significant witness should be interviewed in a location where the interviewer has the psychological advantage. For example, a witness who is interviewed in his office will have a psychological advantage because of his familiarity with the surroundings. He would not have the same advantage in a strange office.

Regardless of the location, the need for confidentiality is essential. Interviews should not be conducted in glass-walled conference rooms or offices. There should be minimum distractions in the room and no interruptions allowed. Cell phones and similar devices should be turned off.

WHAT IS THE MOST PRODUCTIVE INTERVIEW PROTOCOL?

The interview should start with a very general question: for example, "What do you know about the incident?" The interviewee should be allowed to speak without interruption, including the taking of notes. This will allow the interviewer to develop an interview strategy based on the interviewee's knowledge. Following the initial question, the interviewee should be requested to tell the story a second time and notes taken at this time. After the second recital of facts, detailed and specific questions should be asked to fill in informational gaps and develop additional areas for inquiry.

It is important to remember that it is not always the words used by the interviewee but the manner in which the information is stated that is significant. It is also important to identify what the interviewee did *not* say in response to a question. The body language of the interviewee is an important indicator in the evaluation of the information and the interviewee's truthfulness. Body language is a good indicator of truthfulness, as any parent with children will have experienced.

The use of rapid-fire questioning is usually not a productive strategy. It frequently leads to confusion and emotional tension and destroys the established rapport. The long pause–silence–may lead the interviewee to assume you are not satisfied with an answer and to voluntarily provide additional information.

There may be some subtle signs of submission by the interviewee. They include uncrossing arms and legs; neutral facial expression; leaning forward in a slumped position; paying attention to the interviewer's words with occasional nodding, weeping, or a generally defeated look. These are not foolproof indicators because tension or personal problems may produce similar responses.

The manner in which you end an interview will influence future interviews with other interviewees. It is not uncommon for witnesses to discuss their interviews. If interviewees feel that they have been treated with professionalism and respect, it will have an impact on the attitude and cooperation of future witnesses. They will be more cooperative and ready to assist rather than resist future requests for assistance.

Never end an interview with a curt "Okay. Thank you." You should let the interviewees know you appreciate what they have done and that they have performed a valuable service.

USING AN INTERPRETER

Because of the multitude of languages in the workforce, and, in many cases, the limited ability of some workers to speak English, external language expertise will be required. An interpreter is not necessarily a translator nor is the translator an interpreter. An interpreter deals with spoken communications and the translator with written documents. There are also two types of interpretation techniques. A simultaneous interpretation is through an ear piece and is spoken as the interviewee speaks. A consecutive interpretation is one in which there is a pause for the interpreter to repeat what is said by the interviewee. The consecutive interpretation normally takes twice as long, whereas the simultaneous interpretation is more expensive. The consecutive interpretation may restrict the sense of when to probe further in a particular response.

CHOOSING AN INTERPRETER

Your choice of interpreters and their qualifications will significantly affect the quality and quantity of information obtained. The choice of interpreters should not be restricted by the cost. It is important to have their skills and qualifications to meet your requirements. Recommendations for individuals who have previously provided interpretation services should be a significant qualifier. In addition to relying on someone else's judgment, the investigator must personally verify the prospective interpreter's qualifications.

The interviewer should talk directly to the interpreters to determine fluency in both languages. The interpreters should be asked to orally translate written samples into both languages and in both directions. The interview is not the time to decipher a thick accent. It is important to ask for and check professional references and determine if the interpreters have a professional classification or certification.

Language ability is not the only desired qualification for interpreters. Cultural implications must be considered. In many cultures, difficulties may arise if the interpreter's age, ethnicity, and sex are not compatible with the cultural norms of the interviewee. In some cases, a woman, an extremely young person, or someone of a certain ethnicity could be counterproductive.

The procedures to be used during the interview must be completely understood by the interpreter prior to the start of the interview. It is extremely important that the interviewer totally control the interview and not let the interpreter interject extraneous comments or information. A problem may arise when ethnic or cultural norms cause interpreters to fail to provide bad news or some other information that they believe may be insulting to the interviewer or in order to avoid an argument. Interpreters must be required to interpret the words spoken exactly as stated by the interviewee. An interpreter's summary is not acceptable. Interpreters must not add any words to those spoken by the interviewer or explain part of a question to the interviewee. If the interviewee has a question, the interpreter must tell the interviewer in the exact words spoken by the interviewee and not provide his or her own interpretation.

FINDING AN INTERPRETER

Finding a competent interpreter may be difficult. A primary source can be found through the court system. They will know individuals who have the necessary expertise and are competent to testify in court. Other sources are available through commercial interpretation services or hotel business centers. The hotel cost is normally more expensive and depends on the needed language expertise, such as a common European language versus a not so common language, such as Urdu. Costs vary with the language and the source of the interpreter. In the United States an interpreter for a common language costs about $600 per day whereas for a less common language the cost may be $1200 or higher.

In the international environment, the U.S. Embassy business center normally can provide advice on interpretation services. In international areas, the prevailing local rate will be significantly different, depending on the area. Less expensive rates may be obtainable through the U.S. Embassy. If it is necessary to travel with an interpreter, the investigator will be responsible for all expenses, including a possible tip.

On occasion, interviewees may want to use their own interpreter. This can be a money saver for the interviewer but may be problematic. There may be an existing relationship with the interviewee that may taint the accuracy of information transfer. Even if the interpreter is provided by the interviewee, all measures taken to evaluate an outside interpreter should be employed to determine the interpreter's qualifications and impartiality.

The use of a family member or close friend may create problems. Again, the qualifications of the interpreter may be questionable. Additional problems also arise. The neutrality of the interpreter and the confidentiality of interaction are absent. Sensitive issues affecting family relationships cannot be addressed. The interviewee may be reluctant to discuss sensitive issues in the presence of family members and friends because of embarrassment and other reasons. The money paid for an impartial interpreter is well-spent.

OBTAINING WRITTEN STATEMENTS

The written statement is extremely valuable because it requires commitment to a specific set of facts and reduces the probability of later disputes and changes in information. The use of a handwritten statement based on a request to "write down what you know" is unprofessional and leads to much extraneous information to the exclusion of that which is necessary. On many occasions, the handwriting will be undecipherable and confusing, even if prepared by the investigator. In this world of electronics, a laptop or notebook computer with a portable printer is the best approach. The costs of such equipment are not exorbitant and are a worthwhile investment.

The manner in which you obtain a computer-based statement depends on your computer skills. Ideally, the statement is taken simultaneously with the spoken word. Otherwise, it may be taken from notes or through a slower process of reducing the interviewee's words to writing. Whenever possible, the words spoken by the interviewee should be used. When a clarification is required, an additional question should be asked. The use of unfamiliar terms and idiomatic anomalies needs explanation. The interviewee's language should not be sanitized because of vulgarity, profanity, or insulting language. Remember, it is a statement by the interviewee and not the investigator.

The statement must stand on its own and include all information necessary for proof in a court or litigation. Any notes taken during the interview, regardless of the type of statement, must be safeguarded for court purposes. If the investigator is a notary public, the interviewee may be asked to swear or affirm that the information is true and correct to the best of his or her knowledge and belief.

WHAT IS AN APPROPRIATE STATEMENT FORMAT?

The statement should include the beginning and ending time and date of the statement. This information can be placed either at a single location within the parameters of the statement form or separately at the beginning and ending of the statement. It should also show the location where the statement was taken. The page number and total number of pages should be reflected on each page.

The following recommended statements should appear on the statement form:

- As an introductory paragraph: *"I (interviewee), residing at (complete address), telephone number (work, residence, and cellular), date of birth, having been informed by (investigator's name) that he is a private investigator and not a law enforcement officer and is conducting an inquiry on behalf of (client's name), freely and voluntarily make this statement. No offer of any benefit or reward has been made to me and no one has threatened me to make this statement."*
- On top of each continuation page: *Statement of (interviewee) taken at (location), dated (current date) continued*
- At the end of the final page: *"I have read this statement that begins on Page 1 and ends on Page __. This statement is true and correct to the best of my knowledge and belief. I have initialed all corrections and signed the bottom of each page."*

- If the statement is notarized:
State of _____
County of _____
"Sworn and subscribed to before me (Notary's Name), at (location) by (interviewee's name), this ____ day of month, year."
Printed name and signature of Notary, Notary Stamp and My Commission expires (date).

SUMMARY

The art of successful interviewing is not easily learned. It requires practice and interaction with many different personalities and situations. Using an interpreter creates additional problems. An understanding of the interviewee's culture, education level, and environment will facilitate rapport with, and cooperation from, the interviewee. The use of confrontational techniques should be a last resort.

Chapter 11

PRODUCING A PROFESSIONAL REPORT

WILLIAM F. BLAKE

S uccess as a businessperson can be difficult to achieve and very easy to lose. Many elements contribute to success. The primary elements include experience, appearance, and reputation. Experience and appearance are easy to define and develop. A reputation as a competent professional is much harder to define and achieve. One aspect of your reputation that is frequently overlooked is the quality of the reports and other documents you use to report your activities. A few words of praise are quickly forgotten, a poorly written report will be around to haunt the writer for a long time. Producing a professional-quality written report is critical to success.

WHAT DOES YOUR REPORT TELL THE
READER ABOUT YOU AND YOUR COMPANY?

- What and how you write are primary indicators of your professionalism. It tells many tales that are not explicit in writing.
- If your report is sloppy in appearance, you are lazy and careless.
- If it is incomplete, you are incompetent.
- If it contains poor English or grammar, you are not too smart.
- If it contains misspelled words, you are depending too much on Spell-Check and should use a dictionary. Spell-Check can be wrong.

If you are content to allow the preceding assumptions to be part of your reputation, you will fail as a businessperson. By following a few suggestions, your written reports can do much to enhance your professionalism and business success.

WHAT CAN YOUR REPORT BE USED FOR?

The primary purpose of any report is to provide the reader with factual information concerning a project or problem area. There are many other uses for your report, some of which may not be evident at the outset. Once the report is finalized, it cannot be retrieved for correction or alteration–the final report is "final." Your report also has other uses.

- Your report can be used as evidence in a criminal or civil court proceeding.
- The information in your report can be used to impeach your reputation and the validity of the information, within both the corporate structure and the court system.
- Your report becomes a permanent part of "your record." Good reports are easily forgotten, but bad reports will remain a part of "your record" for many years.
- A professional-quality report will demonstrate your abilities, not only to the original recipient but also to everyone who has an opportunity to see it. This is a prime marketing strategy and may lead to future referrals.
- It is critical to remember that anything you write will be subject to critical review and may end up in front of a jury or arbitrator.

REPORT CONTENT

The specific content of any report, of course, is determined by the type of investigative or consulting matter and the ultimate purpose of the report. Regardless of the type of matter being reported and the purpose of the report, all reports should have common features.

The report should contain comprehensive and complete statements of all opinions or conclusions to be expressed. The opinions and conclusions must be written in terms easily understood by the layperson. Reports are not written to impress the experts; they are written to inform the client. The excessive use of obscure or unexplained technical terms does not inform the reader. Each report must be written on a level comprehensible to the reader. A report prepared for an attorney may contain legal terms not familiar to the business executive; this type of report would be clear and concise for one person and confusing for another person with a different background.

Just stating opinions and conclusions is not adequate. The most valuable information is that which is used to substantiate the opinions or conclusions. Without substantiation, opinions and conclusions are just statements; with substantiation, they become of value to the client.

The data and other information relied on as the basis for opinions and conclusions must be identified. Credibility comes from using appropriate sources of information. These sources, whenever possible, should have first-hand information. If secondary sources are used, they should be identified as such. Copyright restrictions must be considered when using information published by others than the report author.

Exhibits used to support opinions and conclusions must be succinctly identified and appended to the report. How the exhibits are used and reported is determined by the writer for overall clarity and their contribution to understanding the report.

All key issues and elements, as determined by the nature and purpose of the report, must be identified. All criminal and civil matters have legal elements that must be proven in court. It is suggested that the report be written in a manner that adequately addresses each element in a logical order.

Finally, the authenticity and validity of the report must be acknowledged by the signature of the writer. Facsimile signatures and signature stamps should not be used. The professionalism of a report is dramatically reduced if it does not have an original author's signature.

SAMPLE REPORT COMPONENTS

For ease of reading and comprehension, the various components of your report should follow a logical order from initiation of the inquiry to the presentation of opinions or conclusions. These components include the following:

PREDICATION. It provides a recitation of why and when the inquiry was initiated. For example, "On July 24, 2011, Mr. John Smith, Human Resources Director, The Widget Company, Any Town, CO, requested that an investigation be conducted of a physical assault on a company supervisor by an employee.

SYNOPSIS OR EXECUTIVE SUMMARY. This is a concise recitation of the facts in the "Sgt. Friday" mode: "Just the facts, ma'am." At 9:30 AM, Tuesday, July 18, 2011, in the Maintenance Department, Room 201, The Widget Company, 1234 Main Street, Any Town, Colorado 80895, James Smith, a welder, struck Joseph Jones, Welding Maintenance Supervisor, on the right side of his head with an eighteen-inch piece of angle iron during an argument over the quality of welding done by Mr. Smith. Mr. Jones received a six-inch laceration on the right side of his head and was transported to the Community Hospital Emergency Room by the Any Town Rescue Squad, where he received twelve sutures in his head and was released.

SUBSTANTIATION. How do you know the circumstances surrounding the incident? This is a listing of the various documents and information generated during the inquiry, including the source and the content of the information received. It also may include a synopsis of various documents used to determine the facts: for example, photographs of injuries; medical reports; witness statements; investigator's statements concerning information developed by the investigator that is not in another document, in other words, investigative observations of the incident location or a review of HR disciplinary records.

EXHIBIT LIST. This is a listing of the documents obtained during the inquiry listed in a logical order: for example, statement of Joseph Jones, dated July 24, 2011, relating the circumstances surrounding being struck by Mr. Smith and medical report of Dr. James Andrews, MD, dated July 24, 2011, describing Mr. Jones' injuries and treatment. Photographs of Mr. Jones' injuries taken by Investigator Jack Green, Ajax Investigations, on July 24, 2011.

WITNESS LIST. Each person with information concerning the incident must be identified for possible contact at a future date. Each individual should be identified with his or her complete legal name (Joseph William Jones), residence address (101 Buttercup Lane, Apartment 101, Any Town, Colorado 80895), and residence and work telephone numbers. An alphabetical listing is preferable for ease of locating information.

WRITTEN STATEMENTS

When the inquiry is a complicated matter or the information source has valuable and extensive information critical to substantiating your conclusions, a written statement may be advantageous. Obtaining a written statement with the questions and answers documents the information provided by the source and is helpful in preventing contradictory information from the source at a later date.

A written statement based on questions originated by the investigator is the superior method for ensuring a comprehensive and useable statement. In this method, the investigator asks questions of the source and reduces the answer to a written format. All information necessary to substantiate your conclusions can be obtained through proper questioning.

Asking an individual to write out a statement leads to many difficulties, primary of which is the quality of the individual's handwriting. Statements that cannot be read are of little value. Additionally, the average witness does not know what information is relevant and needs to be included in the statement.

This is the individual's statement and not that of the investigator. Extreme care must be undertaken to ensure that the investigator does not influence the information provided by the source. The witnesses' terminology should be used even if an additional question must be asked to obtain an understanding of the terminology. To the extent possible, slang should be avoided.

When the information source is asked to initial or sign the bottom of each page of a statement, it impresses upon the source that this is his or her information and identifies a given set of facts. If the source provides conflicting information at a later time, the written statement can be used to impeach the source at trial.

FORMATTING THE REPORT

The value of your report is directly related to the report's ability to persuade the reader to whom it is directed. It is more likely to persuade the reader if it is easy to read and has a professional appearance. Professional reports should not be written on copy paper or ruled pads. The appearance of your report is an indicator of your professionalism and competence. The most complete investigation, poorly reported, is perceived as a poor and incompetent investigation.

RECOMMENDED FORMATTING

Your report should never arrive on the client's desk without a letter of transmittal. Professional business correspondence requires that any report include a brief letter of transmittal, identifying the recipient and the sender.

The cover page of your report will make a valuable impression on the client if it has a photograph of company facilities or the client company logo, which individualizes the report.

The quality of the paper is important. Reports generated on ordinary copy paper are unacceptable. The report should be printed on high quality twenty-four-pound paper with a high degree of brightness. The higher the quality of the paper, the more professional the report appears.

A twelve-point font with 1.5 line spacing provides an easily read report. The font used should have a professional appearance, such as Verdana, Arial, or Helvetica. Never use script, block letters, or other artistic fonts.

Each section of the report should have a topic heading to correspond with the various components of the report. This facilitates location of desired information.

Lengthy and convoluted sentences confuse the reader. Each paragraph should be short and concise and address only one element or major fact of the inquiry. Your reputation is based on the quality of your report—not the quantity.

DEADLY ERRORS

The value of your report can be dramatically damaged unless extreme care is taken to ensure accuracy. A substantive error can be very damaging to your reputation. In an assault, if the actions of the perpetrator are erroneously attributed to the victim, everything else in the report is suspect.

Poor English or grammar is a reputation killer. Improper capitalization and punctuation are, unfortunately, a common error in many reports.

In the era of modern computers with a Spell-Check feature, there is no excuse for misspelled words or typographical errors. Such errors clearly demonstrate carelessness and apathy.

The best-written report can be easily destroyed by dirt and extraneous markings on the pages. Keep your coffee cup away from your computer!

THE WELL-WRITTEN REPORT

A well-written report is an example of your work that will be seen by many people for many different purposes. It signals to all the quality of your work. The highest quality work with a poorly written report will always be viewed as poor quality work.

State things clearly and directly. You are compensated for the quality of your investigative effort, not for the number of words in your report. Brevity with completeness and clarity are the keys to a well-written report.

Do not speculate or guess. You have been tasked to determine facts and provide accurate data. Anyone can guess and speculate. Why spend money for an investigation just to have someone else do what you can do: guess.

Do not use boilerplate language. Boilerplate language indicates that all situations have common facts that can be expressed in terms that do not differentiate your situation from all others. Each situation is different and should be described in terms unique to the situation.

Avoid absolute words: always and never. It is the rare situation when absolute words can be used without being subject to question. Before using these words, make sure you can justify their use.

Make sure the report is not vague, equivocal, or uncertain. Any report should be factual and specific in detail. If for some reason there is justification for using vague or uncertain terminology, the reasons should be spelled out in your report.

Avoid emphatic language, exclamation points, boldface, italics, and capital letters to emphasize findings or conclusions. Unnecessary emphasis within a report can indicate your personal opinions, bias, and prejudices when your role as an investigator is to simply collect factual data and let others make their own judgment.

Use the active voice: "John hit Joe," not "Joe was hit by John." This shows assertiveness and that you are comfortable with the information you have developed. The active voice is strong as opposed to passive and weak.

Use precise (specific, clear-cut) language. This is another indicator of your confidence in the work produced and reduces the probability of others misunderstanding the facts.

Define technical terms and language. You can never assume that the reader will be familiar with technical terminology. The excessive use of unfamiliar technical terminology confuses the reader and may lead to an assumption that the writer is attempting to display his technical knowledge and belittle the reader—the person who is paying for the report.

Avoid evidence of bias. Nothing will call your report into question quicker than evidence of bias. You have been retained to report facts and not express your personal opinion through apparent biases in your report.

Use confident language; do not hedge words: it seems, could, apparently, or I believe. Failure to use confident language may appear to the reader that you question some of the information being presented as facts.

Use objective (unbiased) language and avoid subjective (prejudiced) characterizations. You cannot be impartial when you use wording such as "Joe Smith, the perpetrator" in your report. Remember you do not provide legal advice. You provide facts and let the reader arrive at their own conclusions.

Avoid commenting on the credibility of witnesses. This is another example of inserting your opinions into the data and not letting the reader evaluate the source of your information. In some cases, this could lead to legal difficulties for the writer.

Ensure internal consistency. Make sure that if "Smith shot Jones" at the beginning of your report, it does not change to "Jones shot Smith" or "Smith shot Johnson" in later parts of the report. This could be embarrassing at the least and devastating to your reputation at the extreme.

REPORT NO-NOs

Never use the words legal or legally. Remember, you are an investigator and not an attorney, unless you have a law degree, and then be careful.

When you annotate a report with the title "draft," it announces to others that there are other versions of this report. They will be reviewed for consistency among the reports, and you may be required to explain the differences.

Probable, substantially, and possible are ambiguous words. These words may show that you are not sure of the information contained in your report and should be avoided except in very rare circumstances.

Obviously or clearly are patronizing, condescending, and presumptive words. To many it would indicate that you question the reader's ability to recognize obvious facts. Insulted clients do not return for additional insults.

"Appears," "presumably," "supposedly," "is said," and "evidently" imply uncertainty. This is another example of letting others know that you do not have complete confidence in the information in your report. If information is questionable, state that fact in clear-cut language.

The words he, she, it, and they are confusing and uncertain as to identity. It is better to use proper names, such as Mr. Jones or Mrs. Smith to reduce misunderstanding.

One person is writing the report, and using the "royal we" suggests more than one report writer. Using we to attribute success as a combination of individual collaborative efforts is commendable but not acceptable when writing a report that you will be signing.

Complete, thorough, meticulous, and exhaustive are words that are self-serving and hold the investigator to extremely high standards. During the review of your report, other ideas and investigative leads may be identified, thus bringing your "exhaustive" report into question.

SUMMARY

Your written report is a major indicator of your professionalism and will greatly influence your reputation among your clients and contemporaries. Your investigative effort will not be considered a competent investigation if your written report contains numerous spelling and grammatical errors. A more disastrous mistake is a mistake in the facts. There are no innocent mistakes that can be overlooked. It is a wise move to have someone else review your report for factual accuracy and proper report-writing techniques. Your report will be subject to review and critique by executives, attorneys, judges, and a jury. Perfection must be the acceptable standard.

Chapter 12

CONDUCTING INVESTIGATIONS IN CHINA

JACK CHU

CHINA'S COMMERCIAL INVESTIGATION
HISTORY AND CURRENT TREND

China's commercial investigation work has an extremely glorious history. In the Sun Tzu's *Art of War* it is stated, "Know yourself and your enemy, hundred battles are hundred victories." The real modern commercial investigation work begins in 1978, however, the year after China realized the reform and open policy. The new China was established after 1978; before then, no foreign contact was allowed and China implemented the planned economy. All enterprises and businesses were controlled by the state and owned by the country. For economic trade activity and businessmen, regardless of the management in the governmental department or in the enterprise unit, the personal files were to be unified by the government; in this way the possibility of false records would be minimized. The only changes would reflect the person's change of administrative units along with personal changes. In the case of any commercial dispute or when an investigation was needed, the enterprise or individual had to seek support and assistance from the public security department that was responsible for the social order and the economic crimes investigation.

CHINA'S COMMERCIAL INVESTIGATION'S
MARKET DEMAND AND DEVELOPMENT

In 1978, the Chinese government implemented the reform and open policy; massive foreign capital and capital from Taiwan and Hong Kong and private enterprise entered China's economic domain. The massive economic transactions needed verification and investigation services.

Chinese society, as well as the relationships in the family, has also been influenced by the China Economic Development and the Society Transformation, with more and more marriages disintegrating or third parties interfering with the family, which leads to the need for marital background and individual privacy aspect investigations.

Along with the China Economic Development and the blooming of famous brand names, the Chinese market has turned up with more and more counterfeit or parallel import product to present; enterprises are in need of the brand protection investigation and strike prevention.

A lot of economic activities and business operations will need commercial investigation services, but China's public security departments or other governmental department are undoubtedly not adequate to bear the related commercial investigation and security management services. The first China Security management company was incorporated on December 18, 1984, in Shekou, Shenzhen, China. After that, many security management or private investigation companies emerged in China. A few foreign investigation companies or individuals have also carried out commercial investigation services in China. Following the China economic development, a world finance crisis happened; many different enterprises had continuously serious problems due to lack of a security management concept. The entire world's economic footsteps slowed down; everybody stopped the radical attitude making a fresh start and recognized the importance of commercial investigation. The demand for Chinese commercial investigation services is becoming important. Some foreign investors and businessmen are also thinking of moving their nation's services into China. China's enterprises are also more and more concerned with the commercial investigation service.

CHINA'S COMMERCIAL INVESTIGATION INDUSTRY STATUS AND RESTRICTION

Since 1978, Hong Kong and China internally have gradually produced some big and small investigation companies. So far, possibly several thousand investigation companies and more than ten thousand individuals are carrying on various commercial investigation services. As of March 2010, the Chinese governmental departments have not issued any commercial investigation licenses. No matter, big and small companies are using other commercial licenses to carry on the commercial investigation work. The Chinese government opened the market for Security Guarding Service to Chinese enterprises in January 2010. Since the development of Chinese security businesses, the opening of the commercial investigation market is only a matter of time. The opening and strict management of Chinese commercial investigation will provide benefits toward a healthy development direction.

CHINA MARKET NEEDS IN INVESTIGATION SERVICES: COMPANY BACKGROUND INVESTIGATION

Company background investigations may be divided into several types. Some investigations are due to merging or joint venture investment. Mainly because of taking over businesses, it will need comprehensive and thorough verification of the information provided because some enterprises in the process of selling will provide false information to the purchaser. Therefore, the investigation goal is to:

- discover as far as possible the real situation on the related enterprise and to provide fair objective information to the customer
- carry out the checking or investigation, which includes the enterprise's industrial and commercial registration status
- determine its management and actual operation situation; the business management team's specialty level, prestige, and personal integrity; the employees' quality and energetic condition; as well as their management level opinions and whether there is hidden debt or possible questions (for example, after taking over the operation, is there any possibility for the worker to go on strike or to slow down operations?)

- discover whether part of the enterprise's properties are being transferred to any individual
- the management level and the concerned local government department have very good relationships, which may lead to a bribe in order for the enterprise to obtain some benefits

Before the foreign enterprise buys a Chinese enterprise or investment, a thorough, careful, and responsive examinations will be needed. If this is neglected or has not been completed properly, after the investment is made, lots of problems may arise. Experience has shown that if a complete investigation has been conducted, fewer problems occur after the investment. If the investigation has not been done or has been done improperly, problems may soon arise after the investment. This kind of investigation is not merely reading the related articles but also understanding the related company's situation and more importantly being familiar with the management team from a thorough and detailed analysis.

The company-registered information with the local Administration Industry and Commerce Bureau should include incorporation date, shareholder information and share proportion, the registered capital, legal representative's situation, management team, and annual return with turnover and profit and loss data.

Conclude the preceding information with generalized analysis appraisal; review of the related company's media link, blog discussion, and so on; and related company's references and comments from same industries.

A site visit to the operation place is necessary to:

- identify if the workplace is rented or purchased, number of employees, office condition, main products and services, main customer and service location, and other information
- exchange comments with employees

A company background investigation may also involve false documentation verification. This type of company background investigation will be difficult. Generally, the created false company information will be uploaded on the Internet to advertise the business reputation. The infringed party or the interested party to take over the product or the investor or any of them would like to conduct an investigation on the company. With this kind of counterfeit company, some of them may have a business registration with a governmental department, some possibly may not register. Moreover, they may not have any fixed and legitimate operation office in place. For this kind of investigation, you must be extremely careful and make sure not to alert the investigated party. Some individuals have experience in creating false impressions and have counterdetection abilities. Moreover, they employ mostly their relatives or friends. Through investigation, you must target the individual's personal registration information, and operation location and gather as much detail as possible on the individual's background information. For this kind of investigation, you must discover their real situation while collecting the relative evidence that is as detailed as possible in order to further report to a governmental department to consider a raid or seizure. You have to also pay attention to the operator's collected relevant personal and family information and their operation method, location, tools, storage, and logistic arrangement of counterfeit samples and their sales channels.

PERSONAL BACKGROUND INVESTIGATION

The personal background investigation also has several goals. Some clients are prepared to hire a person and would like to carry out a thorough verification on the provided information before confirming the appointment. This will aim at the individual's trustworthiness, integrity, and employment history check, including a family background check. Some individuals may take part in a publicly listed company or act as a shareholder, so their declared information will need to be verified in order to locate any reported derogatory or negative information. Some personal background investigations may involve a litigation court case; the other party may need a thorough background information on the plaintiff, especially current activities, personal and family assets (e.g. property, vehicle, yacht, and debenture) tracing. Of course, some personal background investigations may try to locate the defendant in order to arrange for service delivery of court-written notice.

INFORMATION VERIFICATION

Some international organizations and the stock market request that the personnel who hold a trustee position submit verification of their background information: namely, education, family background, and current address; employment unit and experience; as well as a media search on their negative record and so on. The key point for this kind of investigation is to verify if their submitted information is accurate. If the investigation comes up with errors, then the investigator should try to provide the reason why as far as possible.

INSURANCE CLAIM INVESTIGATION

THE DEATH INVESTIGATION. Some insurance companies will carry out thorough investigation and verification of proposed death claims, some of which are fraudulent. Under these circumstances, the investigation must concentrate on the real death situation and the truth, as well as the claimant's witness and evidence documentation provided. Some death evidence may have been provided by the claimant's contacts in the relevant department, for example, the hospital, the funeral parlor, or the notarized false death certificate. The author has received requests from several foreign insurance companies to conduct the investigation, and he eventually discovered that the claimant had provided a false death certificate, but the "dead" person was still alive in China.

PERSONAL MEDICAL INSURANCE CLAIM INVESTIGATION. Some insurance companies have provided medical safeguard service for their clients; some individuals may not be injured seriously but keep taking treatment from the hospital and continue to claim compensation from the insurance company. Therefore, some insurance companies entrust the investigation company to conduct tracking on the individual's current situation in order to get a clear picture of health status. The author does not suggest meeting the doctor at the hospital because doctors may advise their patients and expose related investigation work to the claimant.

TRAFFIC ACCIDENT INSURANCE CLAIM INVESTIGATION. Some individuals have purchased automobile insurance but have made a false traffic accident claim to the insurance company. This kind of investigation needs the claimant to provide evidence while the investigator contacts the related traffic department of the public security bureau and the witness for interview. The Chinese Public Security Bureau will request an authorization letter from the insurance company before accepting this kind of investigation.

TRAVEL LOSS BAGGAGE INVESTIGATION. Some foreigners have purchased travel insurance locally; after their trip back to their hometown from China, they will report loss of baggage to their insurance company. This kind of investigation will need to pay attention to verifying if they reported the loss to the Chinese Public Security Bureau on site immediately. If they have made the report, the Public Security Bureau should have the record. If not, very possibly there may be fraudulent practice, and a thorough investigation will be a necessity.

ASSETS AND REAL PROPERTY INVESTIGATION

Many legal proceeding cases will need to carry out the related asset and real property investigations on the defendants' assets and real property conditions. If assets and real property are located, after winning the court cases, the plaintiffs will request the court to preserve the defendants' asset and real property. For this kind of investigation, if the other parties' asset and real property information are known, verification can simply be conducted; if not, then they must act according to the concrete case situation and conduct a thorough investigation. At present, China does not have a full package of an electronic database system for the checks, but according to the individual (or company) residential address may be used to conduct a thorough investigation. You may be able to start the investigation with an inquiry from the family housing or the company address. This kind of investigation needs to consider that the property may have been shifted under the relative friend's name; therefore, the investigator must pay attention to the related property for the shift direction.

Checking an automobile number or whether the individual has any automobile registration will be investigated by cities. No national computer retrieval system is available.

There is also no unified computer system in the nation for the yacht and other high-end luxury accessories registration situation. Needed manual checks are required by relevant cities.

SEEKS INDIVIDUAL INVESTIGATION

Some counterfeiters and other criminal offenders, in order to avoid penalty, debt, or any of a number of reasons, leave their original housing and their workplace and cover their surname to live incognito. This kind of investigation is very difficult. The Public Security Bureau does not accept some cases as a result of the human resources and because of the expense. The customer can entrust the investigation company to carry on seeking the related individual's workplace. This kind of investigation may result from the individual's telephone contact, the hotel accommodations registration, the airline boarding pass, the media search, as well as their connections with relatives and so on.

BRAND PROTECTION INVESTIGATION

At present, the most popular investigation in China is the brand protection investigations. These include some types listed below:

MARKET COUNTERFEIT INVESTIGATION. Through some region on certain counterfeits brand market survey, you may understand the relevant local brands' counterfeits against genuine articles on the ratio, the pricing, the sales volume, and so on. You also may conduct a technical appraisal on the counterfeits to discover the counterfeiters' level of technique and if there is only one or many. Based on the market survey foundation regarding sales at the vacation store, the personnel desires to carry on a thorough investigation. It is necessary to conduct a thorough investigation of the counterfeit shops and the counterfeiters to discover their warehouse, transportation means, and supply channel.

COUNTERFEIT FACTORIES AND COUNTERFEITERS SITUATION. Investigation of counterfeiters and the counterfeit factories are quite complex and involve great difficulties. Because the time involved in counterfeiting and anticounterfeiting is quite long, counterfeiters have accumulated lots of counterdetection experiences. Their organization is quite strict; moreover many of them make use of their relatives or friends to conduct related counterfeit work, counterfeit places are quite covert, the counterfeit goods transport mode is quite flexible, and the counterfeit warehouses are difficult to discover. If investigation and raid action are not organized strictly and professionally enough, the counterfeiters possibly escape and get away.

Chapter 13

A FEW WORDS ABOUT
INVESTIGATIONS IN EUROPE

MARY CLARK FISCHER

A colleague contacted my partner and told him he needed a due diligence in Texas and wanted to know how much it would be and how fast he could get it. Yesterday would be perfect! My partner said it would generally be no problem, and he would be happy to help. Then my father gave him a little geography lesson: Texas covers about 637,000 square miles of territory, has five of the twenty largest cities in the United States and 254 counties, more than any other state in the United States. So, he would need to know where precisely the due diligence needed to be done to know how difficult it might be and what it might cost. He also needed a brief description of what the colleague's definition of due diligence entailed.

Texas and Europe are not as far apart as you might think when it comes to investigation. Like Texas, Europe is big—and diverse. The European Union (EU) alone—which is not all of Europe—comprises twenty-seven countries, each with its own laws, customs, and language. It covers more than 1.7 million square miles and has more than 500 million citizens. Asking for an investigation "in Europe" or even in a single country, say Germany, brings some of the same challenges as those my colleague faced in Texas. A request for a company check "in Germany" has the same effect on the investigator as a similar request for a check in Texas might. Is the investigation in Hamburg in the far north, in Munich in the south on the Austrian border, or in Berlin in the east? Each of these places may be several hundred miles from the investigator and require a day or more of travel. Each is in a different state with slightly different regulations. How much will it cost? How long will it take? It depends on where it is and what kind of information the client wants—details, details, please.

Location is only one of the issues, however. Let us look at a few others up close and see what you, as a U.S. investigator, can do to ensure your client understands what the request entails and what information is needed from the client to get the best and fastest results your foreign counterpart can deliver.

RECORD AVAILABILITY AND ACCESS

Without exception, European investigators cite misunderstandings over records and accessing them as the number one problem they have with their U.S. counterparts. Information that is public and accessible to everyone in the U.S. can often be called up on the Internet for free or from a database for a one-time fee or subscription. The same information in Europe may not be public or can only be accessed with a letter to the office concerned or by a visit in person or a combination of the two. An e-mail will not suffice. What may take less than an hour in the United States may take several days elsewhere. In some countries, public officials can be unhelpful, even rude, or expect "personal compensation" for their assistance.

Company and financial records are now available online in many countries, particularly in Europe and the EU, but the amount and quality of information may vary widely. A company check in the Czech Republic, for example, can usually be done quickly online; the information is detailed, thorough, and up-to-date—but only available in Czech. In a neighboring country, Hungary, online searches can also be done, but the amount of detail is limited and especially in cities outside Budapest the information is often not up-to-date. Regulations and rules that hinder inquiries are constantly changing. For example, as of January 1, 2010, in Hungary, business owners are not obliged to provide the Company Courts with their residence. Having their permanent address enabled an investigator to do research based on this information (for example to obtain information on the number of companies in which a subject has business interests). Now, it is extremely difficult to identify a subject's interests, especially in the case of a very common Hungarian name like Kiss, Nagy, or Kovacs (equivalent of Jones, Smith, etc.). There is no free online search. Only basic information is available free of charge (name of the company, contact details, scope of activity), which is totally inadequate for a background check or due diligence.

Continuing with Hungary as an example, for a thorough due diligence outside Budapest, an investigator must travel to the county registry and review the files in person or ask a trusted associates to review the information. A personal review of the files is often the only way to ensure that important information has not been missed. Local company courts have different regulations on accessing the files, however. Some want you to fill in a form giving your personal details, the company's name, and the purpose of the request before you can get the dossiers. In many places, taking pictures of the files is allowed; other courts prohibit it; and still others permit photos if you submit a written request to the judge and he or she approves it. Such quirks in retrieving documents are prevalent throughout Europe and result in delays.

Online searches, which are fast and relatively inexpensive in the United States, can be expensive in Europe. An online search in Hungary carries charges for every click at approximately U.S. $5–6. In addition, this service is only available for companies established within the last five years. Older companies' files have not yet been scanned, so the hard copy must be reviewed in the county court or company registry. The complete company record is available on CD, issued monthly. It, too, is expensive, but it enables searches based on a variety of criteria. On the negative side, the CDs do not consist of scanned documents and are therefore often full of typing errors (especially in foreign names and addresses). In the case of Hungary, the CDs are multilingual (English, German, French), but information such as the scope of activities and professions are either badly translated or not translated at all.

In most countries, the records will be only in the local language, and any comments will need to be translated. More importantly for your client, in many countries the list of companies and owners tells a story of its own that only a local investigator or attorney who knows the players and local situation can interpret, and that information is of far more value than is the list of companies and owners itself. So, although the U.S. investigator may get copies of the file, without an "interpreter" he risks missing important information.

Another constant source of misunderstandings is criminal records checks, a frequent request from U.S. investigators. Criminal records are not public information in the EU or indeed anywhere in Europe with the exception of the United Kingdom (UK), where there is the process of "disclosure," a process basically introduced to protect the vulnerable. The Criminal Records Bureau (CRB) thus carries out checks on teachers, those working with children, and vulnerable adults. Nearly anyone can apply for the information, and there are two categories of checks, basic and enhanced. Numerous organizations now require checks to screen their members. For example, all private investigators must now have a CRB certificate before they can join a professional body such as the Association of British Investigators.

In the rest of Europe, such records are inaccessible to anyone except police and the courts. Even lawyers' access is limited. An individual may go in person to the local police and request a criminal check. The check, however, will be a simple yes or no with no details in the event any crime was committed. Therefore, because private investigators are denied any access to criminal records in the EU, investigators are required to do a great deal of footwork and old-style detective work seeking out sources and acquaintances to develop information. Some of you will undoubtedly ask if the information can be gotten illegally. The answer is yes, depending on the country. The penalties for such disclosures are extremely severe in the western EU; in the new accession countries the penalties may not yet be as severe, but the cost of such information is exorbitant and cannot be acknowledged or used, of course. This kind of investigation is time consuming and more expensive, as everyone knows. On the plus side, however, the depth and quality of information on the company and subject are almost always superior to the database searches.

Credit reports, financial records, suits, and civil litigation are likewise limited or in some cases even inaccessible, depending on the country or circumstances. Credit checks on businesses and limited checks on individuals are becoming more common but are far more limited in scope than in the United States. Educational records (diplomas, etc.), as well as employment checks, can be requested with the signed consent of the subject, but often only one person in the company is authorized to give out such information. If that person is away, no answer will be provided until he or she returns, sometimes after a three- to four-week vacation. Again, the request must frequently be in a letter with a copy of the release and may have to be provided in translation to receive a response, which will also come in a letter via the post. Birth and death records, along with family information, are accessible in most countries, but a valid reason and often a letter are required to get copies; the turnaround time is several days. In the Balkans and further east, where corruption is still an issue, getting such records may depend on the good will of staff and a "gratuity." Requests by e-mail throughout most of Europe will delay the process or may simply be ignored.

TIME AND TURNAROUND

European investigators—indeed most international investigators—are frequently frustrated and, dare I say it, angered by the time and turnaround expectations of U.S. clients. Their greatest frustration is often that by the time an investigator can provide an estimate, the U.S. client has canceled the request because it took too long. We all deal with cancellations, but making it clear to U.S. clients that it will take longer than in the United States and explaining why gives everyone a better chance to keep the business and avoid jeopardizing relations with our key contacts.

Why does it take longer? First, most international investigators rely to some extent on local contacts and a network of some kind—but then we all do, do we not? Local contacts do not necessarily share the U.S. attitude toward time and urgency. Your e-mail or phone call may not be answered for a day or two, or even longer if the contact is on vacation or on another assignment. The investigator may need to check where documents are located, thus the importance of providing maximum information in the first e-mail, not in the third or fourth exchange. The client may have provided a location for the company check, but the seat of the company may be elsewhere, and only a preliminary check can determine whether travel will be involved. If the U.S. investigator does not provide sufficient information in the initial e-mail, valuable time is lost getting sufficient detail to provide an estimate. The time difference is a minimum of five hours between Europe and the United States, but more likely it will be six to eight hours or more. Footwork and personal meetings are the norm in most countries outside the United States. Sources are reluctant to talk on the phone in many countries, even "western countries," and will only speak freely in a private meeting with the investigator. Naturally, arranging such meetings takes time and requires travel. All of this adds to the time necessary to do a thorough job. The delays in getting information from official registries lead to frustration on both sides. Holidays and vacations wreak havoc on the best-laid plans. Europeans are entitled to more than thirty days of vacation each year, and they take them religiously. The average vacation is three weeks and often takes place in the summer. Throughout the year there are national and religious holidays that vary from country to country, but it is safe to say that from approximately December 15 to mid-January little will be done in any company or office. During winter holidays, in February or early March, families with children take up to two weeks, and the same is true around Easter.

Unlike most U.S. government offices and companies, it is not standard in Europe to have a back-up person to carry out one's duties. Work may simply wait until the person returns. If that is the case, the investigator's hands are tied until the relevant person reappears. The same may be true in the case of an extended illness. Naturally, this sort of business practice is very difficult to explain to U.S. clients.

RELATIONSHIP WITH POLICE AND AUTHORITIES

Unlike in the United States, police abroad generally consider private investigators to be adversaries, or worse. In some countries, for example, Hungary, the oversight of private investigators is in the hands of police who resent the investigators, whom they imagine make much more money than they do and only interfere with legitimate police work. In other countries, their image is that of spies on cheating husbands and wives. The kind of mutual assistance that occurs between investigators and police in the United States is unknown in Europe. Investigators point out that succeeding in such systems requires a great deal of work, especially in building and maintaining relationships that can be called on when information is needed. Cultivating those sources costs time and money, and one uses them carefully. With regard to authorities in other parts of the government–land and property records offices, hospitals, administrative organs–officials may be more or less helpful, depending on the country. Again, contacts are crucial in acquiring information in a timely fashion or sometimes acquiring it at all. There is no universal attitude that the citizen has a right to certain information.

LANGUAGE ISSUES

The investigators you will contact will almost certainly speak English, but it may not be as fluent as you imagine. Terms that seems obvious to the U.S. investigator, such as due diligence, company background, or employment check, may not be at all clear to the overseas investigator. A case in point is the term due diligence, for which an English native speaker colleague sent me a list of fifteen definitions. Which of those definitions is the right one? Even two U.S. colleagues might have different definitions of the term. Although the investigator may speak English, he or she has no idea what elements should be included in the client's definition of due diligence; you must spell that out in detail.

Beware colloquial and slang terms as well. Your counterpart may have learned English in high school or indeed it may have been on-the-job training, in which case much of the nuance, grammar, and private investigator jargon and vocabulary that you take for granted may be unknown to him or her. Use standard English and clear, commonly used terms and grammar for your inquiry. If the conversation is by phone, slow down; check that your counterpart has really understood what you have said. He may sound fluent but have difficulty understanding your accent, your choice of words, or your instructions and be too embarrassed to say so.

Translation of documents is often required. Although professional translators are often expensive, it is wise to be prepared to spend the money for professional translations if the investigator does not speak English fluently. The overseas investigator may already have a reliable translator but, if not, shop carefully because all translations are not equal.

COST

For all the reasons above, including time, difficulty in accessing records, the need to use local contacts in ministries and offices for information, the cost of an overseas inquiry is frequently more than in the United States. Although the cost of documents themselves may not be prohibitive, getting copies of them, particularly if the file is voluminous, can be expensive. If the investigator works with an attorney, the attorney may be able to send his intern or clerk to copy files, but that cost will, of course, be included in the expenses. Investigator fees can vary widely and in some countries, for example, the Balkans,investigators may charge upwards of 300€/hour, making an inquiry prohibitively expensive. The services of sources and administrative "assistance" must also often be added in to the cost. The weak dollar in recent years has often increased the cost of even a simple investigation 30% to 50% and last but not least the value added tax (VAT) of 16-19% that investigators must usually charge can add substantially to the final bill. Last, but not least, it should be remembered that your European colleague must often work differently. He/she spends many more hours on the street and in personal meetings than before a computer screen.

SHARING INFORMATION

Clients are often reluctant to give the investigator complete information and the investigator is also frequently hesitant to reveal details to his overseas colleague. This delays the process unduly and often results in losing the case because the overseas investigator cannot provide an accurate estimate without a certain amount of detail. So, give the overseas investigator as much background as possible, a clear explanation of what is needed, whether it is a due diligence, a company check or an individual background check and what the ultimate objective is. Give them locations and be as specific about the location, city, and province as possible. The more you tell them about the case, the better, faster and more accurate the estimate and end results will be. Especially when the counterpart is a nonnative speaker of English and has never lived or worked in the United States, a clear, detailed outline of the information expected can speed the work enormously.

You can make the process more transparent and comfortable for the overseas investigator and your client if you all understand what is required to get started and what to expect.

- Be prepared to tell the investigator precisely where the work is located. The more precise, the better.
- Provide the name of the entity in which you are interested if at all possible.
- Be prepared for the investigation to take longer than it would in the United States.
- Expect that there will be some documents that will not be accessible.
- Understand that for a number of reasons, the cost will be higher.

Chapter 14

PROFESSIONAL PRIVATE INVESTIGATORS IN THE CIVIL JUSTICE SYSTEM

Warren J. Sonne

Most if not all civil justice systems around the world provide a forum for settling claims, or disputes among people, and enforcing the government's laws. These systems vary greatly from place to place and can change rapidly over time. King Solomon used the threat of a sword to settle the opposing claims of two would-be mothers; today issues of embryonic cell research and human cloning are part of the modern legal lexicon.

As civil laws have evolved, so have the professions that provide services to assist with the prosecution or defense of the parties involved. Judges and advocates are better educated in the laws; doctors (of both medicine and philosophy), and engineers are called upon to provide advice to their clients, and/or expert testimony based on their years of formal education and experience. New professions, such as computer or cellular forensics, are created as new technologies appear.

Professionalism in the investigative field has kept pace, providing great opportunities for private investigators to work with preeminent clients. It is no surprise that there is no single universal standard or license for private investigators, just as there is no universal license for doctors or lawyers. Through perseverance, however, and aided more recently by the development of the Internet, private investigators have been able to expand their knowledge base; communicate ideas; and improve the local, national, and international professional associations, transcending borders and time zones.

We are indeed a profession, because of the following:

- We have a universal philosophy to honestly seek the truth for our clients.
- We have developed bodies of knowledge that we archive for the use of others.
- We continually publish literature of research, and peer review.
- Our leaders around the world represent us to governments, clients, and the press.
- Our associations have codes, guidelines, oaths, mission, and ethics statements.
- We advocate for licensing, certification, specific initial qualifications, as well as requirements for ongoing education.
- We have formal dispute resolution, complaint, and disciplinary procedures.
- We offer thorough and often highly specialized investigative services.
- We investigate for our livelihoods.

There is a "natural selection" process at work within the civil justice field. Both plaintiffs and defendants seek out the best-qualified attorneys to support their cause. These same clients or their advocates will seek out the best-qualified persons or companies to assist them. If a private investigator is required for either litigation or other issues, clients will look for the most-qualified professional they can find. Nothing builds a long-term relationship like success does. The strong will survive.

Exactly what are professional private investigators within the civil justice system? Let me start with what we are not:

- We are not lawyers, yet we need to know the legal limits of our actions and stay within them. We need to understand the issues and the theories of law that are involved.
- We are not engineers, yet we need to have an understanding of how things work or were designed to work. We need to know the products in question and how they are used. We need to have a good eye for detail.

- We are not paramedics, but we need to have an understanding of what they do at accident or injury scenes.
- We are not automotive mechanics or plumbers, yet we need to have a concept of normal operations, maintenance, and repairs.
- We are not janitors, yet we need to know how and when things get cleaned or maintained.
- We are not firemen, yet we need to know their basic procedures at the scene, as well as their record-keeping procedures.
- We are not handymen or carpenters, yet we need to know how they fix a loose handrail or a step or the proper use of a nail gun.
- We are not the police, yet we need to be especially aware of their actions at accident or injury scenes and their follow-up investigative procedures.
- We are not doctors, auto body mechanics, tow truck drivers, property managers, truckers, or so many of the other professions that we are called upon to investigate or interview during the course of a civil matter.

What we are:

- We are the front line eyes and ears for our clients.
- We are the gatherers of facts; obtainer of records; locator of vehicles and other equipment, or parts thereof; interviewer of witnesses; professional photographer; safe guarder of evidence; liaison with law enforcement; expeditor, report writer and many others things.
- We are the seekers of the truth, the true reporters of certain life events.

"As gatherers of facts it is our responsibility to obtain the most information possible. The term knowledge is power has real-world meaning to our clients. If we are able to provide them with specific facts, or witnesses that are not known to the opposition, it allows our client to better formulate their plan. On the other hand, should the opposition obtain information or witnesses that we are unaware of; it places our client at a distinct disadvantage. You will not keep clients if you continually leave them under-informed."[1]

---

1. Warren J. Sonne, Investigating automotive product liability claims, *PI Magazine, 70,* Nov/Dec 2003.

CIVIL INVESTIGATION

There are three basic differences between criminal and civil matters: (1) in criminal matters, the plaintiff or accuser is the "People of the State" or "of the United States," whereas in civil matters the accuser is overwhelmingly a private individual or business entity who believes that he or she or it has been wronged, (2) the punishment at stake in criminal cases is incarceration and occasionally a fine or restitution, whereas the punishment in civil matters is usually monetary, and (3) the evidence requirements (burden of proof) are much greater in criminal cases than in civil ones. In the United States, the burden of proof in criminal trials is always on the prosecution, who must prove the case *beyond a reasonable doubt,* yet in civil cases this burden always begins with the accuser but may under certain circumstances shift to the defendant and both must only prove the case by a *preponderance of the evidence,* meaning just a little more than their adversary. In some civil cases, the level of proof may require the slightly higher level of clear and convincing evidence that is still well below the criminal requirement. Each state in the United States addresses this burden of proof in its own way. Other nations have developed their own distinct burdens of proof.

Other differences between U.S. criminal and civil matters have to do with the protections that are afforded to the participants under the law. As long as the government or its agents are not prosecuting, civil cases are not filled with issues such as the U.S. Supreme Court's 1966 Miranda decision ("The person in custody must, prior to interrogation, be clearly informed that he or she has the right to remain silent, and that anything the person says will be used against that person in court; the person must be clearly informed that he or she has the right to consult with an attorney and to have that attorney present during questioning, and that, if he or she is indigent, an attorney will be provided at no cost to represent her or him"[2]), or the rules of evidence defined in the Supreme Court's *Mapp v. Ohio* decisions, which decided that evidence in state court criminal cases that was "obtained in violation of the Fourth Amendment, which protects against unreasonable searches and seizures, may not be used in criminal prosecutions in state courts,

---

2. *Miranda v. Arizona* 384 U.S. 436 (1966)

as well as federal courts."[3] This reference to unreasonable searches and seizures only applies to government agents and not to nongovernmental plaintiffs and defendants in civil matters. Nor are there any other constitutional protections under the Fourth (unreasonable search and seizure), Fifth (self-incrimination and speedy trial), and Sixth (right to counsel) Amendments. There is also no double jeopardy issue between the criminal and the civil laws, as demonstrated by the civil prosecution of O.J. Simpson after his acquittal on criminal murder charges.

These differences in the U.S. criminal and civil systems of the law have a significant impact on the manner in which private investigators conduct their business. This chapter is not being written as a legal primer, nor should it be interpreted as legal advice, rather it offers a general overview of the issues that professional private investigators deal with on a daily basis. Investigators are strongly urged to seek the advice of their own attorneys, and/or their attorney clients, and to familiarize themselves with the appropriate laws for their geographic area of investigation, both in the United States and, as applicable, internationally.

For the purposes of this chapter, civil investigations will be considered to be U.S. cases that begin as not criminal, even though they may evolve to reach the criminal threshold. Other countries may have similar or very different concepts. Furthermore, the investigative techniques will be discussed without bias as to plaintiff or defendant clients. The role of the investigator as the seeker of facts applies to all cases, regardless of the nature of the client.

Civil law is an overly broad term because it includes many specialized and diverse areas, such as:

- international law
- constitutional and administrative law
- contract law
- tort law
- property law
- equity and trusts
- labor law

---

3. *Mapp v. Ohio,* 367 U.S. 643 (1961)

- human and civil rights
- immigration law
- social security law
- family law
- commercial law
- admiralty law
- intellectual property
- banking law
- tax law
- antitrust law
- environmental law and other subspecialties.

At some point in time, a private investigator may become involved with cases that touch upon these areas of the civil law, and in fact there are some investigators who specialize in many of these categories. Yet, of all these areas, professional private investigators are more likely to be involved in the area that deals with negligence: tort law.

TORTS

Torts are civil wrongs recognized by law as grounds for a lawsuit. These wrongs result in an injury or harm constituting the basis for a claim by the injured party. . . .

> While some torts are also crimes punishable with imprisonment, the primary aim of tort law is to provide relief for the damages incurred and deter others from committing the same harms. . . . Among the types of damages the injured party may recover are: loss of earnings capacity, pain and suffering, and reasonable medical expenses. They include both present and future expected losses. . . . Torts fall into three general categories: intentional torts (e.g., intentionally hitting a person); negligent torts (causing an accident by failing to obey traffic rules); and strict liability torts (e.g., liability for making and selling defective products). Intentional torts are those wrongs which the defendant knew or should have known would occur through their actions or inactions. Negligent torts occur when the defendant's actions were unreasonably unsafe. Strict liability wrongs do not depend on the degree of carefulness by the defendant, but are established when a particular action causes damage. (Personal knowledge of author)

THE SEARCH FOR NEGLIGENCE

Torts are likely the basis for the majority of investigative man-hours expended in civil cases. A party who believes that he or she was harmed by another party's negligence can institute a lawsuit for the purpose of collecting damages and, in some cases, to prevent the defendant from committing the same type of harm to others. Many times the defendant may also face the risk of additional monetary punishment in the form of punitive damages. Punitive damages (punishment) can be awarded in most states when the jury finds that the defendant knowingly or maliciously harmed the plaintiff(s). In cases such as this both the plaintiff and the defendant may retain the services of private investigators. Automobile accidents, trip and falls, dog bites, and product liability cases are examples of torts.

The goal of the plaintiff in tort cases is to prove the negligence of the defendant. Often plaintiffs will share in the negligence if they have done something themselves to cause the injury or failed to do something that could have prevented or lessened it. Defendants will seek to prove that they did nothing wrong or that the plaintiffs were responsible, or at least partially responsible, for their own damage or injury. This theory of law is known as contributory negligence, and in several states it can prevent a plaintiff from winning any award in a case in which he or she was found to be even the slightest bit negligent.

The degree to which negligence must be proved varies from state to state, and in most jurisdictions any damages that are awarded to the plaintiff may be reduced by the percentage of negligence for which the plaintiff was found to be responsible. For example, if the jury or judge found that the plaintiff's injuries were worth $100,000 but also believes that the plaintiff was 25 percent at fault in the accident, the amount that the plaintiff would be awarded is $75,000. This is known as comparative negligence.

Plaintiffs will try to prove that the other party was responsible, or at least more responsible than the plaintiff is. In most personal injury cases the plaintiff will need to show that the defendant was either the direct cause or, through some negligence, caused the plaintiff to be injured. Often, private investigators will be leading these searches for negligence.

In certain instances, such as product liability cases, the manufacturer or seller may be liable based solely on the faultiness of the product, whether the defect occurred during the design, construction, or packaging of the product or if there was a failure to warn the user about some hazard involved with the product's use. Some notable examples of this theory of law are the Ford Explorer Firestone tires, fifteen-inch ATX, ATX II, and Wilderness AT tires, which suffered from a high-tread separation rate; asbestos or lead paint litigations; or the current (2009–2010) Toyota sudden acceleration cases, which should begin making their way through the courts shortly.

When selling their products, the manufacturer and their entire downstream chain of vendors or resellers may be held responsible for injuries caused by the use of that product. Each state has its own rules regarding the statute of limitations for bringing such law suits, and/or may have enacted a statute of repose. A statute of repose is a statute barring a suit a fixed number of years after the defendant had acted (usually by designing or manufacturing an item), even if the injury suffered by the plaintiff occurred after the period had lapsed.

Warnings and instructions on the proper use of a product, such as using a gas-operated generator only in a well-ventilated area, or wearing seat belts to protect you from injury during vehicle accidents, are now required by law in the United States. In such cases, there is no need for the plaintiff to prove negligence, only that the product was defective or that there were no adequate warnings. Again, the laws governing product liability are determined by each state or country and are not universal.

If the injured party may have been using the product in an inappropriate or reckless way that was not imagined by or designed for by the manufacturer, however, the private investigator's hunt for contributory and/or comparative negligence may be back on. Examples of possible inappropriate or reckless use would be the use of a flashlight to hammer a nail, causing an injury from a broken lens or casing; using the family car to knock down the barn; or using a propane torch to dry your hair. Again, each state treats these issues differently, so private investigators need to know what they should be looking for.

In most cases involving strict liability, meaning that the manufacturer is liable if the product is defective even if the manufacturer was not negligent in making that product defective, there may only be a limited need for private investigators. These cases generally involve plaintiff's experts reviewing the defendant's records that were obtained through the discovery process or that may have been obtained from other attorneys who were successful in bringing similar product cases against the same manufacturer for the same defect. Investigative requirements may only be limited to verification that the injury was caused by the product or confirmation that the plaintiff is who he or she claims to be or that he or she was exposed to the specific product as claimed.

In other cases, such as asbestos, tobacco, and lead paint litigation, the investigations may span back over decades to determine if the plaintiff actually worked with, or was exposed to, products that contained these substances. Asbestos litigation was originally brought against the manufacturers of insulation and flooring materials but has expanded to include the automotive and other industries that used asbestos in frictionable products such as brake pads and clutches. These types of litigations have also expanded to include those who may have been exposed by secondhand means, such as children sitting on their parents' laps when they returned home from work from an asbestos contaminated site or people inhaling smoke from someone else's cigarette.

Another theory of negligence that still exists in some states is assumption of risk where potential plaintiffs sometimes take the risk of injury onto themselves and absolve potential defendants from any liability. Formerly, this was an affirmative defense available to defendants but has since been subsumed by contributory and comparative negligence in most jurisdictions.

Prior to the current workers' compensation laws, the assumption of risk was a common defense used by employers. Now that workers' compensation laws prevent employees from directly suing their employer for negligence, this defense has been all but abandoned.

Many states still follow a related theory of law called the "Fireman's Rule," however. As with the assumption of risk, these laws limit the ability of public employees who are routinely involved in emergencies, such as police and firefighters, to sue for damages based on injuries that they may sustain during the normal scope of their employment. The laws vary greatly, with some states allowing lawsuits based on negligence of the property owner or their contractors, product liability, dram shop laws, and so on.

The investigator of tort claims must be aware of the legal requirements of negligence as it relates to their client's case within the jurisdiction. As a professional private investigator you will find your clients may consist of both plaintiffs and defendants. Although there are investigators who may limit their practice to one side or the other, most will accept cases from both sides of the aisle. As your investigation continues, you must always look for issues relating to negligence.

THE TEAM CONCEPT

As a professional private investigator you are a part of a larger team. Many law firms (both plaintiff and defense) will maintain full-time in-house investigators, some of whom may also function in a paralegal capacity. These investigators will usually get to follow a case from intake to disposition, including assisting the attorneys in the courtroom. Most private investigators will not have this degree of total immersion in the case, yet it is extremely important to become as familiar as possible with every aspect of every matter on which you are engaged.

If you are not an in-house investigator, do not be offended if you are excluded from certain knowledge or certain client meetings. Some attorneys and their clients, especially in product liability defense cases, feel that an independent investigator is not bound by the attorney–client privilege, and they may feel at risk in sharing all of their secrets with you for fear that this knowledge may be used against them in future cases. Although these meetings may be covered under the attorney-client privilege, which protects private communications between them, there still may be resistance to allowing an investigator to take part, even if the investigator has signed a confidentiality agreement.

Regardless of whether or not you are admitted to the inner sanctum, you should check your ego at the client's door. Your experience, knowledge, and suggestions should always be available for the client to consider, but much like a sports team, there can be only one manager.

Investigators must take care not to deviate from the overall investigative plan without first discussing it with the client. Being a team player is all about communicating. There may be issues that you are unaware of, such as reasons not to interview a particular person, for example, for fear of alerting the opposition or worse, damaging your client's case. If your client has instructed you not to take recorded or signed statements at this stage, do not take it upon yourself to do so without discussing it first. There may be good reasons, that you are not aware of, for not memorializing statements at this point. Your obligation is to service your client's needs and to keep them well-informed as you move forward. Communications should be a two-way street, and in a perfect world you would be made aware of changing issues that could affect your investigation. Regardless, you should ask the client for updates from time to time as well, so that you can keep up to speed with the status of the case. The investigative plan is not written in stone; rather it will evolve as the case continues. The plan should evolve as the result of a team effort, however.

PREASSIGNMENT PREPARATION

The initial involvement in a tort investigation will vary depending on the terms of your employment, or your relationship with your client. If you are an in-house investigator for a plaintiff's law firm you may actually become involved before the attorney does. Perhaps you work for a large investigative agency that has a nationwide contract with a manufacturer, or maybe you monitor media reports for any mention of your client or their products, or you may be a sole practitioner who has been retained for the first time by a lawyer or insurance company client. Whatever the retention scenario is, if possible, you should try to learn as much as you can about the matter at hand prior to your initial meeting with the client.

It is rare in tort cases for an investigator to be retained directly by a member of the general public. In fact, if you are approached by an individual to investigate a negligence case directly for them, it may be advisable to recommend that they also retain the services of an attorney. If you report directly to that lawyer, the results of your investigation may then be covered by the attorney-client privilege as attorney work product. You will also be removing yourself from those clients' questions regarding whether or not you have actually discovered negligence and what it means. Those types of opinions and advice should be answered by an attorney, rather than an investigator.

Because you will more than likely be retained by an attorney, insurance company, or perhaps even directly by a manufacturer or other business client, the following pages are written from that point of view.

Good recordkeeping begins with your first involvement with the case. The method by which you maintain case files will determine how you record, safeguard, and document your information and evidence. You may be using a case management software package, Redweld's or other file folders with an index sheet, notebooks, index cards, and so on. Whichever method you use, be sure to document your initial retention in every case, whether it came by phone, letter, or e-mail or in person. A best practice is to obtain a written retention letter.

Come to the initial meeting knowing as much about the incident as possible. If there were media reports, obtain copies for discussion with the client. If you are able to obtain copies of police or other official reports prior to the first meeting, bring them with you as well. If the client has sent you a synopsis or copies of records, you should attempt to find or verify as much information about the case before your first meeting with the client. Client relations are an ongoing process that should be pursued at every opportunity. By your showing initiative and concern for the case at hand your client will quickly develop respect for you and confidence in your ability. On the other hand, you should take great pains not to be overbearing or present yourself as already knowing what the client needs. By collaborating with the client you will be able to develop an investigative plan that should be agreed to by all members of the team.

Be prepared to listen, take notes, and make copies of relevant items within the client's possession, if the client will allow it. Be ready to discuss the information sources that may be available for you to pursue without subpoena, including government sources such as building departments, highway department, county clerks, board of health, motor vehicles, police, and so on. You should be familiar with the types of records that are available from the agencies within your jurisdiction. For example, depending on the size of your local government you may be able to obtain records such as:

- traffic light sequencing reports
- occupational or business tax certificate filings
- food-handler certificates
- as-built plans
- assumed name or DBA filings
- asbestos abatement inspections or filings

- building codes, violations, and inspection records
- deeds and mortgages
- property tax and homestead exemption records
- build permits
- animal licenses
- electrician, plumber, contractor licensing
- hunting and fishing licenses
- workers' compensation claims
- vehicle certificates of origin, title applications, titles, registration records
- driver's license history
- accident or incident reports from police and fire departments

This is far from a complete list of things that you can obtain, yet each could provide valuable information in your search for negligence. These records may be called different names in your location, but their purposes are universal. Many of these records are available simply by asking or searching for them; others may require you to submit a Freedom of Information form in compliance with the laws within your jurisdiction.

THE ISSUE OF WHO

In every case there will be a minimum of two "whos": who is the plaintiff and who is(are) the tortfeasor(s) that they believe harmed plaintiff. A tortfeasor is a wrongdoer, an individual who commits a wrongful act that injures another and for which the law provides a legal right to seek relief, or a defendant in a civil tort action.

As the investigator, you will be looking to gather as much information regarding these parties as possible during this first meeting. Although it may be easier to initially obtain your client's information, it is advisable to conduct a full and thorough background investigation of all the whos you become aware of during the investigative process, including your own client. It is your job as the investigator to ensure that there are no surprises in store for your client. If the opposing parties' investigators unearth something that you should have found or did find but did not tell anyone about that proves to be damaging to your client, you can be assured that you will not be retained by that client in future cases. The investigator's job is not to tell the client what he or she thinks the client wants to hear; rather, it is to tell the client what he or she needs to hear. Most attorneys enjoy hearing good news eventually, but good attorneys want to hear bad news immediately.

The other whos may include the various types of witnesses, businesses, employers, employees, contractors, subcontractors, government agencies, landlords, property owners, pet owners, vehicle owners and operators, emergency workers, experts, and so on. You may not learn of all the whos at one time, so you must be alert to recognize them at your initial meeting and follow-up investigation progresses.

WITNESSES

A word about witnesses: There are several different types of witnesses that investigators may become involved with in a civil case. A custodian of records may be called upon as a witness, but it is highly unlikely that a private investigator would be deeply involved with this process.

Private investigators should be concerned primarily with witnesses who may either be "fact" or "expert" witnesses, but these are rather broad terms. A fact witness is a person with knowledge about what happened in a particular case who testifies in the case about what happened or what the facts are. Fact witness testimony consists of the recitation of facts and/or events as opposed to an expert witness, whose testimony consists of the presentation of an opinion, a diagnosis, and so on.

A fact witness is someone who may provide information about the events leading up to, during, or after the incident. These could include people who may have notified the defendant or the defendant's representative that there was a dangerous condition before an accident occurred (notice witness) or an eyewitness who actually observed the incident take place.

However, police, firemen, emergency medical technicians, tow truck drivers, and so on may also be witnesses who can provide facts and observations. Other nonexpert witnesses may be neighbors, relatives, coworkers, maintenance workers, and so on, who can provide information and observations regarding things that happened before, during, or after the incident. These types of witnesses may tell you about a long-ignored roof leak that may have contributed to the ceiling collapse that injured your client, or you may learn that a plaintiff has been working even though he or she has alleged a disabling injury, or you could find out that the broken ankle that the plaintiff claims happened in the stairwell of your clients building may actually have happened during a weekly basketball game.

An expert witness is a person who possesses some special technical knowledge and who is accepted by the court to offer opinions about the incident as it relates to his or her particular field. These types of witnesses include medical personnel, engineers, scientists, CPAs, and so on. As an investigator you may be asked to accompany your client's expert to accident scenes, attend or tape-record inspections conducted by your client or the opposing party, and to conduct background investigations of both your experts and the opposing experts.

WHO NOT TO INTERVIEW

Every state, as well as the federal government has a code of professional responsibility or rules of professional conduct that prevents attorneys from communicating directly with an adverse party whom they know to be represented by an attorney. This prohibition extends to any agent of the attorney, including investigators.

The following is part the American Bar Association's *Model Rules of Professional Conduct* from which the individual state and federal rules were developed:

> DR 7-104 Communicating With One of Adverse Interest.
> (A) During the course of his representation of a client a lawyer shall not: (1) Communicate or cause another to communicate on the subject of the representation with party he knows to be represented by a lawyer in that matter unless he has the prior consent of the lawyer representing such other party or is authorized by law to do so.

For the private investigator, this means that you should not speak to any adversarial party whom you know is represented by a lawyer in the case that you are investigating without first obtaining that lawyer's consent for you doing so. To do so is not a criminal act, but the potential damage to your client's case could be devastating.

This concept may also apply to employees of an adversarial company but is usually reserved for employees with a managerial or ownership position or those who may have direct knowledge of the incident. In any event, before you interview any employee of an adversarial company who is represented by counsel, you should first discuss this matter with your own attorney-client. If you are uncertain as to whether individuals are represented by counsel, you should ask them about this during your introduction and prior to asking any further questions about the case. If they indicate they have counsel, terminate the interview until you are able to obtain their attorney's consent to proceed.

THE ISSUES OF WHAT, WHY, WHEN, AND HOW

Because this is a tort case, you will be asked to investigate the damage that one party allegedly caused the other party. During your initial meeting, your attorney-client should provide you with his or her legal theory of the negligence involved, from which you will launch your investigation. As the investigator, it is not enough for you to simply learn the legal requirement or threshold of negligence; rather, it is far more important for you to understand what, why, and how the damage occurred from a practical, real-world point of view.

Negligence is the failure to exercise the care toward others that a reasonable or prudent person would do in the circumstances or taking action that such a reasonable person would not. Negligence is accidental as distinguished from "intentional torts" (assault or trespass, for example) or from crimes, but a crime can also constitute negligence, such as reckless driving.

Simply stated, people become negligent when they fail to live up to their obligations by not following reasonable practices and when their actions or inactions cause harm to someone else. So, it is not really actions or lack of actions that are negligent; rather, doing or not doing something only becomes negligent when someone is harmed by it. A tightrope walker can practice thirty feet in the air over a concrete sidewalk without a safety net every day and not be negligent, yet the one time that he falls and injures a passerby below him he will likely be negligent. Why? Because he had an obligation to ensure that no one is injured by his actions. This does not mean that a pattern of reckless or dangerous behavior is not important to demonstrate. Quite the contrary, your attorney-client will be very interested in developing any pattern of bad or risky behavior on the part of the opposing party that you can learn about and relay to the attorney.

Once again, investigators should be aware of differences in state laws as they relate to negligence. "Vicarious liability" is a tort doctrine that imposes responsibility on one person for the failure of another with whom the person has a special relationship (such as parent and child, employer and employee, or owner of vehicle and driver) to exercise such care as a reasonably prudent person would use under similar circumstances. For private investigators in many states, there was little to do in vehicle accident cases in which the defendant was driving a leased or rented vehicle. Vicarious liability in the state of New York was absolute. If you were Hertz, or Ford Credit, you were liable even if your renter or lessee was driving recklessly.

In 2003, as a result of continual vicarious liability litigations, many vehicle manufacturing or leasing companies such as GM, Ford, and Chrysler and nearly every major retail bank and credit union in New York, stopped the practice of leasing vehicles. This changed when the Federal Public Transportation Act of 2005 became law, ending the vicarious liability of automobile leasing companies or rental agencies, which would no longer be held liable for the accidents of their renters or lessees. An unexpected bonus for private investigators was the need to determine liability in automobile accidents involving leased or rented vehicles in the affected states.

It is the attorney's job to prove or disprove that a party to the lawsuit had the legal obligation to act or not act in one way or another and that his or her failure to live up to that obligation caused the injury. It is the private investigators job to provide his client with the real facts of what happened.

You will generally not learn the full magnitude of what happened during the initial meeting with the client, yet you should not leave the meeting without obtaining as much information as possible.

You must also listen for the whys, whens, and hows. You may learn that the injured party fell because there was a crack in the sidewalk, and you may learn of the theory that the crack was caused by nearby construction of a subway station. You may learn that several other people had previously reported that they had tripped at the same place. Not only will you need to learn the time and date of the injury, but you may also need to learn when a dangerous condition first appeared. How something occurred will always be of relevance. Was there a mechanical failure? Was one of the parties distracted? Was the weather a contributing factor? Was it a lack of or improper maintenance? These are all issues that will require further investigation and documentation.

INVESTIGATIVE PLANNING

Now that you have learned everything that your client could or would tell you about the case, it is time to agree upon an investigative plan. It is not necessary to reinvent the wheel for every case; rather it is far better to have a general framework into which you can plug data in each particular set of circumstances, keeping in mind that "thinking outside of the box" is often useful. Using what you have learned from the who, what, why, when, where, and how is a good starting point for your plan. This is also the time for you to discuss your fees and payment arrangements if you have not already done so.

If this is the first time that you have worked with this particular attorney or client you should make him and her aware of the types of background investigations you are capable of conducting on all of the parties, businesses, and witnesses (the whos). At a minimum, background investigations should include:

- verification of the person's pedigree information
- present and prior residences
- employment history
- litigation history
- criminal history
- known relatives
- neighbors
- driver's license history
- professional or specialty licenses
- vehicles owned

- accident reports
- property ownership/history
- business relationships and associates

Other areas of background investigation can include interviews of neighbors, employers, employees, coworkers, shopkeepers; searching for previous insurance claims; conducting surveillance; verifying education, hobbies, areas of expertise, military service, and so on; and the follow-up on any information that is discovered.

For backgrounds on all "expert witnesses" it will also be necessary to verify their education and professional credentials and to uncover any disciplinary actions or complaints against them. Your client may ask you to identify previous cases in which the experts provided testimony so that their testimony can be reviewed.

Background investigations can become quite costly, and they should not be undertaken without preapproval from the client, who may already be in possession of some of this information.

Your investigative plan should contain the names of all persons known to be involved and your investigative obligation regarding them, in other words conducts a background investigation, interview, surveillance, and so on. Because most civil cases take years to reach a final conclusion, you should clearly document your client's instructions regarding anyone that he or she does not want you to speak with or those who should be the subject of a background investigation. Three or four years down the road, your client or another attorney who is assigned to the case may ask you why you did not follow-up on a particular person, and it is best to have these instructions memorialized in your records.

This same practice should be followed with respect to other parts of the investigation. For example, you may recommend obtaining certified copies of all building department violations issued for the premises at which the trip and fall accident occurred or copies of all motor vehicle accidents reported during the past three years at the same location as your case. If your client does not think it necessary, you should record his or her instructions in your investigative plan as well.

Aside from the people involved in the case, there are other things that your investigative plan should contain if you are to be successful in providing your client with a clear picture of the event.

In the case of accidents, the plan should include a visit to the scene so it can be photographed and/or videotaped and measurements taken of the entire area. Accurate information is desired, but you may not have the correct equipment or the expertise required to produce exact measurements or to competently compare your findings to certain specifications. Your best effort to document the approximate distance is all that should be expected of you by the client.

If a more exacting measurement, reconstruction, or determination of certain specifications is required, your client should retain the services of an expert in that particular field. Investigators should only portray themselves as accident reconstruction investigators if they possess the specific knowledge and training to be an expert in that area.

If you are investigating an automobile accident, your plan should include the documentation of all traffic control and roadway markings leading up to and at the accident site, as well as any roadway scars, gouge marks, burns, and so on. Line of sight, visibility, time of day, and weather are all important factors to be documented.

In nonautomobile accident or injury cases, you will need to document issues concerning lighting, visibility, defects, grade, height of steps, hand railings, maintenance schedules and logs, potential attractive nuisance issues, and so forth. The attractive nuisance doctrine is a legal doctrine that makes a person negligent for leaving a piece of equipment or other condition on property that would be both attractive and dangerous to curious children. These have included tractors, unguarded swimming pools, open pits, and abandoned refrigerators. Liability could be placed on the people owning or controlling the premises even when the child was a trespasser who sneaked on the property. The doctrine was intended to make people careful about what dangerous conditions they left untended. Some jurisdictions have abolished the attractive nuisance doctrine and replaced it with specific conditions (e.g. open pit and refrigerators) and would make property owners liable only by applying rules of foreseeable danger, which makes negligence harder to prove.

Your investigative plan will tell your clients what you intend to do and give them the ability to add or subtract from it.

Your plan must take into account the amount of time that has passed since the accident. If the incident was very recent, conditions at the scene may be relatively unchanged. There may still be markings left by law enforcement investigators that you can document or debris or other evidence from the accident that has either been overlooked by the initial investigators or swept aside, such as glass or other parts of a vehicle.

On the other hand, you may be going to the scene days, months, or years after the accident or injury. Things may have been considerably altered, sometimes as a result of the accident itself. You may find that a handrail has been installed in a stairwell; lighting has been added; stop sign or traffic control devices now appear at the intersection where none existed before; the road surface has been repaved, regraded, straightened; buildings have been constructed or demolished, and so on.

Because the scene may have been altered or originally improperly designed or constructed, it is important to obtain all official records, applications, plans, and permits, for a predetermined period of time, both before and after the incident. This should be noted in the investigative plan because it can become a time-consuming process.

Other types of official records include but are not limited to police, fire department, building department, traffic department, design and construction plans (as-built plans), traffic light sequencing, property records, tax records, business records, maintenance schedules and records, and so forth. Some items, such as prehospital care reports and other medical records will require subpoenas, as will most business or insurance records.

At times you may be able to obtain the records of nonpublic companies and individuals simply by asking for them, but if they are not produced voluntarily, a subpoena will be required. Your attorney-client can also obtain certain records from opposing counsel during the discovery process. Discovery is the entire effort of a party to a lawsuit and the attorneys involved to obtain information before trial through demands for production of documents, depositions of parties and potential witnesses, written interrogatories (questions and answers written under oath), written requests for admissions of fact, examination of the scene, and the petitions and motions employed to enforce discovery rights.

If you can think of records that the attorney should subpoena, include them in you investigative plan as well. Once received, you will be able to review those records and follow-up as necessary.

Your investigative plan should also indicate your effort to detect any cameras in the area, such as store security, highway department or police department traffic cameras, and ATMs, and to conduct a canvass for witnesses.

You should already be aware of when the incident occurred or was reported (the when), but there is another when that needs to be addressed in the investigative plan: by when is the information needed? Although this initial meeting may be your first involvement in the case, it does not mean that the incident is recent. You may be called in very near the end of the statute of limitations, the time that a person can legally wait to start a lawsuit, or you may be retained on the eve of trial. You must know your own deadlines in every case.

Once you and the client have discussed and agreed upon the investigative plan, your estimated hours for the completion of this assignment, and your fees, it is time to put the plan into effect. Your first item upon returning to your office should be to document your investigative plan by writing your first report to the client. This report should include the following:

- Acknowledgment of your retention and receipt of any retainer from the client. If you have not obtained a signed retainer agreement, you should restate your fees, billing and terms of payment, and reimbursement of expenses policy at this time.
- A complete summary of the facts as you now know them.
- A list of all persons involved and your investigative obligation toward them, including background investigations, interviews, and surveillances. Include any specific instructions from the client regarding persons not to be interviewed or any investigative recommendation that he does not wish you to do.
- A listing of your investigative assignments; in other words, processing the scene and canvassing for additional unknown witnesses; obtaining records; searching for media coverage; and other accidents at the same location; locating and obtaining vehicles, parts, or other equipment involved in the accident, and so on.
- Any deadlines or your anticipated time for completion of the assignment.
- Any special instructions from the client.

Again, private investigators must be aware of the laws relating to retainers and contracts in their areas. For example, in the state of New York, Title 19 NYCRR states the following:

§173.1 Advance statement of services and charges
(a) No licensed private investigator, watch, guard or patrol agency shall undertake to perform any services on behalf of a client unless such licensee shall have delivered to the client a written statement, signed by the licensee, which shall set forth the specific service or services to be performed and the charge or fee therefore. . . .[4]

However, the statute goes on to say

(b) Anything to the contrary of this Part notwithstanding, the statement provided for in subdivision (a) of this section shall not be required to be delivered if the client and the licensee have entered into an agreement in writing, setting forth the services to be rendered and the fee or charge therefore, . . .[5]

Therefore, in New York, investigators can enter into signed, long-term agreements that describe the services and fees agreed to with the client (and, in the case of an attorney, on behalf of the attorneys-clients for which they retain you) and eliminates the need for individual or separate contracts or agreements in every investigation.

PREPARATION FOR FIELD INVESTIGATIONS

To borrow a phrase from the Boy Scouts of America, "Be Prepared." After you get to your destination is too late for you to start thinking about a camera, audio recorder, tape measures, or even pens and paper. A competent investigator will have the appropriate tools available at all times. The following items compose the minimum investigative tool kit for noncriminal investigations:

1. a serviceable vehicle with a full tank of gas
2. pens and pencils with erasers

---

4. New York State Title 19 NYCRR, §173.1 (a)
5. New York State Title 19 NYCRR, §173.1 (b)

3. notepads
4. graph paper
5. clipboard
6. witness statement forms
7. an audio recorder, a supply of unopened audiotapes or digital recording medium, extra batteries
8. quality digital or 35 mm film camera with flash, and sufficient memory or extra film; extra memory cards; batteries
9. tripod
10. Video camera with extra memory cards or tapes and extra charged batteries
11. tape measures, retractable (25 feet minimum) or measuring wheel, a yard stick, a set of commercially available reference scales that you can place in photographs, and street maps or GPS
12. cellular phone
13. magnifying glass
14. binoculars
15. compass
16. hand tools (scissor, screwdrivers, utility knife)
17. umbrella
18. insect repellant and sunscreen
19. reflective safety vests
20. safety cones
21. a stopwatch or a watch with a second hand
22. tire tread depth gauge
23. magnet

You may never use some of the tools that you have brought with you, but the one time that you need a magnet you will be sorry that you did not bring it along. This is not an emergency response accident investigation kit. You are not a safety or risk manager nor should you be concerned about safeguarding the scene for the police or the Occupational Safety and Health Administration (OSHA) if the incident is no longer subject to their investigations. Neither are you on a demolition project, however. If you do find evidentiary matter that has been previously missed by others at the scene, you should notify your client immediately to discuss your next step.

The majority of the items in your kit are used to document what you find at the scene. You cannot overuse the camera or video camera. If you have taken 500 pictures, take another 500. Take the same picture with and without a flash, even outdoors in bright sunlight, because the flash may eliminate shadows.

Many photographers use a polarized lens cover to assist in eliminating reflections. Learn how to use your camera and its lenses to adjust the depth of field, image exposure, and macro and micro functions. Place reference scales in your pictures or videos to provide distance and scale. Use your audio recorder to make notes as you walk the scene. Record all of your impressions as you see them. Most of the tools in your kit have obvious uses; some are redundant ways to record what you find, and others can be used for your own safety. If or how these tools are used is entirely up to the investigator, but it is a best practice to have them available.

POWERS OF OBSERVATION

The most important tool that a professional investigator can possess does not fit into a tool kit, but it must be brought to every accident scene nonetheless. That tool is the power of observation. Observation is an art that must be developed and reinforced over time. It takes conscious effort to recognize what we see, especially for those who do the same thing every day. The ability to be observant can easily be overridden by the many competing events that we become aware of during these days of information overload. Our senses can become dulled and our minds preoccupied by the multitude of problems that we encounter, in both our personal and our professional lives.

The development of observational skills requires training but can be easily self-taught. In Sir Arthur Conan Doyle's *The Adventure of The Red-Headed League,* Sherlock Holmes makes the following observation to Dr. Watson regarding a gentleman whom he had met only for a moment: "Beyond the obvious facts that he has at some time done manual labor, that he takes snuff, that he is a Freemason, that he has been to China, and that he has done a considerable amount of writing lately, I can deduce nothing else."[6]

6. Sir Arthur Conan Doyle, *The Adventure of The Red-Headed League,* London, 1891

Holmes explained his uncanny ability to deduce seemingly impossible information at a quick glance by telling Watson, "You know my method. It is founded upon the observation of trifles. . . . Not invisible but unnoticed, Watson. You did not know where to look, and so you missed all that was important. I can never bring you to realize the importance of sleeves, the suggestiveness of thumbnails, or the great issues that may hang from a bootlace."[7] Holmes practiced the art of observation with the belief that everything has significance.

You can develop your own powers of observation by practicing them on a daily basis. Ask any golf pro how to put backspin on a golf ball and you will get the same answer: Practice.

Observations are not just what you can see, but what you can hear, touch, smell, and taste as well. At one time or another you will be able to make use of all of your senses as a professional investigator.

Try to set aside a few minutes every day to take special notice of a particular thing, person, or event and list a minimum of ten unique items that you may not have seen without concentration. Start with a familiar setting, let us say the street that you live on, and write down your observations for later review. First clear your mind and prepare to concentrate. Deep breathing, calming thoughts, and yoga are all methods that will help you relax. Walk down your block and take note of the signs you see on the houses, fences, street poles, windows, and stores. What message do these signs send? Advertising? Warning? Directional? Informational?

More than likely you will discover more signs than you ever knew were there before. You may also be able to observe if the signs are effective while engaging several different senses. For example, are there "Curb Your Dog" signs? Or "No Smoking" signs? Or "Quiet, Hospital Zone" signs?

You can practice this same exercise by observing things in your residence, such as the way shadows bend on the walls as sunlight spreads across different objects, or you can practice by paying particular attention to new people that you meet and trying to determine their social status, education, employment in the *Holmesian* traditional by taking note of their grooming (fingernails), jewelry (diamonds, school rings), and language (usage of jargon). If you practice being observant, you will become observant.

---

7. Sir Arthur Conan Doyle, *The Adventure of The Red-Headed League,* London, 1891

Whether you have become a practiced observer or not, you should approach each accident scene with a clear mind. If you are distracted by life events you should come back at another time because you will certainly miss something.

KNOW WHERE YOU ARE GOING

One of my favorite Yogi Berra quotes is, *"I knew I was going to take the wrong train, so I left early."* Prior to leaving your office you should know the directions to all of the locations that you plan to visit. You may wish to check ahead of time to avoid any construction or accident delays. A GPS is a useful tool should you become lost or need alternate route information.

WHAT TO LOOK FOR AT ACCIDENT SCENES

As an investigator, you will be called upon to visit and document many different types of scenes. Accidents and injuries can and do occur everywhere. Auto accidents happen on local streets, superhighways, bridges, and tunnels, inside garages, and on ferries. Nonautomotive accidents happen where people work and play, eat and drink, walk and run. Although these various types of cases require different skill sets, the basic investigative techniques remain the same: (1) identify and locate the scene; (2) document the scene through photographs, video, measurements and diagrams; (3) examine the scene and document any evidence, marks, and so on; (4) safeguard any evidence if necessary; and (5) interview known witnesses, locate cameras in the area that may have recorded the event, and canvass for unknown witnesses.

PREPARE FOR THE FIELD

You have now learned everything that the client could or would tell you about the incident. You may have done some preliminary research to prepare for your initial meeting with the client. You have an investigative plan that is approved by the client. You have your investigative tool kit. You know where you are going. So, where are the keys to the car? Not yet. Perhaps there is more to learn about the incident before you get to the scene. Who else may know something about what happened. Before you leave you may want to check or recheck the media sources, which may have covered the story. Perhaps there is a follow-up story or something that you missed the first time. Searches of print, broadcast, and electronic (Internet) news and blog resources or social networking sites may provide additional accounts of what happened. New witnesses can be identified, photographs or videos located, defects identified, all adding to your existing base of knowledge. You may learn of people who could be allies or adversaries of your client.

REVIEW THE POLICE REPORTS

Police are usually dispatched by 911 operators to the scenes of accidents along with an ambulance. If you have been able to obtain a copy of the police incident or accident report you should review it in detail, including any coded cover sheets. If an interview of the reporting police officer is on your investigative plan, you may wish to see if that officer is working, and, if so, you may want to call him or her before you leave. He or she may just consent to meet you at the scene.

> By starting with the Police Accident Report (PAR) you can confirm the date, time, and exact location of the accident. You will be able to identify all of the vehicles that were involved by the registration plate numbers, sometimes Vehicle Identification Numbers (VIN), owner's name and address. You will learn the names, addresses and dates of birth of all the involved drivers, and at least, the names, ages, and positions, and types of injuries to the passengers of all the vehicles. The names and contact information of witnesses are usually included in accident reports as are the identities or badge number of other police officers such as accident investigators who may have responded, EMS personnel, tow truck operators and fire departments that responded. Traffic summonses are usually listed on the Police Accident Report, giving you the opportunity to obtain a copy of the summons, and if a hearing has been held, to obtain a copy of the transcript. Additionally, most Police Accident Reports have now been designed to assist Motor Vehicle or Transportation Departments

to accumulate statistical data such as lighting, weather, road surface, roadway character, the number of other accidents at the same location, whether there were traffic control devices at the scene, whether the vehicle's occupants were wearing seat belts, if there was an airbag deployment, and other details that may not be written in the body of the report. There will usually be an area where the reporting officer can draw a diagram of the accident, or at least select from a standard list of accident types, i.e.; both vehicle traveling in the same direction, head-on, making turns, etc.[8]

Police incident reports are also prepared in nonmotor vehicle accidents and can also contain much of the same information. In addition to learning the identities of the officers involved, you will get the officers' narrative of who told them what. If the officers were eye-witnesses, so much the better, but it is more likely that you will be reading a story that has been related to the officers by someone else. The officers may also include their observations, measurements, and opinions. You may find out from the report if photographs of the scene were taken.

Were there any other incident or accident reports prepared by OSHA, employer, building manager, fire department, or building department? It would be a big advantage for the investigator to know about the existence of such reports and to attempt to obtain a copy before going to the scene for the first time. All of these reports may contain witness statements, lines of sight and distance to the incident, and a host of other information that will be useful to corroborate or dispute your client's position.

INVESTIGATION, FOLLOW-UP, CASE CLOSED

With the preparation and planning now completed, the investigator should be ready to proceed with the established plan. The investigative techniques involved with interviewing, documenting the scene, report writing, evidence, and so on, have and do merit their own chapters or books, so suffice it to say that with a good eye for detail, a good

---

8. Warren J. Sonne, Investigating automotive product liability claims, *PI Magazine, 70,* Nov/Dec 2003.

ear for answers to questions, and the determination to follow up on the investigative plan, every investigator should be capable of discovering the facts and accurately reporting them to the client by verbal and formal report writing. Verbal reporting and communication with the attorney-client cannot be overstated. Since the private investigator's obligation is to his or her client, the client must be made aware of the findings, both good and bad. This should be done verbally, prior to the issuance of a formal report because there may be certain issues that the client does not want to have memorialized in a formal report.

Investigators should continue communicating with the client on a regular basis, and preparing reports as events dictate rather than saving everything for one massive final report. Every interview has the potential of creating additional investigation. Every record that is received has the potential of creating new persons to be interviewed or additional sources to be explored. Every deposition that is taken can produce new avenues of investigation. With the authorization of the client, every new lead should be followed up until there is no investigation remaining.

The private investigator's involvement with the civil justice system does not end with the preparation of the final report. The vast majority of civil cases settle before or at the beginning of the trial. Often, the information that was uncovered by private investigators is the reason for one side or the other agreeing to a settlement, and we can be proud of that as investigators.

On occasion, a civil law suit will go to a trial, and the investigator may be required to give testimony regarding his or her findings. Well-written and -documented reports will enhance the investigator's ability to provide testimony, often several years after the investigation was conducted. In civil matters, the investigator's case is closed only temporarily until the litigation is finally settled.

Chapter 15

THE COMPLEXITIES OF INTERNATIONAL INVESTIGATIONS

WILLIAM F. BLAKE

United States private investigators frequently receive requests from clients that require the assistance from private investigator in other countries. For a myriad of reasons, some of these requests result in unnecessary problems for all parties concerned due to a failure to recognize problems unique to other countries. It is the responsibility of the requesting investigator to educate his or her client on the problems involved in conducting an international investigation.

Among the many issues is the financial cost. It is unrealistic to expect that international hourly rates will be similar to, or lower than, rates within the United States. The decline of the dollar against the Euro and other currencies has dramatically increased the costs of an investigation. The current average minimum hourly rate for international investigations is in the $150 to $200 range.

Another issue is the manner in which international records are maintained and the bureaucratic roadblocks to speedy compliance with requests. In the United States, the vast majority of records and documents are accessible via computer with the generation of immediate results. It should be remembered that more than 90 percent of the world works under old-fashioned investigative standards and practices and has draconian secrecy laws for all investigations, including asset searches and background checks. In some instances, the bureaucracy requires that only a limited number of individuals have access to records. This could mean an extended response time when the designated person is unavailable to process the request. Many public records are only accessible to indigenous law enforcement agencies.

Another issue in the international arena is the additional travel time required because of the distance involved in getting to records storage locations at distant locations. The poor quality of the transportation system in some countries dramatically increases the travel time required to complete a project. In non-English-speaking countries, there is also the cost and time required for translations. The actual and incidental bureaucratic costs of obtaining records on a timely basis must also be considered. In some foreign venues, nonnative requests for information are not given the same priority as requests from indigenous personnel.

In addition, corruption can be a factor in some developing countries. This has to be included in any pricing arrangements. When a client or fellow investigator is quoted a fee from an overseas provider estimated to be in the $150 to $200 per hour range, the potential customer often decides to get a quote from several other local providers in the country concerned. Fair enough. Sometimes local providers will be in a better position to quote lower prices than those from an international provider, usually based on lower overhead but sometimes based on issues of corruption.

Transparency International ranks many countries in the developing world much higher on the list of corrupt countries than it does those in the western world. That occasionally trickles down into our industry. Unfortunately, some local providers, although not necessarily the majority, may discard your legal papers in a process service and prepare a fraudulent affidavit of service. They may engage in ghost writing negative results, never having followed the required leads in the first place, taking your money for a little literary effort.

Minimizing the costs and time delay for completion of international requests is contingent on the preparatory actions of the requesting investigator. It is incumbent upon the requestor to advise the client of the difficulties encountered in international jurisdictions. Of primary consideration should be the explanation that foreign privacy and secrecy laws are considerably more restrictive than are United States laws. Records that are commonly available in the United States may not be available in other countries. Secondarily, the client needs to be advised that it normally requires additional time to complete an international investigation because of the unique political and judicial situation in each country.

There are certain steps that the requesting investigator can accomplish to facilitate the investigation.

- Consider the international investigator an integral part of your investigative team and take him or her into your complete confidence, providing all pertinent details surrounding your client's request. The requesting investigator may be required to obtain the client's consent and have the international investigator execute a nondisclosure or noncompete agreement if necessary. The international investigator may be able to suggest leads unique to his country.
- The approach to information disclosure should be to "tell everything, as if you were handing over the case to a new investigator." This approach allows the international investigator, who is uniquely acquainted with the local culture and bureaucratic structure, to analyze the request and prepare an investigative plan in accordance with the laws of the foreign area. It is essential to solicit advice from the international investigator, who may be able to provide direction to an area not known to the requester.
- The agreement with the client should document the explanation of problems encountered in other countries, such as record-keeping systems, translation problems, and travel. The agreement should also specify the approximate turnaround time, costs and budget limits, and reporting standards, in other words, the need for official documents and signed statements and translation responsibilities.
- When considering time constraints, it is important to coordinate with the foreign investigator to arrive at a reasonable and manageable time line.
- The cultural and ethnic background of the chosen private investigator must also be considered. In some cultures, women are not allowed to talk to men who are not part of their family. This would prevent or impede the information transfer unless a female private investigator was utilized. In some cases, because of cultural and ethnic differences, the private investigator may not be

allowed to talk with members of another ethnic group. In some cases, there may be a difference in language dialects that could cause confusion in translation.

Appropriate prior planning will prevent misunderstandings and unanticipated results.

SUMMARY

There are many influences that must be considered before maximum information and cooperation can be obtained from sources in other countries. National privacy protection laws as well as nongovernmental issues such as corruption and ethnic and cultural differences will influence expected results. Financial costs and time constraints are also a factor.

Chapter 16

CONDUCTING INVESTIGATIONS IN JAPAN

FREDERICK COWARD, JR.

This chapter is designed to guide foreign investigators through key considerations and steps when conducting investigations in Japan. We will suggest basic guidelines but, due to the complexity of the social climate and government systems, investigators should when at all possible, consult investigators who have extensive experience in Japan and who are able to speak, read, and write the language. An established office location and experienced personnel in the country are always beneficial.

Investigators requiring investigative assistance should have an understanding of the 2003 Mutual Legal Assistance Treaty, the Japan Judicial Assistance Treaty, and the Status of Forces Agreement (SOFA) to help facilitate their investigative requests for assistance via either an in-country private investigator or proper legal channels available for assistance.

This chapter will cover privacy, civil matters, service of legal papers, divorce and child custody, database and media searches, individual and corporate background investigations, due diligence (public records, prosecutor's office, criminal checks, credit and bankruptcy checks, sources), financial record search, debt collection, gaming industry, entry into Japan, trademarks, copyright and counterfeit, patent records, phone records, locating heirs to last will and testament, surveillance, SOFA, record searches, Okinawa considerations.

PRIVACY

Japan remains a very closed and secret society with very little transparency. Privacy is entirely different than what we assume it to be in the west. If an investigator attempts to travel to Japan to conduct an independent investigation, it most likely will be fraught with roadblock after roadblock. It is imperative to have in-country sources and Japanese language ability to be productive. Unlike other countries, face-to-face contact is the rule; telephone contact will be unsuccessful and is not culturally acceptable. This stems from the Japanese culture's being a very formality-based culture. The process is not straightforward. It will take more time than traditional investigations and therefore must be budgeted accordingly, and patience is imperative.

In addition to social obstacles, investigators must consider legal obstacles as well, for example, the Personal Information Privacy Act (PIPA). Under Japanese law the rules surrounding the PIPA must be fully understood before any investigator can request this information and of course complied with for a successful investigative result.

CIVIL MATTERS

Like any other investigation conducted worldwide, investigations in Japan require as much detailed background information about the task as possible. Typically, records are not always kept in one location, for example, Tokyo. Most often, records will be stored in other locations outside of Tokyo. Careful planning as well as permission is required prior to viewing them. In this case, travel expenses will be an important component when estimating cost of an investigation. Also, keep in mind that the person who reviews these records must be able to read Japanese and interpret the information contained in the documents. Frequently, the agency or corporation controlling the documents will not allow documents to be copied, which creates an additional obstacle for the investigator.

SERVICE OF LEGAL PAPERS

If legal documents are to be served in Japan, they must be channeled and in line with The Hague Convention guidelines. For example, a complete set of documents must be translated into the Japanese language. The Japanese Ministry of Justice handles any such legal action for their country, so all documents to be served must be delivered to the Japanese Ministry of Justice via the in-country embassy.

It is important to understand the process of serving papers in Japan. Certain Japanese laws are in place that require certain procedures to be followed and should be left to in-country investigators familiar with these guidelines and procedures. In addition to local investigators, a local attorney should be consulted to help facilitate any legal action in Japan.

DIVORCE AND CHILD CUSTODY

These matters are generally the result of marriages in which one of the parties is a Japanese national. Typically, investigators are requested to help locate and return children whom the Japanese spouse has transported back to Japan, leaving the other spouse behind in the foreign country of residence.

If the marriage is registered in Japan, the Japan Family Court has jurisdiction over the case. No other rulings are taken into consideration by any other court outside of Japan. The matter is only viewed from a Japanese point of view. This means all judgments rendered by courts other than Japanese courts are not considered and have no authority in Japan.

No assistance from the Japanese government regarding collecting alimony or custody can be expected to be provided by authorities.

DATABASE AND MEDIA SEARCHES

The *Japan Economic Journal* or the *Nihon Keizai Shinbun* is available online. The Nikkei is a database of news articles and requires a subscription.

Japanese newspapers belong to Nikkei a major compiler and distributor of corporate, national, economic and financial data. These data are compiled from a number of other database providers from national, regional, and local newspapers and magazines.

Media databases are subscription based and available in English and Japanese.

INDIVIDUAL, EMPLOYMENT, AND CORPORATE BACKGROUND INVESTIGATIONS

The Japanese Government recently passed the PIPA, which limits the amount of information that can be obtained on individuals without their permission. Penalties and legal remedies can be applied against individuals for revealing information. As a result, when procuring information on an individual or corporation, established sources are necessary.

The following investigations are available and are limited as to what can be conducted in Japan on Japanese nationals due to the Privacy Act. They can be conducted individually or as one due diligence investigation, depending on what information is required.

Background Check of Individual

This includes reputation (media and industry sources), criminal (police, prosecutors, courts), civil-legal (noncriminal cases), credit and checks for evidence of gang and/or right wing and/or organized crime affiliations.

Background Check of Corporation

Information obtained relates to a corporation and checks with regulatory, tax, and exchange authorities (if the company trades on one of the country's markets).

DUE DILIGENCE INVESTIGATIONS

Individual investigators must do it the old-fashioned way, pure footwork and research, most of which is set out below.

- Individual
- Confirmation of residence: (1) all Japanese houses have a name-plate identifying the occupants; (2) family registration is checked and verified officially with authorities; (3) obtain the house ownership registration.
- Corporation: There is no centralized registry that lists all Japanese corporations.

Public Records

Under the PIPA, credit data are also not to be released to third parties who do not have an established need to know, for example, credit card issuers and banks. Contacts can be made in the three main credit reporting agencies that are willing to give general verbal reports as to whether a subject has credit payment problems, is on a blacklist, or other general information.

All real estate ownership registrations are on file at the Legal Affairs Bureau.

Vehicle ownership can be researched and obtained.

Prosecutor's Office

No database capability exists. All searches are to be done in person, by hand, by the investigator. Data are available in Japanese only.

Criminal Checks

Hearsay is not subject to Japan's Privacy Law so obtaining information from sources, as long as documents are not furnished, is permissible. Foreign-signed release forms for any such information has no standing in Japan.

Civil, Credit, and Bankruptcy Checks

Bankruptcy checks are part of litigation checks. However, credit agencies are willing to confirm an individual's credit records, and no documentation can be obtained.

Civil litigation archives of a subject can be conducted to determine if a subject has ever been a defendant or plaintiff in any past or current cases.

Investigators can check to see if the subject is a listed defendant in the Yokohama District Court (individual) or the Tokyo District Court (individual and corporate).

Courts require that a copy of any lawsuit filed against any subject in any case in which the subject is named as a defendant and/or director of a defendant be sent to the district court serving the subject residence in question. Local and national knowledge is a must to obtain this information.

Organized Crime Sources and Police and Government Sources

These checks are available via established contacts in Japan only. They can be used for a wide array of information gathering. For example, in-country financial sources are well-placed to determine if money laundering activity is ongoing or has a history. Another example would be the gaming industry, in which boat, Pachinko parlors, and horse racing are legal betting activities in Japan. This industry as well maintains established sources.

FINANCIAL RECORD SEARCH

Physical asset searches can be conducted. Certain financial documents are on file with various agencies. As a legal requirement, these agencies are required to maintain these documents in the event of a due diligence investigation.

DEBT COLLECTION

Local law firms are available for any and all inquiries that require legal representation. There is a separate process for Japanese nationals and for expatriates.

ENTRY INTO JAPAN

Before you go and attempt to conduct investigations in Japan, you must consider the complexity of Japan's immigration procedures. For example, you cannot enter Japan as a tourist and conduct an investigation. On the other hand, you cannot enter Japan as an independent investigator without a business license or without having a subsidiary company representation in Japan. So, entry into Japan as an investigator has limitations and if not followed severe implications can result.

TRADEMARKS, COPYRIGHT, AND COUNTERFEIT

Japanese law provides entities the means to completely recover their trademarks, but there is a process. Everything in Japan is about process, and the process is designed to protect the stakeholders first.

Because of Japan's reputation as a country that has a need for brand-name goods, the government has passed legislation that requires investigators, lawyers, police, public prosecutors, and Japanese Customs to work closely together to stop parallel importing, fake licensing, and the import and sale of counterfeit goods. The procedures are clear and simple:

1. In any case of identity theft, counterfeiting, contract fraud, or the like, a Japanese attorney is absolutely necessary. The attorney requests the initial private investigation.
2. Evidentiary reports are provided to the police and the public prosecutor for review.
3. The authority agency will conduct an independent investigation and then report to the public prosecutor.
4. Japanese civil and criminal cases are handled separately individually.

Japanese courts are historically slow and can take years for appeals to be exhausted.

PATENT RECORDS

Patent information must be researched and investigated in person. Direct access to the Patent Office is absolutely necessary to obtain copies of applications and/or approved patents. Obtaining copies can take several working days. In the case of patents issued after 1985, be prepared for a considerable delay.

TELEPHONE RECORDS

In May 2009, the government amended the PIPA to criminalize possession of individual and/or corporate data by any third party without the express written permission of the subject.

LOCATING HEIRS

In order to fulfill the legal requirements in Japan, breaking the PIPA for these types of cases requires a Japanese attorney. The attorney will then lead the process and requirements as per Japanese laws.

SURVEILLANCE IN SUPPORT OF INVESTIGATION

Surveillances are legal in Japan and can be conducted, but investigators need full disclosure of the purpose along with specific instructions as to evidence required for their respective cases. It is imperative, however, that your surveillance team compliments the target as well as the social behaviors and ethnic make-up of the environment of Japan.

STATUS OF FORCES AGREEMENT

SOFA is a document signed by the United States and Japan that governs the role, responsibility, and rights of military members, base employees, and their families while assigned to the country.

Locating military members, service family members, and SOFA employees through military legal channels is always possible.

Service of Documents and Procedures

Base commanders of U.S. military and support organizations require a copy of the complaint for their legal officer (usually from the Judge Advocate General's Corps) before one is allowed to serve a person on U.S. military facilities. Procedures are different for each base. Most bases prefer that a service member or base employee be served while on duty. Hard copy, original docs are typically needed.

IDENTIFICATION NEEDS TO
ASSIST IN ALL INVESTIGATIONS

Investigations will be difficult to impossible without the kanji (Japanese-Chinese characters) of the subject in question for any investigation. The full name along with the kanji characters, date of birth, place of birth, and residence is required to conduct a criminal check in Japan. The Families Registry Law is a method of verification for the subject of interest. Japan residents have an identification with their name and address that is required by the police.

OKINAWA INVESTIGATIVE MATTERS

All laws passed in Japan have an exception clause for Okinawa, which makes it necessary for the Japanese officials to check and approve everything investigators do on the island. Culturally, they view themselves as a separate country in how things are perceived and done on the island.

SUMMARY

As you can see, Japan is a unique and sometimes challenging country to conduct investigations. Laws and practices are very different from what investigators in other countries are used to and are not always patterned after a western approach to conducting investigations.

Chapter 17

INVESTIGATOR LIABILITY

Reginald J. Montgomery

For many private investigators, talking about liability seems as meaningful as watching paint dry. Some dismiss it out of hand; others brush it off saying, "I have insurance." Most investigators came from law enforcement, the military, or other governmental backgrounds, where they were protected from personal liability. In the private sector, however, liability is a real issue—one that can dramatically affect each (and every) private investigator.

Under the American legal system, any person can be sued for any reason. Technically, there is a rule against frivolous lawsuits, but it is rarely imposed. In fact, there are numerous examples of neighbors suing each other simply out of harassment. When litigation is turned on investigators, however, the tide changes. Private investigators sell themselves and their skills, knowledge, contacts, expertise, and, most importantly, integrity. When that integrity is challenged, it costs time, effort, energy, and money to defend.

To protect themselves from liability, many investigators purchase insurance. Is that enough? Actively choosing what services to offer, what clients to work for, and which of each to avoid will have a greater impact on liability than will the presence or absence of insurance. This chapter will explore the risks private investigators face, explore options for managing these risks, and provide recommendations for minimizing exposure.

WHERE WE ARE TODAY

Today private investigators are involved in almost all aspects of legal and business processes. As the profession has grown and matured, professionals have replaced cowboys. The retired part-timers, who once dominated the ranks, are now outnumbered by full-timers.

In the early 1900s, only New York licensed investigators. Today, more than forty states recognize that private investigators are a specialized function and require various combinations of licensing, experience, and continuing education. The emergence of standards also brought about the liability for failing to meet those standards. Then the privacy movement emerged, including criminal and civil penalties for invasion of privacy.

These factors all combine to put private investigators under increasing scrutiny. In the past, issues of trespass or invasion of privacy were rarely mentioned. Many investigators thought nothing of calling buddies to get them inside information. In the last ten years, however, the situation has changed dramatically. Investigators began to be prosecuted, first on the federal level for IRS and Social Security records and then on the state level for records from the Division of Motor Vehicles (DMV). Lately, both federal and state prosecutions have occurred regularly for violations of various privacy laws involving criminal, driving, financial, and other records.

THE INVESTIGATIVE BUSINESS

Today is a far cry from the days when Pinkerton and Burns could operate above the law in the 1880s. Then readers were entranced by the exploits of Sherlock Holmes. Later, people followed the hard - harging actions of Mike Hammer and the incredible investigative powers of Perry Mason and his team. The Wild West has passed on into history, however. Today, the successors to Pinkerton and Burns are guard services companies. Private security functions are highly regulated and increasingly routine. Successful private investigators proudly display credentials, not pistols; state licenses are seen in offices, not whiskey bottles.

Even as the industry grew and matured, the core needs remained the same. People still lie, cheat, and steal. Every day telephones in private investigators offices ring with tales of woe, claims abuse, and demands for justice.

So what does the ethical private investigator do? Is it possible to serve your clients without bending (and sometimes breaking) the law? Are the rewards worth the risks in today's environment? What are the risks? These questions can have very different answers depending on the specific services offered and clients served.

SERVICE RISKS

Investigative services can involve specific inherent risks, and different services, locations, and specialties can greatly increase or decrease the overall risk level. Services that involve no contact (such as document retrieval) generally have the lowest level of risk. Next are services that involve contact with witnesses or other nonconfrontational parties (friendly interviews, locating witnesses, etc.). The highest risks are those that directly involve parties (surveillance, process service, domestic matters) and those that involve sensitive or borderline legal areas, (background investigations, asset searches).

These risks are enhanced depending on your specific service. For example, serving a business is generally very low risk, whereas personal service can be very high risk. Covert surveillance in a high crime area is a considerably higher risk than is open surveillance of a loading dock. Further, these risks are affected by your actions as well. Carrying a weapon dramatically increases the risk level (although it may seem safer).

Providing higher risk services is often part of the job. Some investigators, out of a sense of competition or ego, try to push the limits; by climbing trees, crawling under fences, hiding in bayous, all to get the best possible film. When they do, they may break the law and put themselves in potential jeopardy. Others may decide that the risk required for a certain service is no longer worthwhile. The key is in actively making an informed choice.

CLIENT RISKS

Similarly, some clients are riskier to serve than are others. Investigators who work for corporations are primarily involved in litigation (or potential litigation) matters. Thus, the main risk is being embroiled in the litigation. The more important your role, the more likely you will be named as a party in the case. On the other hand, investigators who work for lawyers or law firms face different risks. The possibility of litigation is much lower because an attorney's agent is often protected, but the risk of violating legal ethics rules (many of which are unknown to investigators) or the risk of not getting paid can increase. Investigators who work for private persons run the highest risks, potentially involving themselves in the improper use of information, charges of conspiracy, and the greatly increased risk of nonpayment.

Choosing to work or not work for certain types of clients has a great impact on a private investigator's risk levels. The previous examples may seem either common sense or farfetched, but they are all based on real-life examples from the past five years. It is important to remember that the entire driver's privacy protection movement began when a private investigator sold driver's license information to a man who then killed an actress. For a simple $50 case, that private investigator has an affect on every other private investigator in the United States.

RISK MANAGEMENT TECHNIQUES

Because each private investigator's clients, services, risks, and tolerances are different, it is impossible to simply spell out a global solution. Rather than guess as to the proper balance, private investigators should utilize risk management techniques to find the best solution for their situation. Risk management is based on a process of controlling risk analytically and its basic formula is RISK=Acceptance, Avoidance, Identification, Measurement, Mitigation, and Transfer.

Identification

Determine what risks you face. These can be caused by location (flood, hurricane, tornado, rebellion, etc.), services (surveillance, repossession, background checks, domestic, etc.), and/or clients (corporations, insurance companies, lawyers, individuals). They can also be caused by your background, history, skills, training, and/or experience. The purpose of this exercise is to ensure that you are aware of the specific risks your business experiences.

Measurement

Next consider the impact of these risks. Some are more likely than others. Some are more devastating than others. Since most private investigators function as small businesses, be sure to address the impact of these events on your family. Are there other income sources? What would happen to your business if you were sued, arrested, or described negatively in the press?

Acceptance

There are some risks that you are willing to accept. For example, there is a possibility that a meteorite might hit you. Although the risk is small, this would certainly be significant. On the other hand, there is really nothing that can be done about it, so the risk must be accepted. Similarly, most private investigators are willing to accept the risks of political instability in the country they live in and other types of risks. File in this category any identified risk that you are willing to accept unchanged.

Avoidance

There are other risks that you are never willing to accept. This may require that you limit your services, location, client types, or other factors. Many investigators will not take a case outside of their comfort zone. That might mean only working local cases, not taking surveillance cases, or turning down interviews with non-English speakers. File in this category any risks that you are unwilling to accept.

Mitigation

For those risks that you are neither willing to accept nor able to avoid, use mitigation techniques to reduce your exposure. For example, if you take cases from individuals, you can reduce your risk of not getting paid by executing a written contract or requiring a deposit payment. Other risks can be mitigated by thorough documentation, use of disclaimers, or obtaining a signed confirmation letter. Use mitigation techniques to reduce risks to an acceptable level.

Transfer

Finally, for those risks that you must take and cannot otherwise mitigate, consider transferring them to another party. For example purchase E & O insurance or execute a hold harmless agreement to move the risk of litigation to your insurance company or client. Similarly, formalizing your business structure by creating a partnership or corporation will shield your personal liability. Remember that all transfer activities involve costs, paying for an insurance policy or hiring a lawyer to create a corporation, for example, but for those costs you receive a layer of protection, wherein another party takes part or all of the risk for you.

STRATEGIES FOR SUCCESS

This brief review of investigative service risks, client risks, and risk management techniques provides a foundation for increasing the success of your business. Follow this process to determine your risk tolerance. Look at your situation and measure your exposure. By focusing on these areas, you can use this risk assessment exercise to not only reduce your exposure but also increase your profitability.

1. What clients do you serve? Where?
2. Do you have employees? How are they controlled?
3. What services do you provide? Why?
4. What are your least favorite services? Can you eliminate them?
5. What are your least profitable services? Can you eliminate them?
6. What are your highest risk services? Can you eliminate them?
7. Have you eliminated any unnecessary risks?
8. Have you mitigated any remaining risks?
9. Have you transferred all catastrophic risks?

To be more successful, give your business a physical. Take a good look at the service/client/risk picture and make sure that you are comfortable with it. Identify any problem areas, poor profitability, high exposure, changing client demand, and so on. Make active decisions about your risks—it does not matter what another investigator's tolerance is; only what your tolerance is. The time to find holes in your liability protection is before the other side finds them for you.

Chapter 18

FOOT AND VEHICLE SURVEILLANCE

Andrew C. "Skip" Albright

For many investigators or investigation firms, there is probably no more important skill to master than that of conducting surveillance. Surveillance is the cornerstone of many investigation businesses, and it is the successful conduct of surveillance that makes or breaks their reputation and, therefore, their ability to make a living.

Surveillance is the surreptitious (unseen) observation of a person, people, or site. Surveillance can be recorded by written notes, dictation, still camera, or video camera. There are numerous elements in conducting a successful surveillance. Many of these will be discussed in detail hereafter, but there are four critical aspects you should always remember, the lack of any of which will render your surveillance unsuccessful. Those four elements are as follows:

1. Locating and positively identifying the subject of the surveillance.
2. Remaining concealed; that is, not getting burned.
3. Operating the camera to produce professional results.
4. Successfully tailing (not losing) the subject.

What follows is very detailed training on the art of surveillance, covering virtually every aspect you will need to make you successful. Learn this well, and you will only succeed in your profession as a private investigator. Ignore it, and you will surely fail.

INTRODUCTION TO SURVEILLANCE

Imagine that you have been given the assignment of conducting surveillance on an important insurance claim. More than $100,000 in potential settlement fees ride on whether you can successfully take a video of the claimant, who is suspected of faking a back injury. You set up across the street from the subject's house in your car. He comes out of the house sometime later and drives away toward town. You follow, barely able to keep an eye on him, let alone see what he is doing. Suddenly he runs a red light, and you decide to follow him. He notices you do it and drives straight home. When he arrives home, he notices your vehicle stopping a few houses down the street. Your surveillance is blown, but what did you do wrong? Everything.

In this training section, we are going to cover the following topics associated with our introduction to surveillance:

1. definition of surveillance
2. scope and purpose of surveillance
3. categories of surveillance
4. methods of surveillance
5. objectives of surveillance
6. presurveillance consideration factors
7. legal considerations

Before we can conduct a successful surveillance, we must first know what it is. In order to learn about the foundations of surveillance, we are going to dissect surveillance operations and see just what surveillance is and is not.

DEFINING SURVEILLANCE

To some degree we all have been involved in some form or type of surveillance activity, but do we really understand what surveillance is? *Webster's Dictionary* defines surveillance as the "close watch kept over someone or something (as by a detective)." For our purposes, we define surveillance as the deliberate, systematic, and continuous observation or monitoring of an area, person, or group of persons by any means without the consent of all persons being observed or monitored. Surveillance is an investigative tool that if properly employed, can bring about a successful resolution to an investigation. Surveillance is quite limited in scope and purpose. Only when we have clearly identifiable surveillance objectives will surveillance operations be initiated.

SCOPE AND PURPOSE OF SURVEILLANCE

The primary purpose of surveillance operations is to gather intelligence. We want to learn what is going on. Once we have gathered intelligence, it can be used to decide what further investigative steps or actions need to be accomplished. Once we have decided that we do in fact need to conduct surveillance, we need to figure out how we want to approach this surveillance. Is it important that the claimant, or subject as we shall call him, not know he is being surveilled? Let us look at the two categories of surveillance.

CATEGORIES OF SURVEILLANCE

There are two general categories of surveillance relating to intensity or sensitivity:

- Discreet Surveillance. The subject is unaware that he is under observation. This is the usual meaning of the term surveillance. The adjective discreet is used merely to distinguish it from what may be termed a close, restraint, or control surveillance. The essence of discreet surveillance is that the subject is unaware of being watched. Generally, the guiding rule is to discontinue surveillance rather than risk actions which make the subject aware of the observation.
- Close Surveillance. A close surveillance is one in which maintaining constant observation of the subject is the paramount objective, even though the subject may become aware of the surveillance. Surveillance to provide protection is frequently of this nature. This type of surveillance can also be used as a preventive measure to deter individuals from committing illegal acts or from fleeing, once they become aware of an investigation or operation.

Private investigators involved in personal protection details are in fact conducting "close surveillance" of their principal.

So now that we have decided which category of surveillance we want to employ, how are we going to go about this? We will now look at the five methods of surveillance available to us.

METHODS OF SURVEILLANCE

The following are the types of surveillance methods that are used most often:

- Fixed Point: A fixed surveillance point is one in which the surveillance remains in a relatively fixed position to observe the activities at a specific location. These fixed points are usually predetermined locations selected after extensive analysis of the subject and his or her activities.
- Moving: In a moving surveillance, the investigator follows the subject from place to place to maintain continuous watch over his or her activities. The movement may be on foot or by vehicle and include land, water, air, or any combination of these.
- Technical: This type of surveillance is accomplished by the use of technical visual devices, electronic listening devices, vehicle trackers, and signaling devices.
- Photographic: Often considered part of technical surveillance, the term technical implies that the agent must be a technician or electronics expert to accomplish the task. However, all investigators must be able to accomplish photographic surveillance coverage, which is why we treat this as a separate method.
- Combination or Mixed: A combination of technical, fixed, moving, and photographic surveillance is usually the most expensive in terms of money and investigative effort but will often achieve the best results. In almost all surveillance operations, we employ a combination of the different types of surveillance methods.

From what we have said so far, it is easy to see that surveillance might be confused with an undercover operation, but there are some definite differences between the two.

OBJECTIVES OF SURVEILLANCE

Surveillance is employed by investigators as an aid in achieving investigative objectives that vary with the requirements of the case and the particular circumstances prevailing in a given place at a given time. Some of the most common objectives of surveillance are as follows:

- Obtain information or develop leads
- Obtain evidence of a crime that has been committed or to observe a crime actually being committed
- Check the reliability of informants or their information
- Check the loyalty of employees
- Monitor the movements and activities of subjects
- Determine if a subject is frequenting a certain establishment or location
- Establish a subject's habits, such as his or her hangouts, associates, or place of employment
- Confirm a subject's whereabouts

These are not the only considerations we should take into account before we initiate surveillance, however. There are other factors we should consider.

PRESURVEILLANCE CONSIDERATIONS

Knowledge of the case and the subject is necessary prior to initiation of the surveillance. In many cases, fragmentary information concerning activities, habits, and routine of a subject will be available through information, documentary evidence, records reviews, and similar means. The necessity for surveillance is frequently determined on the basis of a picture created by this fragmentary information. Careful study of the information by the investigators will enable them to visualize activities, determine the type of surveillance, consider the proper methods to use, minimize the chances of error, and save time that might otherwise be devoted to useless action. Surveillance is often the most costly, boring, monotonous, and unrewarding investigative technique in which you will ever be involved. Careful consideration must be given before surveillance is initiated. Continuous surveillance is difficult at best. To accomplish surveillance, the recommended approach is to carefully case the area, study and analyze the subject, exploit all developed information, and then plan and execute the surveillance.

Prior to conducting a surveillance, and indeed critical to the decision of whether one will be conducted at all, is the area of legal and policy considerations. Just as there are rules, regulations, laws, and policies that direct our actions in all other phases of investigations, they exist to guide us in the conduct of surveillances.

LEGAL CONSIDERATIONS

Physical surveillances may usually be conducted where there is no reasonable expectation of privacy. Surveillances conducted where a reasonable expectation of privacy exists, such as a technical surveillance, may be a violation of law. Therefore, surveillance must be conducted in the least intrusive manner possible. When surveillance is deemed necessary, it will be conducted within the scope of the laws, regulations, and guidelines set forth to direct it. Prior to conducting surveillance, it is imperative you understand what you legally can and cannot do during the course of the surveillance.

AREA CASING AND SUBJECT STUDY

If you knew there was something you could do that would make the rest of the work you do easier and would greatly increase your chances for success, you would probably do it. Well, what we are going to be talking about during this block of training is exactly that: something that can definitely make your surveillance operation easier and will help you achieve success.

In preparation for conducting a physical surveillance, the first step is to carefully case the area and study the subject. Without this careful planning it is doubtful a successful investigation and surveillance could be conducted. Casing the area in which the subject resides, works, or participates in leisure activities provides the investigator with valuable information on the subject's environment, leading to a better understanding of character, personality, and motivation. Knowledge of the area in which the subject resides provides information on the mode of living, and may help provide the necessary background information for planning the development of the investigation and surveillance if necessary. We will examine the following areas:

1. area casing
2. other area factors
3. maps and map reading
4. subject study
5. informant recruiting in surveillance

Area Casing

This is the complete and systematic study and analysis of the environment in which the subject resides and works or travels to and from. The purpose of the area casing is to learn as much as possible about the subject's environment and associates so that adequate planning can be accomplished to further an investigation or to conduct a physical surveillance.

The saying that there is no substitute for experience is especially applicable to conducting surveillance. There is no way to become competent as an investigator other than by actually participating in surveillances. Even though training can go a long way in offsetting the setbacks that inexperienced investigators face, investigators may conceivably be faced with conducting surveillance in a major investigation with some personnel who do not have much actual experience. One way to help overcome this shortfall is a very detailed casing of the area. Knowledge of the area (subject's environment) complements experience, and if an investigator has both, she or he will likely have the confidence needed to conduct a successful surveillance and ultimately a successful investigation.

One of the most important things to consider when conducting your area casing is those things that will impose limitations or problems during your surveillance operation. We call these things as they pertain to the area "environmental limiting factors." Some environmental limiting factors to consider include:

• geography
• distance

- topography/terrain
- local culture
- language
- customs
- racial/ethnic differences
- transportation
  - public
  - traffic density
  - quality of roads
- population density and type of buildings
- local authorities and laws
- availability of quarters/facilities
- weather
- presence of opposition/countersurveillance (to include capabilities)
- home turf

Aside from these environmental limiting factors, there are also some other things that must be considered when conducting the area casing.

Other Area Casing Factors

The type, nature, and amount of information to be gathered will depend on the nature of the investigation or allegation and what use is to be made of the information once it is collected and evaluated. The following, although not all inclusive, are factors to consider when casing an area:

- Area where that subject resides, works, and spend leisure time.
- Public transportation (taxi, railway, air, underground, rental cars, bus). This analysis should also include hours of operation, fares, and types of coins needed or special fare cards utilized.
- Local customs, laws (including traffic), and business hours.
- Roadways, traffic flow, and construction.
- Location of nearest police, fire, and medical/emergency facilities.
- Local police coverage and patterns.
- Identification of friends and associates.
- Location of telephones, types of coins or credit cards needed, instructions on use.

- Location of mail boxes, post offices, mail pick-up schedule for subject.
- Threat posed by subject (if any) to include ability to monitor communications and conduct countersurveillance.
- Weather and climate conditions and time of daylight and darkness.
- Nature, location, and types of buildings that may be encountered, to include floor plans, addresses, operating hours.
- Gas stations used by subject.
- Banks and stores used by subject.
- Communications. Check your communications in the area of operation to determine coverage patterns and range and note any problems that may be encountered.
- When possible, obtain maps, diagrams, photographs, sketches, and floor plans of the subject's work location and places frequented, as well as facilities which may be used to conduct the surveillance.

Information should be updated as required. Investigators who are new to the case should be required to review the area casing study and familiarize themselves with the area as soon as possible. Consideration should be given to the possible risk of compromising your investigation during the area casing stages. The value of the information being gathered must be weighed against the possible risk of exposure in collecting it. Consideration should be given to the advantages and disadvantages of briefing other police, investigative, or security personnel. It may be possible to provide a limited briefing or some plausible cover story if necessary. It may be that the entire casing effort and any follow-up investigative activity or surveillance is done without the knowledge of other local police or security personnel.

Nighttime surveillance offers unique limiting factors that must also be taken into consideration and planned for. Some of those include the following:

- Street lights: location of lights and when do they come on and go off?
- Bars: Times they open and close?
- Sensitive buildings: jewelry stores, banks, and so on.

- Male and female teams: very versatile.
- Rural areas: people notice strangers at night.
- Urban areas: Busy, but they may go dead at night.
- Extremely difficult to recognize subject at night.
- Get to know the rear light pattern of subject's car at night.
- During acquisition of the subject, pass anything that might be strange about the car lights onto the other surveillance vehicles.
- If you need to confirm the subject, make sure you have a back-up investigator (if you have one) to take the subject so you can peel off right away.
- At night you must keep your eyes on the subject at all times because peope are so easy to lose.
- Equal spacing of vehicles is very dangerous at night and very easy to see.
- Night surveillance is extremely tiring.
- Consider use of headlight cut outs (dimmers), but use out of sight of the subject or third party.

When conducting the analysis of the area, it must be remembered that the subject is familiar with the area and his or her daily habits and you are not. The better you know the area and the subject, the more successful you will be. In planning and training investigators to work in the area, emphasis should be given to the places the subject goes and things that the subject does. If the subject should become "lost" to the surveillance team, it would be nice to know that she or he stops at a bar or the local post office at a specific time. Investigators should know the area well enough so that they are not led down one-way streets or dead-end roads or into closed stores, or some other area where the surveillance operation can be burned. If the investigation or surveillance is to be conducted over an extended period of time, consideration should be given to locating a room or apartment near the subject's residence to be used as a listening/target acquisition post, as well as locating a suitable command post. Investigators conducting the area casing must have suitable cover stories and documentation to avoid compromise.

Now we know the area in which our surveillance is going to take place as well as we think we need to. We took all the limiting factors and other problems that might occur into consideration. How do we ensure that we will know where we are, and how to explain to others where we are or where the subject is? The answer is the surveillance map.

Maps and GPS Devices

Your ability to stay on the subject during surveillance is greatly enhanced by the use of maps, your ability to read a map, and the use of a GPS device. Knowing where the subject is and where you are is important. Your ability to relay that information to other members of your team, when applicable, is paramount for continued surveillance coverage. If you do not know where you are or how to explain that information to others, you may as well close up shop and go home.

If there is one thing that is key with regard to maps and surveillance, it is that you *must* be able to competently read the maps you have. So many times, investigators are confused when reading their maps, and they end up in the wrong place, or it takes them far too long to find out where they are supposed to be. You cannot be *too* familiar with your maps.

GPS devices are amazing at letting you know exactly where you are. This is particularly useful in cases in which you have other surveillance investigators in the chase, and you need to let them know where you or the subject is located and the direction of travel. Here again, knowing how to use your GPS device properly is crucial. Many of the GPS devices available have unique and helpful features that will aid in your being able to conduct a successful surveillance. For instance, if you are in an unfamiliar area, many of the GPS devices available can point out the closest restrooms, burger joints, gas stations, and so on, so that you do not have to waste time getting to such places if you have to get back in the chase or back to a fixed-point surveillance spot.

Our area casing is done, and our maps and GPS are ready to go. The only thing we do not know too much about is our subject. How can we be just as prepared from that standpoint as we are with the area–through the subject study.

Subject Study

A subject study is the complete and systematic study and analysis of the subject of your investigation. The purpose of the subject study is to learn as much as possible about the subject's character, personality, habits, lifestyle, finances, activities, and motivation, so that adequate planning can be accomplished to further an investigation or to conduct surveillance. In our investigations, much of this information is provided to us by our clients, and other aspects of the subject are learned by database searches conducted before the surveillance begins.

In conjunction with area casing, a complete study of the subject must also be accomplished to understand how he or she fits into the environment. The following are some factors to consider but are not all inclusive, depending on the type of investigation:

- Detailed physical description of subject and her or his clothes and shoes. Photographs are extremely helpful, especially from the back and sides.
- Finances, credit cards, spending habits, and location of banks used.
- Mannerisms, personal habits, walk, gait (emphasis should be on peculiarities contributing to ready identification, particularly from a distance or from the sides and rear of the subject).
- Description of any vehicles owned or used by subject, friends, relatives, and associates.
- Transportation habits and routes used.
- Hobbies.
- How does subject spend leisure time?
- Daily habits and routines.
- Work habits and schedule.
- Assessment of the probable degree of suspicion the subject may have toward being under investigation or surveillance.
- Personality.
- Motivation and ambition.
- Character.
- Arrest record and database checks.
- Travel history and currency of passports.
- Names, addresses, locations, and identities of associates and places frequented. An attempt should be made to fully identify all persons contacted by subject.

As investigators, we are taught from the beginning that one of the most important aspects of an investigation usually is or can be the effective use of informants. It is no different in surveillance operations.

As you can tell from what we have discussed here, preparation is certainly one of the key ingredients in a surveillance operation, and knowing how to adequately prepare for that surveillance and then doing it will go a long way toward making your job both easier and more successful.

MINIMUM MANPOWER FOR SURVEILLANCE

Having a team of trained investigators available to conduct a surveillance operation is great, but in almost all of the surveillances we conduct, we are forced to use only one investigator, or sometimes two, to conduct surveillance. It is a simple matter of economics. There is no reason we cannot conduct a successful surveillance just because we have limited manpower. Although it does reduce our flexibility in many instances, most often it is still done successfully. As proof, we do it every day.

Foot and vehicle surveillance are the keys to many surveillance situations encountered. In almost every surveillance operation, even the sparsely manned ones, we will be required to conduct some type of foot and vehicle surveillance coverage or, at a minimum, be prepared to conduct each type of surveillance if it becomes necessary.

Although surveillance could be conducted by a single investigator, the success of this will depend solely on the ability of the investigator and often on good fortune. The distance between the subject and the investigator is usually either too great or too far, and the subject must be kept in view at all times by the single investigator, which increases the risk of being identified as surveillance. A one-person surveillance does not provide for any flexibility.

The subject study is especially important in one-person surveillance operations. Knowledge of what to expect from the subject (i.e. where he or she normally goes, does, etc.) will help decrease face time with the subject and allow the investigator to increase the distance between herself or himself and the subject. One-person surveillances are usually most effective in situations in which countersurveillance or suspicion of surveillance by the subject is unlikely.

Very often it is advantageous to conduct a fixed-point surveillance with one person because it will often attract less attention than two people. There are some obvious drawbacks, however, such as no relief, more demand on concentration and therefore fatigue of a single investigator, and single-witness problems should the subject be observed doing something illegal. We try to overcome that problem through the capturing of the subject on videotape.

The use of at least two investigators greatly increases the chances of success because the second agent does allow for some flexibility. With two investigators, the position of an investigator directly behind the subject in a moving surveillance can be changed as often as possible and allows for relatively close positioning of the investigator behind the subject. The use of two investigators affords greater security against detection and reduces the risk of losing the subject. In foot surveillance, both investigators would normally be on the same side of the street as the subject, with the first being fairly close behind the subject. The second investigator is positioned behind the first with more distance between them. On streets that are not crowded, one investigator may walk on the opposite side of the street. Unfortunately, we are seldom afforded the luxury of a second investigator, and it is therefore extremely important that each investigator be the best investigator he or she possibly can be.

SURVEILLANCE VULNERABILITIES

Surveillance does not mean that we just simply follow a subject. This is only one facet of surveillance activity. Surveillances should be conducted in a manner in which we try to make our subjects predictable, yet we avoid being predictable ourselves. Fortunately, subjects are human and therefore make mistakes on which we can (hopefully) capitalize.

In this section, we will discuss vulnerabilities, both ours and theirs. Although we may sometimes encounter countersurveillance, many vulnerabilities are common to most surveillance operations and may be exploited to our advantage. We will look at the following areas related to surveillance vulnerabilities:

1. keys to detecting surveillance
2. surveillance dry cleaning
3. subject vulnerabilities

We will examine some of the areas that the opposition will focus on and review some of the possible ways we might be able to exploit the subject's perception of our methods.

Keys to Detecting Surveillance

As a general rule of thumb, a lesson we learned from international counterintelligence surveillances is that foreign intelligence officers marked a person as surveillance if they spotted the person (or vehicle) three times, separated by time and distance. This does not mean that they did not mark people as surveillance the first time they were spotted if they were careless and obviously conducting surveillance, but the third time spotted was an automatic mark. You can also assume that even in insurance, criminal, and fraud surveillances, if the subject spots you three or more times, you are probably burned. To help detect surveillance, the subjects "key" on several areas:

- Commonalities. A lesson we learn from counterintelligence surveillances is that subjects look for things that do not change. Examples could be an investigator who changes his jacket and pants but not his shoes or glasses. Each investigator should carry at least one complete change of clothing to reduce the things that are obvious and do not change. Always consider belt buckles, jewelry, and shoes. Make your change complete. Hats and glasses are an excellent addition that makes an investigator look completely different. If a claimant is getting used to the way you look, these items can give you a fresh look and make you unrecognizable to a subject.
- Uniforms. For some reason, if a group of investigators were gathered together and told to prepare for a surveillance operation tomorrow, the majority of them would report wearing the "uniform": blue jeans and sneakers and if it was winter a flannel shirt and in summer a T-shirt with a logo emblazoned across the chest and a baseball cap. Surveillance does not mean dressing down. However, many of our subjects look for the "typical" surveillance

uniform worn by investigators because they know this is how surveillance people dress. Common sense will tell you that subjects also know that we dress down for surveillance work, because they watch television and see the uniform. We can exploit this weakness by changing our uniforms and dressing appropriately for the environment and the subject. It is the responsibility of each investigator to decide what he or she will wear on any given day of a surveillance operation. Because subjects often travel through a variety of environments, the investigators will want to ensure that they are not always dressed the same but that a variety of dress styles or "classes" are represented so that they can move freely in those particular environments.

- Long Stays/Short Stays. The subject may stop in a building, movie theater, store, restaurant, and so on, where it is anticipated she or he will remain for a period of time. Investigators "collapse" around the building waiting for the subject to reappear. While everyone is waiting, investigators become bored, thirsty, and lonely, often moving, changing positions, and often "bunching up." Investigators usually anticipate the subject will be making a long stay, and they will not be detected. Subjects often depart before the investigators think they will, and the investigators are caught off guard. The investigators scatter in an attempt to resume their positions.

- Vehicles. It is often hard to disguise cars. Make your surveillance vehicles have a personality. Add car seats, trailer hitches, and bumper stickers. Keeping your surveillance vehicle ultra-clean and highly waxed or extremely dirty may draw more attention to it than if it has a normal amount of road dirt on it.

- Vehicle Usage. Remember, many of our subjects are involved in illegal activity; that is, they are defrauding the insurance company. As such, many of them are highly suspicious of surveillance, because they know it can cut off their supply of money from the insurance company. Subjects look for the investigator by looking for cars turning in behind them from the right. They will put themselves in your shoes and look for the most logical place for you to be. In vehicle surveillances, they expect you to make a right turn into traffic to follow them since this is easier for you to accomplish than to cross against traffic. Psychologists tell us that subjects will be more conscious of surveillance during the first 10 percent of their trip and the last 10 percent of their trip. In other words, the longer you can delay the pickup, the less likely you will be burned in surveillance.

- Highway Courtesy. If you drive with extreme courtesy during surveillance you will most likely be marked as surveillance. For example, if you are trying to keep a car between you and the subject, but traffic is light and you keep slowing down at highway entrance ramps to let cars pass and get in front of you, you call attention to yourself. You must be natural and normal in driving, and in some cities, being courteous is not the norm for drivers.
- Peeking. Finally, you manage to get a vehicle in front of you, but it just happens to be a bus. You cannot see what your subject is doing or where he is going. So you ease out gently, just enough to peek around the bus at your subject. Once you are satisfied he or she is still in front, you ease back in behind the bus and breathe a sigh of relief. After a short distance, you become worried because you cannot see the subject and you peek again. Peeking will get your surveillance blown in a very short time.

Some of the activities we spoke about before now can result in the inadvertent or accidental disclosure of the surveillance to the subject. However, there are subjects who will purposely act to try to identify surveillance following them.

Surveillance Dry Cleaning

Subjects may attempt to identify or shake surveillance when they begin movement. This activity is known as "dry cleaning." Some of the tricks that they may employ (and could be employed by any subject who has read a novel or watched a movie about spies or the police) include the following:

A. In and Out. Buildings, stores and shops are used by the subjects to go in and come out quickly. This activity often forces the investigator to follow the subject in and out of those same buildings, and therefore become familiar to the subject.
B. Ducks in a Row. Basically there are four maneuvers used by the subjects to draw out surveillance and line them up like "ducks in a row."

1. Stops (*see* Long and Short Stays)
   a. Expressway Turn-Off. Counter-surveillance will be sitting near the ramp ready to identify all the vehicles coming off behind the subject, or the subject will simply observe who follows them off the highway.
   b. Reverse. The subject will drive into a park or housing area where he knows the road just loops around and comes out the same way. With only one way in and out, any surveillance vehicles which follow him in will be easily identified by him as he drives out.
   c. Choking. The subject will try to find a bridge, tunnel or road where the surveillance team has no alternative but to line up and follow–a chokepoint. At the other end, counter-surveillance will be waiting to identify surveillance vehicles as they come out of the chokepoint.
2. Windows. Subjects will look in the window reflections to spot surveillance. Another favorite trick is to enter a store and then look out the window. It is difficult for the surveillance team to look in, but the subject can easily see out.
3. Stores. Subjects will go straight to the back of a store and browse from back to front. They can then try to spot surveillance as it enters. Normally people will enter and browse from front to back.
4. Restaurants. Subjects use time as the main factor to detect surveillance. If anyone follows them in, they believe it to be surveillance. If you decide to follow the subject into a restaurant, ensure that if you order food, you order something which can be received quickly, so that the subject does not leave without you. If you see the subject leave before you receive your food, leave your food behind and follow the subject. You can be reimbursed for the money you wasted, but losing the subject may result in a tremendous loss for us and the client.

C. Movement/No Movement. Another favorite technique of subjects is to draw surveillance into a place where there is a great deal of movement (a busy street) and then just stop. The opposite would be to draw surveillance into an area where there is no movement and then quickly move through the area. They are looking for movement when there should be none and no movement when there should be movement.

D. Out of Uniform. The subject will start off in one venue or part of town, but quickly move to another where the clothes you are wearing may not be appropriate. A favorite trick is to go from a business district (i.e. where business suits are appropriate) to a park (where suits are not appropriate), or from the hotel restaurant to the pool.

E. Change of Venue. This is similar to Out of Uniform. Basically, the subject will try to draw out surveillance by moving into different areas to make it more difficult for the surveillance to cover them, force decision making process and communications.

F. Eyes. The subject will walk down a very busy street. Suddenly, he will stop and turn around very quickly, looking at the people following him. He is looking for the one set of eyes that are looking away because everyone else will probably be looking at them since they stopped abruptly.

G. Throw-Aways (bait). Subjects will throw an item away in plain view. This diverts your attention and eyes. While you are looking one way, they may be noting the numbers on a telephone pole the other way. If someone stops to pick up the bait, counter-surveillance may then burn the surveillance.

The basic philosophy behind all of these tricks is to force the investigator into making a decision. Foreign intelligence services used to say that they believed that if they forced the decision-making process, the investigator would make the wrong decision 50 percent of the time.

Remember, however, we are not the only ones who make mistakes. The subject is just as likely to make mistakes as we are, and very often we can take advantage of those mistakes.

Subject Vulnerabilities

The subjects themselves often create vulnerabilities that can be exploited by investigators. In other words, they are human too, and humans make mistakes. However, if we do not know whether these vulnerabilities exist, we cannot take advantage of them. The following are some basic considerations we must be aware of:

- We must know all we can about the subject prior to the surveillance. There is often a great deal of information readily available to us about the subject that we can gain through our subject study mentioned previously.
- We must think from the subject's perspective. We need to keep our "face" (surveillance) as small as possible.
- We must "freeze the scene" on every surveillance. We should plan and conduct our surveillance so that we always come away with something. We must gather all available information and then analyze and exploit the information.
- Think Beyond Placement. We often develop good surveillance plans and place investigators in good locations but fail to think beyond the initial placement. Each investigator should know exactly what she or he is supposed to do, observe, and record whilein place, and where she or he is supposed to go when activity occurs.
- Come out of the subject area the same way you went in. If you go in covertly, then come out covertly. We very often terminate a surveillance only to have a client come back later and request more work be done. If we "heat up" the subject, we are only making our job harder.
- Anticipate the unexpected. Plan, plan, plan.
- Always assume there is countersurveillance, regardless of what type of investigation you are conducting. Subjects in all types of investigations have been known to have friends or accomplices observe the area or transactions to detect if any police or investigators are present.

No matter what type of subject you are surveilling, there are always going to be mistakes by the subject that you may be able to exploit. At the same time, we must guard against making mistakes ourselves. If we plan for our own movements and actions and watch for mistakes made by the subject, we can increase our chances to conduct a successful surveillance and achieve the objectives we set out to achieve.

DETECTING AND ELUDING SURVEILLANCE

Subjects who are suspicious of being under surveillance may resort to trickery in order to verify their suspicions. When subjects resort to such acts, it is good to know the various techniques they may employ to detect and elude surveillance. Some subjects may accomplish this task in very subtle ways, without making it obvious that they are attempting to detect and elude surveillance. On the other hand, their actions may be very obvious.

Investigators must be aware of the various techniques employed to detect and elude surveillance. We must constantly evaluate and assess the subject's actions to determine if positive detection and eluding techniques are being employed.

Many of the areas discussed in this section may seem elementary and perhaps obvious from a commonsense point of view, but it must be remembered that every investigator is at one time inexperienced. Not only do inexperienced investigators fall for some of these obvious and commonsense tricks, but very often so too do experienced investigators. Some of the areas we will explore include the following:

1. testing for foot surveillance
2. testing for vehicle surveillance
3. eluding foot surveillance
4. eluding vehicle surveillance
5. special considerations in avoiding detection
6. recommended actions
7. being made

When actively involved in surveillance it is very easy to become absorbed in what you are attempting to accomplish and to suddenly realize too late that the subject's dry-cleaning efforts have burned you and your surveillance team. Expanding on what we talked about in the section Surveillance Vulnerabilities, we are going to look at some specific methods used to test for surveillance.

Testing for Foot Surveillance

Foot surveillance can be tested for by the following methods:

- Retracing Course. By changing direction of movement several times in a short span of time and retracing their course, subjects may be able to determine if they are being followed. This is the most common and easiest method subjects may employ, but it can quickly burn a surveillance team.
- Window Reflections. In business districts, subjects concerned about possible surveillance may pause in front of a large show window for the ostensible purpose of window shopping and then observe the reflections of passersby to spot indications of surveillance.
- Use of Bait. Subjects may throw away a scrap of paper, an envelope, or some similar item that may be of interest to anyone following them. They will then use window reflections or a similar means of observation or countersurveillance to determine if anyone retrieves the bait.
- Change of Pace. Another very simple and common technique employed, but highly effective, is changing pace. In areas where pedestrian and vehicular traffic is relatively sparse, subjects may detect surveillance by moving very slowly for a distance, then changing to a very rapid pace, and later again, changing to a slow pace. The subjects may couple this procedure with a sudden stop after turning a corner in order to observe the actions of those behind them. This may also be encountered during a vehicle surveillance.
- Public Conveyances. On conveyances, subjects who identify or anticipate surveillance may employ a variety of actions to test for the presence of surveillance:
  - A subject may board the conveyance, pay the fare, and then get off just as the vehicle starts to move, observing the actions of others who have boarded at the same stop to see if anyone attempts to follow.
  - A subject may leave the conveyance in an area with little pedestrian or vehicle traffic and then loiter to determine if the investigator dismounts at the same stop or the next one.
  - A subject may board several successive conveyances along a single route within a short period of time and watch for faces that reappear.

• Convoy. Subjects who recognize they are under surveillance or who anticipates surveillance may employ the services of one or more colleagues to follow them at a discreet distance to determine if they are under surveillance. The assistant is termed a "convoy" (and could actually be several assistants) or more commonly referred to as countersurveillance. Fixed points may also be used, and the subjects will walk a prearranged path within view of the countersurveillance fixed points so that they may detect any surveillance activity. This is a most effective method of detecting surveillance.

Now let us look at some of the techniques used to test for vehicle surveillance.

Testing for Vehicle Surveillance

The following methods are often encountered when subjects are attempting to test for vehicle surveillance:

• Traffic Signals and Controls. If subjects are driving an automobile, they may use traffic signals and other controls to their advantage to determine the presence of surveillance vehicles. For example, they may time their approach to a traffic light so that they will pass through the intersection just as the light turns red or may even run a red light and then watch the rearview mirror to determine if any vehicle commits a deliberate traffic violation in order to follow them. They may also drive the wrong way on a one-way street, feign motor trouble in a sparsely traveled area, or stop quickly after turning a corner or going over the top of a hill. The subjects may drive extremely fast or slow, make U-turns, and park illegally. They may also park frequently in crowded urban areas where parking space is difficult to find. This may be done three or four times, while the subjects carefully watch for any car that repeats the process with them.

• Stops. Subjects may stop in front of a vacant lot or vacant house in a suburban area where houses are few and far between to feign motor trouble. The stops may be in other areas, preselected for the ideal conditions they provide for countersurveillance. You may stop, thinking your vehicle and actions cannot be observed by the subject, but if countersurveillance techniques are being employed, then subjects do not have to watch your actions but can be alerted to danger by countersurveillance personnel.

- Dead-End Streets. Little needs to be said. This is a common practice that is easy to employ and can quickly isolate vehicles targeted as being surveillance.

Many subjects who suspect surveillance or because of the clandestine or illegal nature of their activities expect it will take steps to elude the observation.

Eluding Foot Surveillance

Common and effective measures for eluding surveillance include

- Entering and leaving crowded buildings. In business areas, persons seeking to evade surveillance can usually succeed with little difficulty by hurrying in and out of crowded buildings and taking advantage of multiple entrances and exits found in large city buildings.
- Concealment. Subjects may elude surveillance by dodging into an available entrance immediately upon rounding a corner and disappearing. Entry into apartment buildings for this purpose can usually be gained by pressing a number of bells to the various apartments. At least one person will usually respond and release the entry latch, after which the subject may enter, remain concealed, and later depart using another entrance.
- Confrontation. The subject may stop a police officer or security guard, point out the suspected investigators and have the police officer check them out because they are acting suspiciously.
- Change of Appearance. The same tactic employed by an investigator to avoid becoming conspicuous can be equally effective for subjects seeking to elude surveillance. Changing appearance is particularly effective where, because of crowds or limited visibility, the investigators are forced to rely on color of clothing or silhouette to maintain contact.
- Dodging. Pursuing an erratic course through dense pedestrian or vehicle traffic is always effective, particularly when traffic controls can be used to maximum advantage.

- Decoy. This can be accomplished quite easily, often using another person or vehicle look-alike. This technique has fooled many surveillance teams.

Let us look at some of the specific ways in which subjects attempt to elude vehicle surveillance.

Eluding Vehicle Surveillance

Some of the usual methods of eluding vehicle surveillance are

- Parking in crowded areas, especially where there is only one parking space available and pulling out within a minute or so.
- Operating a vehicle on wrong side of street, driving the wrong way on one way streets, running red lights and committing other violations are successful because investigators will not want to take similar action because it would confirm that they have the subject under surveillance.
- A combination of foot and vehicle surveillance could be used to decoy the investigator. The subject will jump out of the vehicle just after it swings around a corner and out of sight of the investigator. He may proceed on foot or later in another vehicle. The subject's original vehicle, driven by an accomplice, is followed by the investigator and becomes a mere decoy to lead them from the subject and his activity.
- The subject may suddenly turn off the road into a roadside gas station in an attempt to elude surveillance. After the surveillance vehicle has passed the station in an attempt to appear normal, the subject can drive off in a different direction at high speed.

Now let's look at some special situations which warrant attention in the area of surveillance detection.

Special Considerations in Avoiding Detection:
Eluding Foot and Vehicle Surveillance

- Telephone Booths. When the subject enters a phone booth, the surveillance team must consider the following possibilities of gaining information which may contribute to the investigation:

- it may be possible to use an adjoining phone booth to overhear the conversation.
- the subject may leave the phone book open to the page containing the name of the person called or he may note the number on the phone booth wall or a slip of paper which can be retrieved by the investigator.
- the time spent in the phone booth by the subject will afford the investigator an excellent opportunity to take video.
- Entering Buildings. The size, nature and surrounding locale of buildings entered by the subject are significant considerations in determining further action.
  - Small buildings. If the building has exits which can be kept under observation from a discreet outside position, the investigator normally should not enter. However, if the previous pattern of activity indicates that the subject may make a contact or engage in some other action pertinent to the investigation, the investigator should enter by an entrance other than that used by the subject (if possible) or otherwise convey the impression that he has arrived at the building from a different direction than that of the subject.
  - Large buildings. An investigator normally will follow the subject into a large building such as a department store or office building. Within the building, the investigator must take advantage of the building layout to observe the subject without attracting attention to him.
- Elevators. If the subject enters an elevator, the investigator should also enter if there are passengers and the subject is unsuspecting. The investigator may ask for the floor above or below that requested by the subject. Don't loiter. If the subject is the only passenger - don't follow. Remain in the lobby and watch floor indicator.
- Restaurants. When the subject enters a restaurant, the investigator must seat himself out of the direct view of the subject, but with a view of the subject. If the subject is accompanied by others and their conversation is deemed to be of probable interest to the investigation, the investigator should attempt to place himself within hearing distance. The investigator must give attention to the type of service ordered by the subject and govern his own

order accordingly to insure that he will be able to pay his check and depart from the restaurant without disrupting the surveillance effort when the subject leaves. In some instances, the departure of the subject can be anticipated and it may be advantageous to pay the check and leave ahead of the subject, provided that this can be done without attracting the subject's attention.

- Hotel. If the subject registers at a hotel, the investigator should attempt to ascertain the room number by observation of the registration process from a discreet distance. The investigator should exercise caution in seeking assistance of hotel staff personnel to obtain a room adjacent to the subject, monitor his mail or take any other action connected with the investigation. In trying to locate the subject's room, it is often possible to follow the baggage to the room if a porter is used to carry it.

- Motel. If the subject's vehicle enters a motel court, the investigator should not attempt to follow immediately, but from a discreet distance should attempt to observe if the subject registers and to which unit he is assigned or proceeds. Should it then be determined advisable for the investigator to also register, he must exercise caution. He has not only the problem of remaining inconspicuous himself, but he must keep his vehicle from attracting the subject's attention. Especially in the cases of infidelity investigations, motels often offer excellent video opportunities, as many of them have exterior doors and the investigator can set up outside (i.e. in the parking lot) with the door in plain view.

- Railroad, Plane, or Bus Station. If the subject enters a station or terminal and purchases a ticket, the investigator should discreetly attempt to obtain as much information as possible regarding the trip. A position in line one place removed from subject will often afford the opportunity to overhear the discussion between the subject and the clerk without any indication of obvious interest. The limits imposed on the surveillance will govern whether or not the investigator purchases a ticket and follows the subject on his trip

- Aircraft. Of special interest and significance, in planning for vehicle surveillance when it is known that the subject is tail conscious and difficult to follow is the use of planes and/or helicopters. With this type of conveyance, the subject is easily and discreetly followed, regardless of the types of evasive actions he takes or if counter-surveillance techniques are utilized. Not only must you have descriptive data concerning the subject's vehicle but the vehicle must also be "tagged" both for day and night surveillance. Weather, darkness and surrounding cover may impact on the use of this type of surveillance. Normally, air surveillance will be used in conjunction with foot and vehicle surveillance and in particular with fixed point surveillance (i.e. the craft can track movement between the fixed points). This type of surveillance is used for anticipated long trips in rural areas, down interstate highways, mountainous country, and when the subject is expected to move rapidly or attempt to evade surveillance.

Let us briefly look at the following recommended actions investigators should take when the subject attempts to detect or elude surveillance.

Recommended Actions

The best way to avoid being burned by the subject or by counter-surveillance is to be prepared to act when the subject makes certain predictable moves. Although these actions may be innocent enough, they may also be very conscious attempts to dry-clean or identify surveillance. The following are some actions that may be taken by the subject and recommended actions by the investigators in those specific situations:

- Subject: Turns a corner and immediately parks.
- Investigator: It is still better for the investigator to pass the subject and turn off a short distance ahead rather than stopping behind him or her.
- Subject: Drives up to the curb as if to park and then pulls away abruptly.
- Investigator: It is normally best to pass the subject and then later turn off, allowing the subject to pass by and then discreetly move in behind her or him.
- Subject: Uses excessive and/or irregular speeds.
- Investigator: If possible, settle on an average speed.
- Subject: Uses devious routes.

- Investigator: Investigators should remain at as great a distance as possible to avoid detection. Subjects are likely attempting to determine if they are being followed, and a decision should be made as to whether it is better to lose the subject than be compromised.
- Subject: Drives the wrong direction on a one-way street.
- Investigator: During daylight hours, attempt to parallel the subject on the next street, watching at intersections. After dark, consideration should be given to the possibility of following without lights. In the event that the street is only one block long, wait until the subject has made a turn at the far end and then follow either directly or by using a parallel street.
- Subject: Makes a mid-block U-turn.
- Investigator: The investigator should attempt to circle the block or to turn around out of sight of the subject. At night, consideration should be given to the feasibility of maneuvering without lights.
- Subject: Goes through red traffic lights or times his or her arrival at lights so that the subject goes through on yellow; watches the rear view mirror to see if anyone goes through against the red light.
- Investigator: If it is necessary to go through the red light to avoid losing the subject, every effort should be made to accomplish it without the subject observing the action because such an act will serve to alert the subject. If there is a gas station or parking lot on the corner, consider going through it to get onto the street that is running perpendicular so that a turn with the green light can be made.
- Subject: Makes false starts to lure the investigator into making a premature move.
- Investigator: Be sure that the subject does in fact intend to leave before leaving one's position to follow.
- Subject: Rides a bicycle that is too slow for automobile surveillance and too fast for foot surveillance.
- Investigator: This is a most difficult situation to contend with successfully; however, there are a number of methods, all of which leave something to be desired, that may be considered depending on the circumstances. Consider using another bicycle or parallel-

ing with an automobile and spotting the subject at intersections. Also consider dropping off a foot person and picking him or her up frequently or circling the blocks.

- Subject: Drives into dead-end streets to see who follows.
- Investigator: Normally, do not follow the subject onto such streets. In this instance, knowledge of the area is desirable. Fortunately, many such streets are appropriately marked.
- Subject: Stops after descending a hill or rounding a curve.
- Investigator: The investigator should drive past and stop as far away from the subject as possible while still maintaining sight of the subject. When the subject leaves his or her vehicle and walks out of sight, the investigator can reposition her or his vehicle closer to the subject vehicle.
- Subject: Drives at a very low rate of speed, forcing other traffic to pass.
- Investigator: Frequently pull into driveways, parking lots, and other available places from which to keep watch on the subject while remaining essentially out of view of the subject. Also consider the feasibility of driving ahead of the subject.

Being Made (Burned)

One of the most confusing times for investigators is when they think they have been burned by a subject. It is difficult at best to know when a subject "makes" the investigator. Some subjects act normally because they do not want to trade a known surveillant for an unknown one. Never conclude you have been discovered when the subject glances your way, although it is hard to overcome this natural tendency. If the subject obviously discovers an investigator, the investigator should drop off and be replaced. In some cases the surveillance operation may have to be terminated.

For someone just starting surveillance, the first skill to acquire is the ability to stop feeling that you are always getting burned. Surveillance is successful because most people do not expect to be observed. Absent an uncomfortable-looking or unskilled investigator, most people will never know that they are being surveilled. Acquiring this comfortable stature merely takes practice for most people; after a period of time, you will realize that people are not aware of you if you act naturally.

Tailing or following a subject is probably the most difficult aspect of private investigative surveillance, as well as the most dangerous. To the customer, losing the claimant or getting "burned" are both signs that the investigators are incompetent. Getting "burned" is especially dangerous, because it can precipitate a confrontation that can blow the case entirely or even cause an assault. If there is any sign that the subject is getting "hot" or becoming aware of the tail, break off the surveillance. The surveillance can always resume another day with a different investigator.

INITIATING AND TERMINATING SURVEILLANCE

Have you ever heard the story of the old bull and the young bull standing on the hill? They were standing there overlooking a herd of cows. The young bull said "Why don't we run down there as fast as we can and jump on those cows?" The old bull said "Well, if you do that, you'll scare them all away. What we should do is just walk down there at a normal pace and mingle in with them. That way, they won't suspect anything and we can have our pick of the cows!"

Like those bulls, there are two ways you can move into your surveillance position. Like the young bull you can rush in, taking the place by storm and attracting all kinds of attention, at the same time probably blowing the surveillance. On the other hand, you can do as the old bull suggested and walk in as if everything were normal, not creating any suspicion. In this section, we will discuss some of the aspects that need to be considered in initiating and terminating surveillances.

1. by vehicle
2. on foot
3. general considerations
4. terminating surveillance

After the initial survey of the surveillance area has been completed and vantage points selected, it must be determined when the surveillance activity will provide the most desired results. After these things have been decided, the investigator moves into the area. Whether this will best be accomplished during daylight hours or under cover of darkness, by foot or by vehicle, will depend on a variety of factors. In any case, however, the main objective is to move into the area and take up a position in a manner that does not serve to alert others to the fact or to arouse anyone's curiosity or suspicions.

By Vehicle

When moving into an area by car during daylight hours, it is desirable in most cases to drive to one's destination in a manner that would be expected of those who belonged in the area and knew where they were going. In other instances, it is possible to move unnoticed into the area by using an alternate route. The simple appearance of not knowing where you are going or what you are doing attracts attention and will often prompt others to try to assist you or to watch you out of curiosity. Familiarity with the area through presurveillance area casing will eliminate this problem. If you will be taking up a fixed-point surveillance, you must know things such as entrances and exits, locations of particular rooms, whether any doors will be locked, and so on, so that you can project that familiarity you need.

When it is necessary to move by vehicle into a rural area under cover of darkness, it is often desirable to extinguish the headlights a considerable distance away. When nearing the vicinity of the subject, it may be advantageous to reduce the speed of the vehicle to eliminate the tire hum that can be heard at night for a considerable distance. On a gravel road, it may be necessary to reduce the vehicle's speed more than on a hard surface road. The reduced speed is also required for safety purposes when driving without lights. When night driving without lights, it is highly recommended that the investigator begin by pulling to the side of the road for ten to twenty minutes, thus allowing his eyes to readjust to the change in illumination.

Another way you can move a team into position is on foot, and this too warrants attention if you are to do it correctly.

On Foot

When moving into an area on foot, it will sometimes be better to travel at night, sometimes by day. Only judgment and circumstances can effectively help you make this determination. When moving into or through a rural area on foot, it is important that it be done in a manner that will not alert the subject to the investigator's presence. The ability to move inconspicuously logically increases the closer one gets to the subject. In situations in which one will be moving in extremely close to the subject, extreme caution must be exercised. When you get this close, always make sure you are not trespassing or violating the person's expectation of privacy.

General Considerations

- People do not wander aimlessly. Their movement and actions have purpose. What may appear to be a minor or insignificant event at one stage of the surveillance may be of critical importance at a later stage.
- Your actions as an investigator must be nonthreatening at all times.
- Radio communications must be kept to a minimum.
- The use of disguises cannot be overemphasized.
- All investigators must ensure they are dressed appropriately for the venue in which they will be conducting the surveillance.
- Investigators must be very familiar with the area(s) in which they will operate.
- Investigators must be natural.
- Investigators must be flexible.
- All investigators must employ patience.

Another inevitable phase of every surveillance is that of its termination. The dilemma remains, however, when to terminate surveillance. It is a natural choice to terminate the surveillance when the objectives have been met. In many of our cases, defined time limits are placed on how long the surveillance will be conducted. In other cases, you may have achieved the objectives already and feel it is appropriate to terminate the surveillance.

Terminating Surveillance

Some points to consider when pondering the termination of the surveillance include the following:

- Has the objective of the surveillance been met? (i.e. evidence collected, leads developed, intelligence gathered, time expired, etc.)
- Is it likely the objective of the surveillance will be met in an acceptable period of time?
- Has the surveillance been burned and rendered ineffective?
- Is the subject irretrievably lost?
- Has the period of the surveillance exceeded available resources, funds, acceptable time limits, physical or mental stamina of the investigators, and so on?
- Is the subject likely to not conduct the activity you hoped he might?
- Have other operational priorities dictated termination of the surveillance?

These are but a few of the considerations that may have an impact on your decision to terminate the surveillance. You should know what the objectives are from the outset and when those objectives will be met. Care should be taken to withdraw from the area when surveillance termination has been decided with due care. You must consider the fact that you may want to conduct additional surveillance on the same subject in the future, and sloppy withdrawal from the area may reveal the surveillance to the subject or countersurveillance and preclude or reduce your chances for a future successful surveillance.

These are normally the most ignored phases of the surveillance operation, and it is during these phases that many investigators are "burned" or attract so much attention that they blow the surveillance or cannot operate effectively in that area. Remember that initiating and terminating surveillance is sometimes just as important as the actual surveillance itself. They must be planned for and executed properly to ensure a successful surveillance. If you believe you have been burned and rendered ineffective in that case, always check with your supervisor about how to proceed, and do not make a unilateral decision to pull off the case.

RURAL SURVEILLANCE

When we think of surveillances, we normally think of the classic movie-type surveillance that takes place on subways, through city streets, and in crowds of people. In reality, surveillances can and do take us just about anywhere we can imagine. Because of that, we need to be able to operate in almost any environment during the course of the surveillance operation, and that operation must perform in such a way as to not make our presence known to the subject. How do we do that? You guessed it: planning. Although most surveillance operations take place in or near urban areas, occasionally we may be required to operate in a rural environment. Operating in a rural environment causes unique problems and concerns. In all surveillance planning efforts, you must be ready to operate in a rural environment.

The possibilities for vantage points in a rural area are many, and investigators are encouraged to use their imagination. The investigator may dig out a shallow foxhole and lie on a tarp in it. If the foxhole is in an open area, it may be desirable to cover up with a camouflage tarp. Tall weeds, crops, bushes, rocks, and tree stumps are also effective. Large bushes, brush piles, and windfalls can be hollowed out to some degree, in many instances without altering their original appearance, and then used to sit in. They make excellent blinds. Natural contours in the land such as ravines and gullies are often located in desirable places and should be used. Actually, any place people can effectively secret themselves will prove to be effective in most instances. Here again, make certain you are not trespassing or violating any laws.

Care should be taken, however, so that the location selected is not one that is likely to be discovered by the subject, children at play, domestic animals, hunters, and so forth. Additionally, the less movement there is on the part of the investigator, the less chance there will be of anyone becoming aware of him or her. It must be remembered that the human eye is quick to detect movement, but if investigators are dressed in a color that blends well with the predominant color of their surroundings and they remain motionless, it is quite likely that someone looking directly at them would not notice them. Investigators should be prepared to remain in place for several hours, depending on the type of investigation and the objectives of the surveillance.

Depending on the circumstances involved, observations in a rural area can sometimes be made from a motor vehicle. When this is done, it is important to position the vehicle so that it is not in direct view of the subject. It is often helpful to have use a ruse, or cover, to explain why your vehicle is where it is. Such props as a surveyor's sighting device, a magnetic sign on the side of your vehicle that identifies you as a contractor, electrician, and so on, or even having your hood up as if you are having engine trouble can help explain your presence in a rural setting.

When one follows a subject in a rural setting using an automobile, the most appropriate method to use will be governed very much by whether the road is a main road or a back road and whether the surveillance is being conducted during daylight hours or at night.

VEHICLE SURVEILLANCE

If there is any aspect of our surveillances that offers a challenge, it is vehicle surveillance, and particularly moving-vehicle surveillance. This is often the most critical aspect of surveillance and is most certainly the aspect in which most surveillance is unsuccessful. Although training can and does help an investigator become better at moving surveillance, the only real way to become proficient at it is through practice. Consider the following hints:

- When surveilling a house or business, stay back as far as possible while still being close enough to obtain good, useful, in-focus video.
- When waiting for subjects, anticipate when their vehicle will leave the premises so that you can be in line to follow them.
- When driving, you should be a minimum of two to three vehicles behind the subject.
- When following a subject down a lesser street, try not to turn down the same street. Instead, go one street past and reacquire them a few blocks down.
- If you confidently know a subject's routine—he always goes to the 7-Eleven for coffee at 8:32 AM—follow even more loosely.
- When you park, make sure that your driver's side window is in the most likely aspect for taking video—remember to consider the likely departure route too.
- When tailing and filming from outside the vehicle, learn to "quick peek" the camera. This is the practice of pulling the camera into view for the shot and putting it back down below your waist when not filming.

- If the subject drives recklessly or speeds, you should discontinue the surveillance; you may have been burned and the subject could act irrationally.

During daylight hours, distance is perhaps the best cover if traffic is very light. If traffic is reasonably heavy, keeping one or two unrelated vehicles between your car and the subject's car will provide reasonably good cover. As we have already discussed, the best way to know how far to stay back from the subject's vehicle is through experience. The type of road, volume of traffic, lighting conditions, the subject's suspicion of surveillance, and so on, all play a part in deciding how to follow the subject. When the subject is stopped in front of you at a red light, you may want to pull into the gas station or convenience store on the same side corner so the subject does not get used to seeing you. When the light turns green, pull back into the flow of traffic. Only you can estimate whether such a move may be possible.

Using various techniques to alter the appearance of your vehicle and yourself will prove to be advantageous. If you have been following the subject for awhile without a hat, at some point when he or she cannot see you do it, put on a noticeable hat that will completely change the look of the "driver behind the subject"–you. Remember, keeping yourself and your vehicle from becoming familiar to the subject is key in maintaining your ability to continue the surveillance.

By utilizing the techniques we talked about here, you can reduce your vulnerabilities in the operation and thereby increase your chances for success.

COUNTERSURVEILLANCE

Everything may be going right; you may have planned well; done all your homework, subject study, area casing; you know the surveillance methodology forward and backward; you are aware of surveillance detection efforts by the subject; but still your surveillance can be burned and compromised. How? By countersurveillance.

It is foolish to think that some of our subjects do not use countersurveillance to see if they are being surveilled. Remember, many of our subjects make a great deal of money by committing fraud against insurance companies or through other illegal acts, and it is in their best interest to ensure that the flow of money is not going to be interrupted. Many of our subjects know that they may have surveillance conducted on them, and they will take steps to find that out. It is as easy as having their wife, girlfriend, a friend, a coworker, and so on, watch to see if someone follows the subjects when they drive away or if someone parks close by just after the subjects arrive home or at work.

An exceptional investigation and surveillance can be neutralized very easily through compromise. Your surveillance activities could be quickly identified by a successful countersurveillance mounted against you. The sophistication and degree of countersurveillance will vary with the type of investigation you are conducting. You must always assume that countersurveillance is being directed against your surveillance operation.

Let us look at some of the methods of countersurveillance that are likely to be used against you and what you can or should do about it.

Countersurveillance includes all actions designed to detect surveillance activity. The most common and most successful type of countersurveillance involves the use of fixed point locations. The fixed point provides greater security to the countersurveillance team. Subjects may follow a specific path or route and along this route will be the countersurveillance chokepoints. A chokepoint is nothing more than a location through which surveillance members must travel and from which countersurveillance can quickly and easily identify if there is any surveillance. Some examples of chokepoints are the following:

- Passageways between one street and another.
- Stores or buildings with glass walls allowing an unobstructed view of the outside street.
- Homes of acquaintances, family, or friends.
- Stairways and escalators facing in the direction from which the subject has just come.
- Short, narrow alleys.
- Tourist observation points that allow the subject to turn around and take photos.
- Parking lots.
- Department stores.
- Phone booths (anyone approaching the booth while the subject places a call, or soon afterward, is considered a subject).

- Lightly traveled streets and sidewalks.
- Subway stations.
- Change of transportation.
- Bridges
- Highway entrance or exit ramps.

When using these chokepoints, the countersurveillance is basically looking for some very telltale signals or behavior that the investigators will automatically exhibit. Some of these include the following:

- Hesitation or evasion on the part of a person or car.
- The same car or person seen two or more times in two or more different areas or after two or more changes of transportation.
- Vehicles that stop or start when the subjects do, especially behind them, or who pass and make a U-turn, then park.
- Any vehicle with other than a normal antenna.
- Cars that signal a turn and then do not make it.
- After the subject turns, any vehicle that goes slowly through the intersection, rounds the corner slowly, or pokes its nose around the corner and then withdraws.
- Vehicles driving too fast or too slow.
- Any vehicles that follow the subject the wrong way on a one-way street.
- Any car that makes a turn a block before or a block after the subject stops.
- Flashing of lights between cars.
- Any car that maintains the same distance at different speeds.
- Vehicles moving on parallel streets at roughly the same speeds under conditions of light or no traffic.
- Vehicles that slow down and duck behind other cars when the subject slows down.
- Vehicles that hide behind buses or pull out as if to pass the subject's car, then drop back.
- Any vehicle that follows or soon turns onto the street after the subject reverses direction.
- Any person seen talking on a mobile phone.
- Any vehicle following the subject completely around a traffic circle or a city block.

- Any vehicle pausing in a traffic circle until the subject has turned.
- Any vehicle that stops slightly behind and to the side of the subject at a stop light.
- Jumping or running red lights.

On foot, subjects may consider the following as evidence or grounds for suspicion:

- Anyone turning his or her head away or turning around when looked at by the subject.
- Anyone showing hesitation and/or looking around when entering a building that the subject has just entered.
- Anyone crossing the street when the subject doubles back in the direction he has come from.
- Dress out of place.
- Anyone running.
- Anyone entering by a service entrance in a restaurant.
- Leaving or entering a store, restaurant, for example, immediately before or after the subject.
- Making an obvious attempt to get a table or spot behind the subject in a restaurant.
- Special attention paid to people waiting at bus stops.
- Any person who begins to move when the subject does or stops when the subject does.
- Any person who gets out of a car when the subject does.

Another method of countersurveillance is to employ a convoy. The countersurveillance will follow the person they are interested in at a discreet distance and attempt to identify surveillance team members attempting to follow the subject.

You must always be wary of locations, routes of travel, and actions that may place the subject into a location that is ideally suited to conduct countersurveillance. More and more, sophisticated technical devices and countersurveillance techniques are being employed by those involved in illegal activities. The surveillance team must consider that they are always being watched and take no action that would identify them to the countersurveillance team.

It should be obvious that countersurveillance is definitely a force to be reckoned with. If we fail to plan for it, it can ruin months of work in short order

SURVEILLANCE CONCEALMENT

During the process of "previewing" the subject and during the process of taking film, it is vital to remain unobserved. Remaining unobserved is an art and a science. All investigators have their favorite ways of concealing themselves in their vehicles, but here are a few pointers.

- Remaining unseen in your vehicle while conducting surveillance is paramount! You must be concealed from the sight of not only the subject, but also neighbors, passersby, children playing, workers in the area, in short, everyone. If you are seen sitting in your vehicle for a length of time with no apparent purpose, you draw suspicion. People may suspect you are "casing" the area to do a robbery, or you may be a child molester who is waiting for a target of opportunity. You are going to seem suspicious and someone may blow your cover.
- Using sunshades, towels, curtains, dark window tint, window cutouts, or a combination of any of these will greatly assist you in maintaining your concealment in your vehicle. Towels and curtains hung from the interior header trim is especially useful, because it prevents others from seeing into your vehicle, but still allows you to part the screening slightly to observe and film your subject.
- Generally speaking, when you block out three sides of a vehicle, persons outside the vehicle cannot see into the fourth side unless the sun or some other lighting is shining directly into the fourth side. This is especially true when there is a considerable distance between the investigator's vehicle and the subject.

SURVEILLANCE EQUIPMENT

Being prepared to conduct surveillance requires more than just knowledge of the case, of the claimant, and of surveillance techniques.

It requires being prepared to do the job by having the equipment necessary to conduct surveillance. The following is a list of some of the basic equipment necessary to conduct surveillance:

Video Camera	Make sure your camera is in good working order and that you have extra batteries and the batteries are fully charged. Have a supply of fresh videotapes on hand.
Camera Mount	Have a tripod, bipod, or monopod available to assist you in holding the camera still during long-term filming sessions. It does not matter who you are, your hands and arms are going to get tired when you try to hold a camera steady for an hour at a time.
Camera Bag	Having a bag to conceal your camera for use indoors is critical. This is discussed in detail elsewhere in this manual.
Cellular Telephone	Make sure you know how to operate it properly and that your battery is fully charged before you begin surveillance. Make sure the cigarette lighter adapter works properly.
Micro Recorder	Having a recorder is a great way to keep surveillance notes, especially when things are happening quickly or you are driving. Ensure your recorder has good batteries, and you have extra tapes (for tape-type recorders).
Props and Disguises	Investigators worth their salt have a variety of props and disguises to use on surveillance. This may include hats, glasses, long and short pants, wigs, beards and mustaches, jackets, and so on. Do not forget about your vehicle. Items such as blankets or extra clothing to cover your investigative equipment, baby seats, bumper stickers on magnetic tape, sunshades, curtains or towels, and so on are all essential.
Survival Gear	A cooler with ice and drinks, food and snacks, hand warmers, a "potty bottle," a battery-operated fan, and so forth are essential in allowing

	you to conduct surveillance without having to get in and out of your vehicle repeatedly.
Maps and Compass	Even if you think you know your way around, maps and a compass are important. You need to be able to determine your present location, identify possible chokepoints and dead ends, be able to direct another investigator to your location, and so on.
Your Vehicle	It should be in good repair and ready to operate, even over long distances. It does you no good whatsoever if you cannot follow subjects when they drive away, and you are doing a disservice to your client and to outsource investigations. Before you go on surveillance, *always ensure you have at least three quarters of a tank of gas.* If you have to stop for gas while following a claimant, and it causes you to lose her or him, you have hurt all your chances for continued success.

With all of this equipment available, it does you no good if it is not in good working order or if you leave it at home. Additionally, this equipment should be available to you from within your vehicle without having to get out and open the trunk of your car or the bed cover of your truck. It might be more convenient for you in your off-duty hours to maintain your equipment in your trunk, but when you are preparing to perform surveillance, you *must* have that equipment available covertly and immediately.

Chapter 19

EFFECTIVE SURVEILLANCE TECHNIQUES

Christopher Finley

It was a sunny day and the claimant's day had been practically void of any activity. Suddenly, the garage door opened and the claimant's vehicle backed out from the garage and departed the area. Meanwhile, the investigator was still trying to find the keys to his vehicle as the claimant drove out of sight.

A little later across town, the female subject departed the night club as the investigator was returning to his vehicle from a badly needed bathroom break. However, he was too late as he began to record her activities. She had already embraced an unknown male subject and kissed him as they returned inside the club.

Does either of these scenarios sound the least bit familiar? Hopefully they do not, but more than likely, anyone who has conducted surveillance for a long period of time has encountered a similar situation.

Surveillance is an art that can only improve with experience and continuous training. The use of good techniques can minimize situations like these, however, and somewhat limit the amount of unnecessary mistakes made in the field. Utilizing effective surveillance techniques could mean the difference between a standard day of surveillance or getting that long-awaited "money shot" for your client. In this chapter, we will discuss some tips and techniques that can possibly make the difference between getting made or staying undetected and tracking your subject for an extended period of time. Use of these techniques could also mean the difference between calling it quits with no results at all and obtaining additional billable hours from your client on a case well-done.

This chapter will be divided into several parts and address issues that may assist the investigator in certain surveillance situations. We will begin by addressing issues you may encounter during a "fixed surveillance."

FIXED SURVEILLANCE ISSUES

Fixed surveillance can best be described as a surveillance detail from a still or fixed position for an extended period of time. This type of surveillance can come into play in insurance fraud and worker's compensation claim situations, civil and criminal case situations, domestic and child custody situations, corporate investigations, and many others.

Each time investigators deploy for an assignment, they should be prepared for a possible extended surveillance assignment. Good techniques can only be implemented by being well prepared. This means having the proper equipment and power sources for that equipment, water and/or snacks, cash on hand, a fully fueled vehicle, clean windows, and so on. Included in this chapter for reference is a Surveillance Checklist 101. This list is identified as a "101" because most of the information included is basic surveillance knowledge.

However, when someone has been conducting surveillance for years, they sometimes tend to forget the most basic of things that could make a great difference in the way an assignment progresses. When investigators depart for surveillance they never know how long the assignment will be or where the case will take them. It is always a mystery and the investigator needs to be prepared for any situation. Alexander Graham Bell was once quoted as saying "preparation is the key to success." I must wholeheartedly agree.

If not conducted properly, the fixed surveillance can quickly become a situation in which nearby neighbors, businesses, and/or onlookers become suspicious of who you are and what you are doing. Since September 11, 2001, and with the current state of the country's heightened awareness, more and more people are aware of their surroundings and more suspicious of people who look "out of place." A vehicle with the engine idling for hours and with no driver is sure to attract attention.

This can quickly become a situation in which you can be discovered by your subject or, at the very least, forced to move from your position by another suspicious party. These problems can sometimes be avoided by spending some time preparing your equipment, making sure that all possible case information has been reviewed before departing for the assignment. A main focus of the fixed surveillance should be finding a location beneficial for monitoring your subject and to then remain hidden in your vehicle at that surveillance position. Do not sit in the front seat, hang around outside of the vehicle, or be seen inside of the vehicle in any way. This issue will be discussed in another section of this chapter.

Prepared investigators always have their equipment ready to use at a moment's notice. Depending on your vehicle make and model, you should also have several vantage points from which to obtain video from the inside of the vehicle. Make sure to use your vehicle's design to your advantage when it comes to obtaining video and vantage points from which you will observe your subject. No investigator should be on a fixed surveillance assignment without a camera tripod. No matter how long you have been conducting surveillance and no matter how steady you believe your hand to be, a camera tripod will produce maximum results for recording extended video segments.

Another situation that will inevitably occur on a fixed surveillance is the opportunity, or lack thereof, to relieve oneself. Fortunately, we do not have to be as creative as in the past and there are now several manufacturers that do make portable "potties" that are convenient for this type of work. There is no excuse for leaving your post on a fixed surveillance, and this should be avoided at all costs. The more often you move, the greater your risk of being spotted by the subject or arousing suspicion of a third party.

Another issue that must be dealt with is the elements of nature. Depending on your geographic location, there will be times when the temperature inside your vehicle will be in excess of 100 degrees. There are also times when the inside of your vehicle will be well below 0 degrees. Allowing the vehicle's engine or auxiliary power to run in order to keep warm or cool for comfort is an unacceptable practice and will appear suspicious to others in the immediate area. There are so many gadgets and comfort systems available today that this should not be an issue. There are portable hand and feet warmers, cooling gel vests and jackets and personal cooling systems. Although it is important to make yourself comfortable in order to perform your investigative tasks, please do not let the comfort become a distraction. Remember, the more comfortable you get, the more likely your focus can become compromised.

Another issue to deal with during a fixed surveillance is equipment power. It goes without saying that every investigator should carry extra batteries and tapes or disks for recording. The current availability of hard-drive camcorders has negated the need for 8-millimeter tapes, mini digital video (DV) tapes and disks.

Investigators should also be prepared with an alternate power source and even a secondary camera for backup, should your main camera malfunction. A lack of equipment, memory space, or power for that equipment should never be an excuse for not returning excellent video results to your client.

Another issue during fixed surveillance assignments that some investigators may not think about is things that are sometimes brought upon us. Today's comforts can sometimes be a distraction when in the field. Do not get lured into reading books and magazines or newspapers. Do not listen to digital music players or watch movies. Your client is paying you for a reason, and you are there to do a job. Be prepared and keep your eyes open and alert. Your attention should remain with the subject at all times. You should check your equipment periodically and make sure everything is functioning properly and ready to be used, however. If you cannot sit on a fixed surveillance for an extended period of time without having to do something to pass the time, you may be looking at the wrong career path.

DISCREET VEHICLES AND APPROPRIATE SURVEILLANCE LOCATIONS

In a white sedan with no tinted windows, the investigator parked on the side of the street in the residential neighborhood and patiently waited for his subject to leave the residence. A short time later, the local police department was dispatched to the area due to a "suspicious person in a vehicle."

Across town, a black sport utility vehicle with dark tinted windows sat a short distance from the claimant's residence. As the claimant exited her home to walk the dog, she noticed the vehicle and quickly returned inside her home, not to be seen again on that day of surveillance.

Again, here are two likely scenarios. Use of a discreet vehicle is a must during fixed and mobile surveillance situations. Often in the private sector, the client will only authorize the use of one investigator on the case. This means the investigator must remain unseen as much as possible in order to remain undetected.

The most comfortable and most practical type of vehicle for an extended surveillance is a van or sport utility vehicle. This type of vehicle will allow the investigator room not only for the needed surveillance equipment but also to move around and set up the equipment and still remain undetected. The vehicle should also be one that has a color that blends into normal traffic and neighborhood surroundings. Obviously, colors such as white, yellow, red, and other bright colors should be avoided. Also, black may look naturally suspicious because more and more people associate these "blacked out" vehicles with detectives and government surveillance due to movies and television scenarios.

Also, things such as bumper stickers or objects hanging from the rear view mirror should be avoided. Major dents, dings, and burned out bulbs should be repaired as soon as possible so they are not noticeable signs of the vehicle. Surveillance vehicles should remain as "factory" and plain as possible in appearance in order to blend into the natural environment of other vehicular traffic.

A nice technique, however, is to have a local automobile mechanic install a relay switch for each headlight so that one or the other can be turned off at any given time, allowing for different looks during nighttime surveillance assignments. Window tint can also play a big part in remaining undetected as you sit in the rear of the vehicle. Remember, having the front side windows tinted sometimes makes the vehicle look more suspicious and is also illegal in some states.

Vans and sport utility vehicles should have not only tinted windows but also some type of thin black curtain in the rear of the vehicle. Many investigators believe that it is necessary to spend hundreds or even thousands of dollars and/or many hours of time to install a proper and effective curtain system in the back of a vehicle. This is simply not true.

A very effective curtain system can be made from buying rolls of black cloth and cutting them to the correct length of your windows. The cloth can then be slid into the head liner trim or pillar frames of the vehicle or attached with anything from paper clips to Velcro® or double-sided tape. This system is not only very economical but also very effective and provides little or no alteration to the inside of your vehicle.

Another good idea is to have a stand-alone battery booster in your trunk or storage area. Battery boosters are relatively cheap in cost and can be a case saver should your vehicle battery lose power as your subject is driving away. These units will allow you to jump-start your vehicle without the use of another vehicle battery.

As for an effective surveillance location, some of these issues can be addressed from the office and before the investigator is even in the field. All investigators should prepare for each and every surveillance case by looking at satellite images of the area of surveillance where you will be working. The availability of free programs such as Google Maps street view and other free and paid web site services has changed the way preparation for surveillance can be done. Directly from the computer and in the comfort of one's office, an investigator can now obtain a street level view or a bird's-eye satellite view of the immediate area in which the surveillance is to be conducted. This will allow the investigator to review local business locations and crossroads for any possible fixed surveillance locations. These satellite images can also assist the investigator in determining possible routes of departure from the subject's home and/or place of business.

This research should assist the investigator and help to ascertain the best possible location(s) for possible setup. Once on the scene, this will allow you to obtain the best location to remain undetected and still monitor your subject and/or his or her routes of departure. You do not want to arrive on the scene and spend several minutes and drive-bys attempting to determine the location where you will set up. This only makes you look suspicious and allows more time for you to be noticed by the locals and possibly the subject.

Once a position is chosen, the investigator should set up and then return to the rear of the vehicle in order to remain undetected. As we discussed earlier, a van or sport utility vehicle would be ideal for these types of situations. However, if a passenger vehicle is all that is available, the investigator should still sit in the rear seats and behind tinted windows.

Once you have positioned yourself in the rear of the vehicle and are out of sight, stay there. Do not move your position in order to go to the bathroom, go get a snack or eat lunch, jump into the front of the vehicle to answer your phone or turn on or off the radio or roll the windows up or down. These things need to be addressed before you are on the scene. Do not let a minor mistake ruin your day of surveillance and then have to explain your mistakes to your client.

Investigators should design their vehicles so that they have all of their equipment and supplies prepared and know where they are at all times. This allows the investigator to be aware of their surroundings because they may be in a fixed position for an extended period of time or the surveillance position could change at any time. And always, always have your camera system within arm's reach and ready to go at a moment's notice.

If, during a fixed surveillance assignment, an investigator must be relieved of duty by a second investigator, the detail switch must be as discreet as possible. If possible, the second investigator should utilize the same surveillance vehicle as the first investigator used, and the vehicle should remain in the same fixed position. If a different surveillance vehicle must be utilized, these vehicles should not be parked in the same position.

One technique the second investigator can use to relieve the first is for the second investigator to enter the vehicle from the most discreet and hidden side of the vehicle. The first investigator should then exit the vehicle a short time later and depart the area. This should obviously be done after monitoring all surrounding areas to make sure that there is no activity and no one appears to be watching the area. Ideally, this should be done when there is no outside activity.

Each fixed surveillance position is a different situation and all aspects of the setup and surroundings should be taken into consideration. Investigators should use the utmost discretion and attempt to remain as discreet as possible during a detail change.

The most appropriate surveillance location is one where your subject can be monitored and you will not be noticed by the subject or others in the immediate area of the subject's location.

WHAT'S YOUR STORY?

As the investigator arrived in the area, he parked on the side of the street and turned off the engine of the vehicle. As discreetly as possible, he then slid between the seats and began to set up his camera equipment in the back of the van. A short time later, the resident of a nearby home exited his home and approached the van. He then proceeded to knock on the driver's side window and asked "Hey buddy, can I help you?"

Another issue that will undoubtedly come about during fixed surveillance is the nosey neighbor. Close-knit neighborhoods (often higher income areas), cul-de-sacs. and mobile home parks will more than likely bring out those nosey neighbors. When people see a vehicle that is not normally there or seems out of place, the neighbors naturally become suspicious. How suspicious could depend on you and the techniques you have employed.

Here are some questions to ask yourself: Is your vehicle marked in any way? Did you circle the area several times before you set up surveillance? Did you park near someone's property or near mutual property lines? Are you hidden in your vehicle? Does your type of vehicle fit into the surroundings?

If you can answer these questions in a positive manner, you should be confident that you are off to a good start. However, this still may not be enough to thwart the nosiest of neighbors.

You have to remember that you are in their neighborhood. The area in which you are conducting surveillance may have just had a rash of burglaries, attempted child abductions, a local peeping Tom or who knows what other type of situations in their area. They may have valid reasons to be suspicious, so you must try to fit in to the best of your abilities.

If so, the investigator should be prepared with one or more believable stories. These stories should be rehearsed and believable. Having several stories ready to use at any time allows the investigator to utilize the one that may work best, depending on the person who approaches you and the situation at hand. If you are using a story that requires documentation (such as road or traffic surveys), make sure and have the proper forms ready to produce, be it business cards, survey forms, and so forth.

If you cannot convince the nosey neighbors that you are not a threat and that you are there for a legitimate purpose, they can and probably will cause you problems. When the nosey neighbors return to their homes and proceed to contact each and every neighbor they know, as well as the local police, your day may end fairly quickly or worse, your subject could be alerted that you are in the area.

If you can convince the nosey neighbor that you are not a threat and that you do have a legitimate purpose to be in the area, however, you may be able to obtain some invaluable information, such as the subject's patterns and work schedule, vehicle information, alternate employment situation, hobbies, marital and home status, and so on. Remember, this is the nosey neighbor, and he or she usually keeps tabs on the neighbors and what is going on in the area. As well, they typically like to talk about it and show others how much they know.

One way to get nosey neighbors on your side is to find something in common with them or maybe even compliment them in some way. This could be done by assessing their home or vehicle or maybe even the way they are dressed and then making a favorable comment, or you may derive a commonality from something that they say during your initial conversation.

One main point in dealing with nosey people is that you have to be courteous and you have to sell your story. It should be well-rehearsed and something that you are knowledgeable about. A good rule is to keep your story about 90 percent true and change what you need to in order to maintain your anonymity and not compromise your mission. This way, you can usually keep the conversation going for a while and possibly obtain additional information. One of your main goals when speaking with nosey neighbors should be to make them feel comfortable. Under no circumstance should you ever reveal the true reason of your presence or reveal any information regarding the subject of your investigation.

One way to avoid being surprised by someone while on surveillance is to remain alert. One of the most effective techniques to stay alert and ready is to play the "what if" game. You should always be thinking "what if my subject leaves out the side door . . . what if my subject takes out the trash . . . what if my subject goes out for a jog . . . what if someone picks up my subject and they go to the park . . ." and so on. This game and this mindset will hopefully keep you alert and ready for any situation that may arise during a surveillance detail.

USE OF REMOTE SURVEILLANCE SYSTEMS AND COVERT EQUIPMENT

A child custody case is often a very emotional situation, and one thing that is usually asked of investigators is to find out who is visiting the home when the child is present or whether anyone is staying the night and possibly cohabitating with the ex-spouse.

Most clients cannot afford to pay for twenty-four-hour surveillance for multiple days at a time and most investigative agencies do not have the manpower to cover a twenty-four-hour assignment for multiple days at a time. A nice arsenal of equipment will allow today's investigator to monitor the home for multiple days at a time without actually being at the home and still obtaining the evidence the client is seeking.

Another aspect of fixed surveillance assignments is the use of a remote surveillance system. These systems can be configured in many different ways with a variety of equipment, but we will discuss the most common types in this section. Remote surveillance systems are unmanned systems consisting mainly of a camera and recorder that typically monitors the subject's home area or a location that the subject is known to visit on a regular basis.

These surveillance systems can be set up covertly by parking a vehicle on the street or near the target location and configuring the recording system inside of the vehicle. This can be done by placing a covert camera on the dash or near the headboard of the vehicle so that it is virtually invisible. You can also place a camera in the front grill or at other locations of the vehicle. These cameras are then connected to a recording device hidden somewhere inside or on the vehicle. The cameras and recorder are then typically connected to a set of deep cycle marine batteries or gel cell batteries that are also conveniently hidden in the vehicle. This configuration will usually provide approximately three to four days of continuous recording, depending on the type of equipment used for the setup. Extreme temperatures can also play a factor in determining battery life and recording conditions.

Another available type of remote surveillance systems is small, all-inclusive recording devices with the video camera and miniature DV recorder included. These units can be configured and custom built into a variety of styles and enclosures. Most all-inclusive units record the video to a memory card that can then be inserted into a card reader so the video can be viewed on the computer. These files can then be e-mailed to the client or stored in a digital file.

A favorite of this author's is the rear view mirror camera and video recorder. This unit is disguised as a vehicle's rear view mirror and has one to five covert cameras installed. The cameras can be positioned to record video at almost any location around the vehicle. This unit records the video onto a memory card that can then be used just as described.

One factor that should be taken into consideration when setting up this type of system is the weather. If inclement weather such as rain or snow is present or direct sunlight is an issue, you want to make sure it does not compromise your video and/or the camera lens. Investigators should first test the configuration and make sure that recording will be optimal. This allows the investigator to prepare for any changes that need to be made prior to actual deployment of the system.

One nice thing about the remote systems is that their design is only limited by the user's imagination. These systems can be placed in plastic construction cones, birdhouses, faux rocks; attached to trees; and attached to utility poles or fences and a host of covert configurations. Camera enclosures can be customized for indoor or outdoor situations, depending on the investigators needs.

Something that the investigator should always take into consideration when deploying remote surveillance systems is the amount of battery time available and the amount of recording space the system is configured for. Regardless of the specifications and ratings of electronic systems, they should always be tested to determine the true parameters of each unit. The advantage to remote surveillance systems is that there is no investigator on site to be detected, and they can be configured to give twenty-four-hour surveillance coverage. This can be a firm selling point for the client, knowing that the area and/or subject can be continuously monitored for multiple hours at a fraction of the cost of having an investigator in the field.

The downside to these systems is that they can only cover the area that they are originally configured for and battery life and recording time can be an issue. Depending on the equipment used, these systems can be set up to record only for motion detection in order to extend battery life and memory space. However, the motion detection configuration should be tested by the investigator to make sure the settings are correct and as they should be. Do not rely on the default settings of the system.

Another problem is that this is an electronic system, and anything can go wrong at any time. These systems must be tested time and again so that when you deploy these units, you are confident that your efforts will be successful. You do not want to be left guessing and worrying that something may go wrong while you are not there. Even worse, you do not want to return to retrieve the unit, only to find that nothing has recorded or that the recording has been lost due to some type of system error.

These systems may obtain exactly the evidence you are looking for. The main use of remote surveillance systems should be a starting point for building a profile of the subject's schedule and activities that might be conducted at a certain time of day or night. Then, more billable time can be designated to the client by placing an investigator on site for a more targeted surveillance assignment. The investigator should now have an advantage when in the field, because the subject's schedule has most likely been determined by the use of the remote surveillance system. Now, maximum results are more likely to be obtained from the physical surveillance attempts.

Another aspect of covert surveillance that should not be overlooked today is body-worn covert camera systems. Body-worn systems are a must for every serious surveillance investigator. Today's incredible technology allows for cameras, recorders and all-inclusive devices (as discussed earlier) to be customized in a multitude of items that can be easily carried and concealed in everyday wear. With the variety of items available and the number of manufacturers to shop with, the price of equipment makes it possible for every investigator to possess possible multiple units without being economically pressured.

Covert devices today are built for low-light situations such as bars and restaurants and can be disguised in everyday items such as key fobs, cell phones, eyeglasses, and the like. Many covert devices do not have a built-in monitor. If no monitor is available to observe what is being recorded, the investigator must be skilled with the unit he is utilizing in order to obtain acceptable covert video. Investigators should often "practice" with the covert cameras they will be using in order to learn the unit's strengths and weaknesses, as well as the angles and field of view of the cameras. This practice must be conducted in order for the investigator to obtain maximum video results for the client

Surveillance is undoubtedly one of the most difficult aspects of the investigator's responsibilities. Continuing education and training will give the diligent investigator a needed edge in today's world of surveillance.

Implementing effective surveillance techniques such as the ones we have discussed in this chapter will not only allow the investigator additional options to rely upon while in the field, but will also greatly improve the investigator's chances of success. Regardless of where we find ourselves, success is the ultimate goal.

SURVEILLANCE CHECKLIST 101

Emergency or first aid kit	_____	Fuel vehicle	_____
Check engine fluids	_____	Clean windows	_____
Alternate power (inverter) for video camera	_____	Check tires	_____
Extra camera batteries	_____	Video camera	_____
Extra video camera and batteries	_____	Binoculars	_____
Tripod and quick release mount	_____	Voice recorder	_____
Covert video camera and batteries	_____	Notepad and extra pens	_____
Camouflage clothes or attire	_____	Extra change of clothes	_____
Clear plastic bags (for rain)	_____	Baseball cap(s)	_____
Water and healthy snacks	_____	Car battery jumper kit	_____
Cell phone and charger	_____	Cash and coins	_____
Case file and maps	_____	Fictitious forms	_____
Navigation system and/or maps	_____	Videotapes/CDs	_____

Chapter 20

EMPLOYING A COMPETENT SUBCONTRACTOR

WILLIAM F. BLAKE

It is Monday morning and the start of another work week. The business owner was looking forward to a productive day in the office. After the regular staff meeting, the company accountant asked to speak with the owner on a sensitive matter. He is told that the person responsible for accounts receivable has disappeared after a domestic violence issue with her husband over the weekend and an unknown amount of money and accounting records are missing from the company safe. It is believed that she may have fled to Mexico. The owner decides to withhold notification of law enforcement authorities until he has more information on what occurred and how much money is missing. This action will also reduce the possibility of adverse public relations issues. The matter has been referred to the outside counsel where you are employed as a paralegal. Your attorney asks you to locate private investigators to look into the problem. The question is, how would you handle this problem?

One area where a private investigator is particularly valuable is the investigation of internal incidents within a corporate structure. The use of in-house personnel to conduct an internal investigation will always be subject to claims of prejudice or self-serving interests. The private investigator with no connection to the corporate entity can easily refute such claims.

There may be occasions when an individual or business entity needs the services of a private investigator to assist in resolving a civil, criminal, or business matter. The utilization of a professional private investigator is not a matter to be undertaken lightly. There is a significant financial investment and a threat to personal reputations that should not be ignored. The investigator is the agent of the employer and if not chosen properly can do much damage to the employer's reputation and financial holdings. The problem for the employer is finding a competent professional investigator who will provide the assistance needed without creating problems of credibility and competence.

IDENTIFYING A COMPETENT INVESTIGATOR

There are numerous factors to be considered in identifying a competent investigator. The reputation of the investigator cannot always be determined by the source from which you obtained his or her name. Using the telephone directory yellow pages as the source for investigative support is a dangerous approach. Although the telephone directory may provide names of individuals advertising investigative services, additional inquiries must be made. The sole criterion for telephone directory advertising is having a business telephone number listed under the category of private detectives or investigators. The telephone company makes no inquiries as to the validity or competence of the business.

It is important to remember that private investigation associations have a variety of qualifications for membership. Membership in a private investigation association, by itself, does not necessarily equate to competence. In some cases it is nothing more than filling out an application form and having the registration fee. In other cases, such as INTELLENET (www.intellenetwork.org), there is a minimum requirement of ten years of verifiable investigative experience, a thorough and extensive vetting process, and a personal recommendation of an Intellenet member to apply for membership. INTELLENET qualifications and experiences greatly exceed the vast majority of other similar associations, providing an appropriate return on financial investment.

LICENSING AND INSURANCE REQUIREMENTS

Another important factor is the private investigator licensing requirements for the various jurisdictions. Some states have stringent requirements to obtain a license as a private investigator. One state has a requirement of a minimum of 3000 hours of experience under the direct supervision of a qualified investigative supervisor before being authorized to operate a private investigation business.

Some states have lesser qualifications and may or may not require continuing education credits to maintain a license. At the other end of the spectrum are those states that have no licensing or minimum standards, such as Colorado, Idaho, Mississippi, South Dakota, and Wyoming. This provides a situation in which a convicted felon can perform investigative services without having to endure the scrutiny of a background investigation or criminal records check. In Colorado, for example, any business should be registered with the Colorado Secretary of State Office but this obligation is not always enforced. In many subordinate jurisdictions even a business license is not required. Many states do not require any form of professional insurance, E & O, automotive liability, or workers' compensation insurance. In the event of misconduct or injury, the financial obligations of litigation and awards may be transferred to the individual hiring the investigator.

HIRING THE INVESTIGATOR

What is a prudent way to hire a competent, trustworthy, and professional private investigator? The most important criterion should be actual and verifiable experience of the investigator. What skills should this person have to best meet your needs? An individual with twenty years of experience entirely as a traffic accident investigator probably is not a good choice in an arson investigation. It is also known that someone with twenty years' experience as a prison corrections officer may not have the necessary investigative skills. The actual skill of the investigator is important, and the employer should not rely on the published skills listed in an advertisement. The employer should conduct a personal interview with the investigator to assist in determining the actual experience and skill sets of the investigator. Professional references should be obtained and inquiries made of these references.

An area often overlooked is the professional certifications of the individual investigator. An important aspect is whether the certification was earned or awarded without examination of abilities. PCI® of the ASIS is an internationally recognized certification based on a minimum experience level, an initial investigative content examination, and periodic recertification through a continuing education requirement. ASIS also awards a CPP® certification with similar qualification in the security consulting arena. CFE awarded by the Association of Certified Fraud Examiners is a similar certification with an emphasis on the investigation of financial fraud. These certifications require continuing education credits.

Another criterion to be identified is the ability of the investigator to conduct the necessary activities. Will the investigator personally perform your investigative requirements or will he or she be subcontracted to another individual? This can create a potential problem: What are the qualifications of the subcontractor? To comply with IRS requirements to be a contractor or subcontractor, the employer or contractor cannot direct the subcontractor to conduct the investigation in a particularly defined manner. The task is given to the contractor and the contractor determines how the task is to be accomplished.

When interviewing a potential investigator, it is prudent to determine the extent of investigative resources available to the investigator. The question is, "What are the qualifications" of the individual from whom the investigator may obtain investigative assistance. This is especially important if portions of the investigation will be conducted in other states or countries.

INTERNATIONAL INVESTIGATIONS

Conducting investigations in an international environment involves problems not normally encountered in the United States.

Among the many issues is the financial cost. It is unrealistic to expect that international hourly rates will be similar to, or lower than, rates within the United States. The recent decline of the dollar against the Euro and other currencies has dramatically increased the costs of an investigation. The current average minimum hourly rate for international investigations is in the $200 to $250 range.

Another issue is the manner in which international records are maintained and the bureaucratic roadblocks to speedy compliance with requests. In the United States, the vast majority of records and documents are accessible via computer with the generation of immediate results. It should be remembered that more than 90 percent of the world works by old-fashioned investigative standards and practices and has draconian secrecy laws for all investigations, including asset searches and background checks. In some instances, the bureaucracy requires that only a limited number of individuals have access to records. This could mean an extended period of response time when the designated person is unavailable to process the request.

Another issue in the international arena is the additional travel time required because of the distance involved in getting to records storage at distant locations. The poor-quality transportation system in some countries dramatically increases the travel time required to complete a project. In non-English-speaking countries there is also the cost and time required for translations. The actual and incidental bureaucratic costs of obtaining records on a timely basis must also be considered. In some foreign venues, nonnative requests for information are not given the same priority as requests from indigenous personnel are.

In addition, corruption can be a factor in some developing countries and thus has to be included in any pricing arrangements. When a client or fellow investigator is quoted a fee from an overseas provider, the potential customer often decides to get a quote from several other local providers in the country concerned. Fair enough. Sometimes local providers will be in a better position to quote lower than an international provider, usually based on lower overhead but sometimes based on issues of corruption. Transparency International ranks many countries in the developing world much higher on the list of corrupt countries than those in the western world. Unfortunately, that occasionally trickles down into the private investigation industry. Some local providers, although not necessarily most may discard your legal papers in a process service and prepare a fraudulent affidavit of service, or they may engage in "ghost writing" negative results, never having conducted the required leads in the first place; taking your money for a little literary effort.

How to minimize the costs and time delay for completion of international requests is contingent on the preparatory actions of the requesting investigator. It is incumbent upon the requestor to advise the client of the difficulties encountered in international jurisdictions. Of primary consideration should be the explanation that foreign privacy and secrecy laws are considerably more restrictive than United States laws. Records that are commonly available in the United States may not be available in other countries. Secondarily, the client needs to be advised that it normally requires additional time to complete an international investigation because of the unique political and judicial situation in each country.

There are certain steps that the requesting investigator can accomplish to facilitate the investigation.

1. Consider the international investigator as an integral part of your investigative team by taking the investigator into your complete confidence and providing all pertinent details surrounding your client's request. This could require that the requesting investigator to obtain the client's consent and having the international investigator execute a nondisclosure or noncompete agreement, if necessary.

2. The approach to information disclosure should be to "tell everything, as if you were handing over the case to a new investigator." This approach allows the international investigator who is uniquely acquainted with the local culture and bureaucratic structure to analyze the request and prepare an investigative plan in accordance with the laws of the foreign area. It is essential to solicit advice from the international investigator who may be able to provide direction to an area not known to the requestor.

3. The agreement with the client should document the explanation of problems encountered in other countries, such as record-keeping systems, translation problems, and travel. The agreement should also specify the approximate turnaround time, costs and budget limits; reporting standards, in other words, need for official documents and signed statements, and translation responsibilities.

4. When considering time constraints, it is important to coordinate with the foreign investigator to arrive at a reasonable and manageable time line.

Appropriate prior planning will prevent misunderstandings and unanticipated results.

TIMELY EMPLOYMENT OF THE INVESTIGATOR

A problem can arise for the employer and the investigator due to the timeliness of employment of the investigator. The investigator should be employed as soon after the incident as possible and prior to the filing of a complaint with the court. There are basically two reasons for this employment time line. First, witness perceptions may change based on public statements of law enforcement officers during their investigation. Fact retention may also be hindered through aging and people's desire to remove the offensive facts from their memory.

Secondly, many times the investigator can provide additional investigative leads or information to the employer based on the investigator's experience. It is basically that two heads are better than one because they see a situation from different angles.

COSTS AND FEE SCHEDULES

A major concern anytime a private investigator is retained is the hourly cost of investigative activity. Again, there is a cliché that states "you get what you pay for." The more experience and expertise that an individual has in a specific area or specialty will have an impact on the hourly cost. The average cost for a highly qualified investigator in the United States is $150 to $200 per hour. Mileage costs are usually equal to the IRS allowance and other expenses are at actual costs. Per diem lodging and meal reimbursement should be equal to the General Services Administration allowances for the area.

The employment of a private investigator should be subject to a written fee schedule or contract that outlines in detail the expectations and responsibilities of each party, including fees, expenses, hourly rates, time requirements, and report criteria as a minimum.

SUMMARY

Obtaining quality professional investigative services is vital to a successful conclusion to your case. To obtain a proper return on your investment in investigative services, there are several issues for consideration:

1. Make sure the investigator is reputable and experienced in the specifics of your inquiry.
2. Determine the scope of the inquiry and the fee schedule at the outset.
3. Ensure that the investigator is available to testify in court, if required.
4. Ensure that the investigator has no conflict of interest in your investigation.

INDEX